JESUS

THE WAY, THE TRUTH, THE LIFE

An account of the life and ministry of Jesus
that reveals what he was like, what he taught and did,
and how you can benefit.

TABLE OF CONTENTS

6 JESUS' FINAL MINISTRY

THE WAY, THE TRUTH, THE LIFE

[handwritten: Endures to the end will be saved]

You likely are pleased to get good news. And there definitely is very good news for you and your loved ones.

This good news is in the Bible, a book that the Creator of the universe, Jehovah God, caused to be written years ago. In this publication, we will focus on four Bible books that contain very good news for all of us. They are identified by the names of the men whom God used to write them—Matthew, Mark, Luke, and John.

[handwritten: message or story] Many refer to these four accounts as the four Gospels. All four relate the gospel, or good news, about Jesus—that he is God's means for salvation and that as King of God's heavenly Kingdom, Jesus will bring permanent blessings to all who exercise faith in him.—Mark 10:17, 30; 13:13.

WHY FOUR GOSPELS?

[handwritten: last 100 times coming / era of God's kg rule - all]

You may have wondered why God inspired four accounts of Jesus' life and teachings.

There are benefits to having these separate accounts of what Jesus said and did. To illustrate, imagine that four men are standing near a famous teacher. The man standing in front of the teacher has a tax office. The one on the right is a physician. The man listening from the left side is a fisherman and is the teacher's very close friend. And the fourth man, located at the back, is an observer who is younger than the others. All four are honest men, and each has a distinct interest or focus. If each writes an account of the teacher's sayings and activities, (the four records would likely feature different details or events) By considering all four accounts, bearing in mind the varying perspectives or objectives, we could get a complete picture of what the teacher said and did. This illustrates how we can benefit from having four separate accounts of the life of the Great Teacher, Jesus.

Continuing the illustration, the tax man wants

[handwritten: good teacher... what I must do to inherit ell?]

[handwritten: no one has left true disciples / vs flattery]

to appeal to people of a Jewish background, so he groups some teachings or events in a way to help that primary audience. The physician highlights the healing of the sick or crippled, so he omits some things that the tax man recorded or presents them in a different order. The close friend emphasizes the teacher's feelings and qualities. The younger man's account is briefer, more succinct. Still, each man's account is accurate. This well illustrates how having all four accounts of Jesus' life enriches our understanding of his activities, teachings, and personality.

People may speak of 'the Gospel of Matthew' or 'John's Gospel.' That is not inaccurate, for each contains *"good news* about Jesus Christ." (Mark 1:1) However, in a larger sense, there is but one overall gospel, or good news, about Jesus—available to us in the four records.

Many students of God's Word have compared and harmonized the events and facts found in Matthew, Mark, Luke, and John. About 170 C.E., the Syrian writer Tatian endeavored to do so. He recognized these four books as accurate and inspired, and he compiled the *Diatessaron,* a harmonized account of Jesus' life and ministry.

Jesus—The Way, the Truth, the Life does similarly, but it is more accurate and complete. That is possible because we now better understand the fulfillment of many of Jesus' prophecies and illustrations. This understanding clarifies the things he said and did, as well as the order in which events occurred. Archaeological discoveries have also shed light on certain details and on the writers' perspectives. Of course, no one can be dogmatic about the sequence of every event.

But *Jesus—The Way, the Truth, the Life* presents what is reasonable and logical.

THE WAY, THE TRUTH, THE LIFE

As you read and enjoy this book, try to bear in mind the primary message for you and your loved ones. Recall that Jesus Christ himself told the apostle Thomas: "I am the way and the truth and the life. No one comes to the Father except through me."—John 14:6. — *mediator*

Jesus—The Way, the Truth, the Life will help you to appreciate how Jesus definitely is "the way." Only through him is it possible to approach Jehovah God in prayer. Moreover, Jesus is the way for us to be reconciled to God. (John 16:23; Romans 5:8) Hence, only through Jesus can we have an approved relationship with God.

Jesus is "the truth." He spoke and lived in harmony with truth; it was as if truth arrived in the person of Jesus. He fulfilled scores of prophecies, which became "'yes' by means of him." (2 Corinthians 1:20; John 1:14) Such prophecies help us to see his central role in the outworking of God's purpose.—Revelation 19:10.

And Jesus Christ is "the life." By means of the ransom, his giving up his perfect life and blood, he made it possible for us to gain "the real life," that is, "everlasting life." (1 Timothy 6:12, 19; Ephesians 1:7; 1 John 1:7) He will also prove to be "the life" for millions who have died but who will be raised to life with the prospect of living in Paradise forever.—John 5:28, 29.

All of us need to appreciate Jesus' role in God's purpose. May you enjoy learning more about Jesus—"the way and the truth and the life."

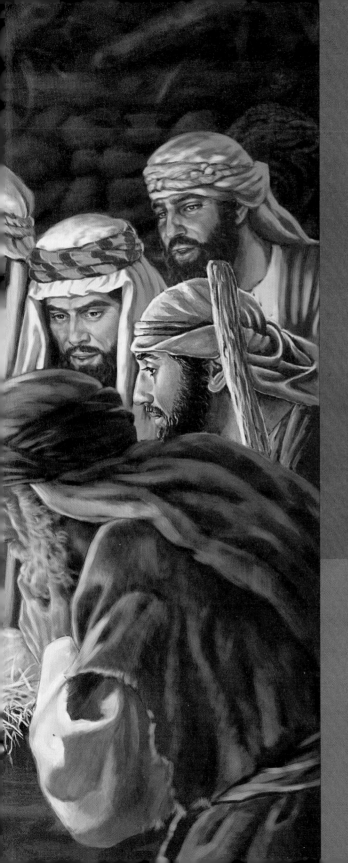

LEADING UP TO JESUS' MINISTRY

"THIS ONE
WILL BE GREAT."
—LUKE 1:32

TWO MESSAGES FROM GOD

LUKE 1:5-33

We can consider the entire Bible to be, in effect, a message from God. Our heavenly Father has provided it for our instruction. Consider, though, two special messages that were delivered over 2,000 years ago. They were delivered by an angel named Gabriel, who "stands near before God." (Luke 1:19) What were the circumstances under which the angel provided those important messages?

It is about the year 3 B.C.E. Where does Gabriel deliver the first message? In the Judean hills, probably not far from Jerusalem, there lives a priest of Jehovah by the name of Zechariah. He and his wife, Elizabeth, are no longer young, and they have no children. It is Zechariah's turn to serve as a priest at God's temple in Jerusalem. While Zechariah is at the temple, Gabriel suddenly appears near the incense altar.

Understandably, that frightens Zechariah. But the angel calms Zechariah's fears, saying: "Do not be afraid, Zechariah, because your supplication has been favorably heard, and your wife Elizabeth will bear you a son, and you are to name him John." Gabriel adds that John "will be great in the sight of Jehovah" and will "get ready for Jehovah a prepared people."—Luke 1: 13-17.

To Zechariah, that seems unbelievable. Why? Because of his and Elizabeth's age. So Gabriel tells him: "You will be silent and unable to speak until the day these things take place, because you did not believe my words."—Luke 1:20.

Meanwhile, the people outside are wondering why Zechariah is taking so long inside. Finally he comes out, but he cannot speak. Zechariah can only make signs with his hands. It is evident that he has seen something supernatural while in the temple.

After Zechariah finishes his service at the temple, he returns to his home. Soon thereafter, Elizabeth becomes pregnant! For five months, while awaiting the birth of her child, Elizabeth stays at home away from people.

Then Gabriel appears a second time. To whom? To a young unmarried woman named Mary, who lives up north in the region called Galilee, in the city of Nazareth. What does the angel tell her? He says: "You have found favor with God." Gabriel goes on to tell Mary: "Look! you will become pregnant and give birth to a son, and you are to name him Jesus." Gabriel adds: "This one will be great and will be called Son of the Most High, . . . and he will rule as King over the house of Jacob forever, and there will be no end to his Kingdom."—Luke 1:30-33.

You can appreciate how privileged Gabriel must feel to deliver these two messages. As we read more about John and Jesus, it will be clear why these messages from heaven are so important.

◊ Who delivers two important messages from heaven?

◊ To whom are the two messages delivered?

◊ Why, do you think, are the messages from heaven so difficult to believe?

JESUS IS HONORED BEFORE HIS BIRTH

LUKE 1:34-56

true meaning of his name is 'kill' an able bodied man

After the angel Gabriel tells the young woman Mary that she will bear a son who will be named Jesus and who will rule as King forever, Mary asks: "How is this to be, since I am not having sexual relations with a man?"—Luke 1:34.

"Holy spirit will come upon you," Gabriel answers, "and power of the Most High will overshadow you. And for that reason the one who is born will be called holy, God's Son."—Luke 1:35.

Perhaps to help Mary accept his message, Gabriel adds: "Look! Elizabeth your relative has also conceived a son, in her old age, and this is the sixth month for her, the so-called barren woman; for no declaration will be impossible for God."—Luke 1:36, 37.

Mary accepts what Gabriel has said, as we see from her response. "Look! Jehovah's slave girl!" she exclaims. "May it happen to me according to your declaration."—Luke 1:38.

Once Gabriel leaves, Mary prepares to visit Elizabeth, who lives with her husband, Zechariah, near Jerusalem in the Judean hillside. From Mary's home up in Nazareth, this is a trip that might take three or four days.

Mary finally arrives at Zechariah's house. As she enters, she greets her relative Elizabeth. At that, Elizabeth is filled with holy spirit, and she says to Mary: "Blessed are you among women, and blessed is the fruitage of your womb! So how is it that this privilege is mine, to have the mother of my Lord come to me? For look! as the sound of your greeting reached my ears, the infant in my womb leaped for joy."—Luke 1:42-44.

Mary then responds with heartfelt gratitude: "My soul magnifies Jehovah, and my spirit can-

not keep from being overjoyed at God my Savior, because he has looked upon the low position of his slave girl. For look! from now on all generations will declare me happy, because the powerful One has done great deeds for me." We can note that despite the favor she is shown, Mary directs all honor to God. "Holy is his name," she says, "and for generation after generation his mercy is upon those who fear him."—Luke 1:46-50.

● In inspired prophetic words, Mary continues to praise God, saying: "He has acted mightily with his arm; he has scattered those who are haughty in the intention of their hearts. He has brought down powerful men from thrones and has exalted lowly ones; he has fully satisfied hungry ones with good things and has sent away empty-handed those who had wealth. He has come to the aid of Israel his servant, remembering his mercy, just as he spoke to our forefathers, to Abraham and to his offspring, forever."—Luke 1:51-55.

For about three months, Mary stays with Elizabeth, likely being of assistance during these final weeks of Elizabeth's pregnancy. How fine it is that these two faithful women, both carrying a child with God's help, can be together during this time in their lives!

And take note of the honor that Jesus was paid even before he was born. Elizabeth called him "my Lord," and the child in her womb "leaped for joy" when Mary first appeared. That is so different from how others later treat Mary and her yet-to-be-born child, as we shall see.

◇ What does Gabriel say that helps Mary to understand how she will become pregnant?

◇ How is Jesus honored before he is born?

◇ For how long does Mary stay with Elizabeth, and why does she do so?

SOMEONE TO PREPARE THE WAY IS BORN

LUKE 1:57-79

Elizabeth is almost ready to have her baby. For three months, her relative Mary has been staying with her. Now it is time for Mary to say goodbye and make the long trip north to her home in Nazareth. In about six months, she too will have a son.

Soon after Mary leaves, Elizabeth gives birth. What joy there is that the birth is successful and that Elizabeth and the baby are in good health! When Elizabeth shows her little son to neighbors and relatives, they rejoice with her.

God's Law to Israel said that on the eighth day after his birth, a baby boy must be circumcised, and he was also named then. (Leviticus 12:2, 3) Some feel that Zechariah's son should be named after him. However, Elizabeth speaks up, saying: "No! but he will be called John." (Luke 1:60) Recall that the angel Gabriel said that this baby should be named John.

The neighbors and relatives protest: "Not one of your relatives is called by this name." (Luke 1:61) Using gestures, they ask Zechariah what he wants to name his son. Zechariah asks for a tablet and writes his answer: "John is his name."—Luke 1:63.

With that, Zechariah's speech is miraculously restored. You may recall that he lost his ability to speak when he did not believe what the angel said—namely, that Elizabeth would have a son. So now, when Zechariah speaks, his neighbors are amazed and ask themselves: "What will this young child turn out to be?" (Luke 1:66) They see God's hand in the way John was given his name.

Then, filled with holy spirit, Zechariah declares: "Let Jehovah be praised, the God of Israel, because he has turned his attention to his people and has brought them deliverance. And

14

he has raised up a horn of salvation for us in the house of David his servant." (Luke 1:68, 69) By "horn of salvation," he means the Lord Jesus, who is yet to be born. By means of that One, Zechariah says, God will "grant us, after we have been rescued from the hands of enemies, the privilege of fearlessly rendering sacred service to him with loyalty and righteousness before him all our days."—Luke 1:74, 75.

Regarding his son, Zechariah foretells: "As for you, young child, you will be called a prophet of the Most High, for you will go ahead of Jehovah to prepare his ways, to give knowledge of salvation to his people by forgiveness of their sins, because of the tender compassion of our God. With this compassion a daybreak will visit us from on high, to give light to those sitting in darkness and death's shadow and to guide our feet in the way of peace." (Luke 1:76-79) How encouraging that prophecy is!

By this time Mary, who evidently is not yet married, has arrived home in Nazareth. What will happen to her when it becomes obvious that she is pregnant?

◇ What is the difference in age between John and Jesus? *6 mo*
◇ What happens when John is eight days old? *Circumc.*
◇ John will have what assignment from God? *to bring repentant ones back to Jehovah via Messiah*

MARY—PREGNANT BUT NOT MARRIED

MATTHEW 1:18-25   LUKE 1:56

3 mo - then returned home

MT 1:18 promised in marriage was a binding arrangement viewed as already married

Mary is in the fourth month of her pregnancy. Recall that she spent the early part of her pregnancy visiting her relative Elizabeth in the Judean hills to the south. But now Mary has returned home to Nazareth. Here, her pregnancy will soon become public knowledge. Imagine how distressing the situation is for her!

What makes matters worse is that Mary is engaged to marry a local carpenter named Joseph. And she knows that according to God's Law to Israel, a woman who is engaged to one man but who willingly has sexual relations with another man is to be stoned to death. (Deuteronomy 22:23, 24) Hence, even though Mary has not been immoral, she probably wonders both how she can explain her pregnancy to Joseph and what will happen.

Mary has been away for three months, so we can be sure that Joseph is eager to see her. When they meet, Mary likely tells him of her condition, doing her best to explain that her pregnancy is by means of God's holy spirit. Yet, as you can imagine, this is a very difficult thing for Joseph to understand and to believe.

Joseph knows that Mary is a good woman and that she has a fine reputation. And he loves her dearly. Still, despite what she claims, it seems to Joseph that she could only be pregnant by some other man. Joseph does not want her to be stoned to death or to be disgraced publicly; hence, he makes up his mind to divorce her secretly. In those days, engaged people were viewed as married, and a divorce was required to end an engagement.

MT 1:20 spirit - first occurrence of Gk word pneuma - God's active force

16

Later, while Joseph is still weighing these matters, he goes to sleep. Jehovah's angel appears to him in a dream and says: "Do not be afraid to take your wife Mary home, for what has been conceived in her is by holy spirit. She will give birth to a son, and you are to name him Jesus, for he will save his people from their sins." —Matthew 1:20, 21.

When Joseph wakes up, how grateful he is that the issue is now clearer! He does not delay in doing what the angel directed. He takes Mary to his home. This is a public action that serves, in effect, as a marriage ceremony, giving notice that Joseph and Mary are now a married couple. Nevertheless, Joseph does not have sexual relations with Mary while she is pregnant with Jesus.

Months later, Joseph and Mary, who is heavy with child, must get ready for a trip away from their home in Nazareth. Where do they need to go at a time when Mary is about to give birth? ?

◊ When Joseph learns that Mary is pregnant, what must he think, and why?

◊ How could Joseph divorce Mary when they are not yet married?

◊ What public action establishes that Joseph and Mary are a married couple?

JESUS' BIRTH—WHERE AND WHEN?

LUKE 2:1-20

*interesting
angels
appear to
shepherds . . .*

Caesar Augustus, the emperor of the Roman Empire, has decreed that everyone must be registered. So Joseph and Mary must travel to the city of his birth, the city of Bethlehem, south of Jerusalem.

Many people are in Bethlehem to register. The only place that Joseph and Mary can find to

stay is a stable, where donkeys and other animals are kept. Jesus is born there. Mary wraps him in strips of cloth and lays him in a manger, the place where food for the animals is put.

God must have seen to it that Caesar Augustus made this registration law. Why? Because this made it possible for Jesus to be born in Bethlehem, the hometown of his ancestor King David. The Scriptures had long before foretold that this would be the city where the promised Ruler would be born.—Micah 5:2.

What an important night this is! Out in the fields, a bright light gleams around a group of shepherds. It is Jehovah's glory! One of God's

angels tells the shepherds: "Do not be afraid, for look! I am declaring to you good news of a great joy that all the people will have. For today there was born to you in David's city a savior, who is Christ the Lord. And this is a sign for you: You will find an infant wrapped in strips of cloth and lying in a manger." Suddenly, many more angels appear and say: "Glory in the heights above to God, and on earth peace among men of goodwill."—Luke 2:10-14.

When the angels leave, the shepherds say to one another: "Let us by all means go over to Bethlehem and see what has taken place, which Jehovah has made known to us." (Luke 2:15) They go in a hurry and find the newborn Jesus just where the angel said they would. When the shepherds relate what the angel told them, all who hear about it are astonished. Mary cherishes all these sayings and draws conclusions in her heart.

Many people today believe that Jesus was born on December 25. But in the area of Bethlehem, December is rainy and cold. On occasion, it even snows. At that time of the year, shepherds would hardly be out in the fields overnight with their flocks. Also, it is unlikely that the Roman emperor would have required a people who were already inclined to revolt against him to travel for days in the dead of winter to register. Evidently, Jesus was born sometime in October.

◇ Why do Joseph and Mary have to go to Bethlehem?

◇ On the night Jesus is born, what marvelous thing happens?

◇ Why is it not reasonable to think that Jesus was born on December 25?

THE CHILD WHO WAS PROMISED

LUKE 2:21-39

Joseph and Mary remain in Bethlehem rather than return to Nazareth. When Jesus is eight days old, they have him circumcised, as God's Law to Israel commands. (Leviticus 12:2, 3) It is also the custom to give a baby boy his name on that day. They name their son Jesus, as the angel Gabriel had directed.

More than a month passes, and Jesus is 40 days old. Where do his parents now take him? Up to the temple in Jerusalem, which is only a few miles from where they are staying. The Law says that 40 days after giving birth to a son, a mother is required to present a purification offering at the temple.—Leviticus 12:4-7.

"THE TIME CAME FOR PURIFYING THEM" When Israelite women gave birth, they were considered ceremonially unclean for a time. At the end of that time, a burnt offering as a cleansing sacrifice was to be presented. All were thus reminded that imperfect, sinful life had been passed on. The infant Jesus was perfect and holy. (Luke 1:35) Still, Mary and Joseph "brought him up to" the temple "for purifying them" as required by the Law.—Luke 2:22.

Mary does that. As her offering, she brings two small birds. This tells us something about the economic situation of Joseph and Mary. According to the Law, a young ram and a bird should be offered. But if the mother cannot afford a ram, two turtledoves or two pigeons will suffice. That is Mary's situation and what she offers.

At the temple, an aged man approaches Joseph and Mary. His name is Simeon. God has revealed to him that before he dies, he will see Jehovah's promised Christ, or Messiah. This day Simeon is directed by holy spirit to the temple, where he finds Joseph and Mary with their infant son. Simeon takes the baby into his arms.

While holding Jesus, Simeon thanks God, saying: "Now, Sovereign Lord, you are letting your slave go in peace according to your declaration, because my eyes have seen your means of salvation that you have prepared in the sight of all the peoples, a light for removing the veil from the nations and a glory of your people Israel."—Luke 2:29-32.

Joseph and Mary are amazed to hear this. Simeon blesses them and tells Mary that her son "is appointed for the falling and the rising again of many in Israel" and that sorrow, like a sharp sword, will run through her.—Luke 2:34.

Someone else is present on this day. It is Anna, an 84-year-old prophetess. Actually, she is never missing from the temple. In this very hour, she comes to Joseph, Mary, and the baby Jesus. Anna begins thanking God and speaking about Jesus to all who will listen.

You can imagine how Joseph and Mary rejoice over these events at the temple! Surely, all of this confirms to them that their son is the Promised One of God.

◇ When was it the custom to give an Israelite baby boy his name?

◇ What was a mother required to do when her son was 40 days old, and what does Mary's response reveal about her economic situation?

◇ At the temple, who recognize the identity of Jesus, and how do they show this?

ASTROLOGERS VISIT JESUS

MATTHEW 2:1-12

Some men come from the East. They are astrologers—men who study the position of stars, claiming that by doing so they are able to tell the meaning of events in people's lives. (Isaiah 47:13) While at home in the East, they saw a "star" and followed it hundreds of miles, not to Bethlehem, but to Jerusalem.

When the astrologers get there, they ask: "Where is the one born king of the Jews? For we saw his star when we were in the East, and we have come to do obeisance to him."—Matthew 2:1, 2. *King of Jews - a rival*

King Herod of Jerusalem hears about this and is very upset. So he calls the chief priests and other Jewish religious leaders and asks them where the Christ is to be born. Basing their reply on the Scriptures, they answer: "In Bethlehem." (Matthew 2:5; Micah 5:2) At that, Herod has the astrologers secretly brought to him, and he tells them: "Go make a careful search for the young child, and when you have found him, report back to me so that I too may go and do obeisance to him." (Matthew 2:8) However, Herod actually wants to find the young child to kill him!

After the astrologers leave, an amazing thing happens. The "star" that they had seen when they were in the East travels ahead of them. Clearly, this is no ordinary star, but it has been specially provided to direct them. The astrologers follow it until it stops right above the house where Joseph and Mary are now living with their young son.

When the astrologers enter the house, they find Mary with a young child—Jesus. At that, the astrologers bow down to him. And they give him gifts of gold, frankincense, and myrrh. Afterward, when they are about to return to Herod, they are warned by God in a dream not to do that. So they leave for their own country by another route.

Who do you think provided the "star" that guided the astrologers? Remember, it did not guide them directly to Jesus in Bethlehem. Rather, it led them to Jerusalem, where they came in touch with King Herod, who wanted to kill Jesus. And he would have done so had God not stepped in and warned the astrologers not to tell Herod where Jesus was. Clearly, it was God's enemy, Satan, who wanted Jesus killed, and he used this means to try to accomplish his purpose.

◇ How do we know that the "star" the astrologers saw was no ordinary star?

◇ Where is the young child Jesus living when the astrologers find him?

◇ Why can we conclude that Satan guided the astrologers?

THEY ESCAPE FROM A WICKED RULER

MATTHEW 2:13-23

Joseph wakes Mary up to give her urgent news. Jehovah's angel has just appeared to him in a dream, telling him: "Get up, take the young child and his mother and flee to Egypt, and stay there until I give you word, for Herod is about to search for the young child to kill him."—Matthew 2:13.

Right away, Joseph, Mary, and their son make their escape by night. They do so just in time, because Herod learns that the astrologers have tricked him. He had told them to report back to him. Instead, they left the country without doing so. Herod is filled with rage. Still wanting to kill Jesus, he gives orders to put to death all the boys in Bethlehem and its surroundings who are two years of age and under. He bases this age calculation on what he learned earlier from the astrologers who had come from the East.

The slaughter of all the boys is a horrible thing! We cannot know how many young boys were killed, but the bitter weeping and wailing of the bereaved mothers fulfills a Bible

prophecy given by Jeremiah, God's prophet. —Jeremiah 31:15.

In the meantime, Joseph and his family have fled to Egypt, and they continue living there. Then one night Jehovah's angel again appears to Joseph in a dream. "Get up, take the young child and his mother," the angel says, "and go into the land of Israel, for those who were seeking the life of the young child are dead." (Matthew 2:20) So Joseph now concludes that the family can return to their homeland. In this way another Bible prophecy is fulfilled—God's Son is called out of Egypt.—Hosea 11:1.

Apparently, Joseph intends that his family

settle in Judea, perhaps near the town of Bethlehem, where they were living before they fled to Egypt. But he learns that Herod's wicked son Archelaus is now the king of Judea. In another dream, God warns Joseph of the danger. So Joseph and his family travel farther north and set-

tle in the city of Nazareth in the territory of Galilee, away from the center of Jewish religious life. Jesus grows up in this community, which fulfills another prophecy: "He will be called a Nazarene."—Matthew 2:23.

As spoken through the prophets.

app Gods name

◇ When the astrologers do not return, what does King Herod do, and how is young Jesus protected?

◇ On returning from Egypt, why do Joseph and his family not go back to Bethlehem?

◇ What Bible prophecies are fulfilled during this period of time?

my son

GROWING UP IN NAZARETH

MATTHEW 13:55, 56   MARK 6:3

Jesus is growing up in Nazareth, a rather small, unimportant city. It is located up north, in the hill country of an area called Galilee, to the west of the large lake known as the Sea of Galilee.

When he is perhaps two years of age, Jesus is brought here from Egypt by Joseph and Mary. It seems that at this time, he is their only child. Later, however, his half brothers are born —James, Joseph, Simon, and Judas. Joseph and Mary also become parents to girls, Jesus' half sisters. Yes, Jesus has at least six younger brothers and sisters.

Of course, Jesus has other relatives. We already know about Elizabeth and her son, John.

He lives many miles to the south, in Judea. Living close by in Galilee is Salome, who is apparently Mary's sister and thus Jesus' aunt. Salome's husband is Zebedee. Their two sons, James and John, would seem to be Jesus' first cousins. We do not know whether Jesus spends much time with these boys while they are growing up, but eventually they become his close companions, serving as two of Jesus' apostles.

Joseph has to work very hard to support his growing family. He is a carpenter. Joseph raises Jesus as his own son, so Jesus is called "the carpenter's son." (Matthew 13:55) Joseph teaches Jesus to be a carpenter too, and he

[handwritten margin note: son - & cousin / α > ADELPHOS or / ADELPHE]

learns well. In fact, people later say about Jesus: "This is the carpenter."—Mark 6:3.

The life of Joseph's family is centered on the worship of Jehovah. In keeping with God's Law, Joseph and Mary give their children spiritual instruction 'when they sit in their house and when they walk on the road and when they lie down and when they get up.' (Deuteronomy 6:6-9) There is a synagogue in Nazareth. We can be sure that Joseph regularly takes his family along to worship there. It is later said that "according to his custom on the Sabbath day," Jesus went to the synagogue. (Luke 4:16) The family also finds great enjoyment in regular trips to Jehovah's temple in Jerusalem.

◇ Jesus has at least how many younger brothers and sisters?
◇ What secular work does Jesus learn to do, and why?
◇ Joseph provides what vital instruction for his family?

[handwritten note: Last mention of J. is at temple when Jesus is 12 - and entrusts mother to John (19: 26, 27]

[handwritten note on image: Tender comfort from hands]

JESUS' FAMILY TRAVELS TO JERUSALEM

LUKE 2:40-52

3 x / year, all males should appear b/4 Jehovah G.

It is springtime. Thus, it is the time for Joseph's family, along with friends and relatives, to make their yearly trip to Jerusalem. They go there to celebrate the Passover, as the Law directs. (Deuteronomy 16:16) From Nazareth down to Jerusalem is a trip of about 75 miles. It is a busy and exciting time for all. Jesus, now 12 years old, is looking forward with special interest to the festival and the opportunity to be near the temple again.

like Reg.

To Jesus and his family, the Passover is not just a one-day event. The day after the Passover, "the first day of the Unleavened Bread," is the beginning of the seven-day Festival of Unleavened Bread. (Mark 14:12) It is considered part of the Passover season. The trip from their home in Nazareth, the stay in Jerusalem, and the return to their home takes about two weeks. But this year, because of an incident that involves Jesus, it takes a bit longer. That has to do with a problem that is discovered on the return trip from Jerusalem.

While they are traveling, Joseph and Mary assume that Jesus is among the group of relatives and friends traveling northward together. However, when they stop for the night, they do not find him. So they go looking for him among their companions, but he is not there. Their boy is nowhere to be found! Joseph and Mary then head back to Jerusalem to look for him.

For a whole day, they search without finding him. Nor do they find him on the second day. Finally, on the third day, they locate their son in the temple, with its many halls. They see Jesus sitting in the midst of some Jewish teachers. He is listening, asking questions, and amazing them with his understanding.

"Child, why did you treat us this way?" Mary asks. "Here your father and I have been frantically looking for you."—Luke 2:48.

Jesus expresses surprise that they did not know where he would be. "Why were you looking for me?" he asks. "Did you not know that I must be in the house of my Father?"—Luke 2:49.

Now that they are reunited, Jesus returns home to Nazareth with Joseph and Mary and continues subject to them. He goes on progressing in wisdom and in physical growth. Though still young, he has the favor of God and men. Yes, from his childhood on, Jesus sets a fine example not only in seeking spiritual interests but also in showing respect to his parents.

OBEDIENT

JOYFUL TRIPS Trips to Jerusalem for the three annual festivals were joyful events for all. (Deuteronomy 16:15) During those travels, Jesus would see different parts of the land, learn about its geography, and meet fellow worshippers from other regions. What memorable trips to make!

Jesus drew conclusions in her heart

◇ What springtime trip does Jesus regularly make with his family, and why?

◇ When Jesus is 12 years old, what do Joseph and Mary realize while returning from Jerusalem, leading to what discovery?

◇ Jesus set what good example for youths today?   *Regular mtg attendance but also paying attention helped him learn many things*

JOHN THE BAPTIST PREPARES THE WAY

MATTHEW 3:1-12   MARK 1:1-8   LUKE 3:1-18   JOHN 1:6-8, 15-28

Some 17 years have passed since Jesus at 12 years of age was questioning the teachers in the temple. It is now the spring of 29 C.E. Many are talking about Jesus' relative John, who is preaching in all the country on the eastern side of the Jordan River.

John is quite an impressive man, both in appearance and in speech. His clothing is made of camel's hair, and he wears a leather belt around his waist. He eats locusts—a type of grasshopper—and wild honey. What is his message? "Repent, for the Kingdom of the heavens has drawn near."—Matthew 3:2.

John's message excites those who have come out to hear him. Many realize their need to repent, that is, to change their attitude and ways, rejecting their past course of life as undesirable. Those who come to him are from "Jerusalem and all Judea and all the country around the Jordan." (Matthew 3:5) Many of those who come out to John do repent. He baptizes them, immersing them in the waters of the Jordan. Why?

He baptizes people in symbol, or acknowledgment, of their heartfelt repentance for sins against God's Law covenant. (Acts 19:4) Not all qualify, though. When some religious leaders, Pharisees and Sadducees, come to him, John calls them "offspring of vipers." He says: "Produce fruit that befits repentance. Do not presume to say to yourselves, 'We have Abraham as our father.' For I say to you that God is able to raise up children for Abraham from these stones. The ax is already lying at the root of the trees. Every tree, then, that does not produce fine fruit is to be cut down and thrown into the fire."—Matthew 3:7-10.

Because John is receiving much attention, has a powerful message, and is baptizing many, the priests and Levites are sent out to ask him: "Who are you?"

"I am not the Christ," John confesses.

"What, then? Are you Elijah?" they inquire.

He answers: "I am not."

"Are you the Prophet?" they ask, meaning the great Prophet whom Moses said would come. —Deuteronomy 18:15, 18.

"No!" John replies.

They become insistent: "Who are you? Tell us so that we may give an answer to those who sent us. What do you say about yourself?" John says: "I am a voice of someone crying out in the wilderness, 'Make the way of Jehovah straight,' just as Isaiah the prophet said."—John 1:19-23.

"Why, then, do you baptize," they want to know, "if you are not the Christ or Elijah or the Prophet?" He gives a meaningful answer: "I baptize in water. One is standing among you whom you do not know, the one coming behind me."—John 1:25-27.

Yes, John acknowledges that he is preparing the way by getting people in a proper heart condition to accept the foretold Messiah, the one who is to become King. Of him, John says: "The one coming after me is stronger than I am, whose sandals I am not worthy to take off." (Matthew 3:11) In fact, John even says: "The one coming behind me has advanced in front of me, for he existed before me."—John 1:15.

Thus, John's message "Repent, for the Kingdom of the heavens has drawn near" is indeed appropriate. (Matthew 3:2) It serves as a public notice that the ministry of Jehovah's coming King, Jesus Christ, is about to begin.

◇ What sort of man is John, and what is he doing?
◇ Why does John baptize people?
◇ What is John's message, and why is it appropriate?

THE BEGINNING OF JESUS' MINISTRY

'SEE, THE LAMB
OF GOD WHO
TAKES AWAY SIN.'
—JOHN 1:29

JESUS GETS BAPTIZED

MATTHEW 3:13-17   MARK 1:9-11   LUKE 3:21, 22   JOHN 1:32-34

Some six months after John the Baptist begins preaching, Jesus, who is now about 30 years old, comes to him at the Jordan River. For what reason? It is not merely to pay a friendly visit. Nor does Jesus simply want to see how John's work is progressing. No, Jesus comes to ask John to baptize him.

Understandably, John objects: "I am the one who needs to be baptized by you, and are you coming to me?" (Matthew 3:14) John knows that Jesus is God's special Son. Recall that while still in his mother's womb, John had jumped with gladness when Mary, pregnant with Jesus, visited John's mother, Elizabeth. No doubt John's mother later told him about this. And he would also have learned about the angel's announcement of Jesus' birth and about the angels who appeared to the shepherds on the night Jesus was born.

John understands that the baptism he is performing is for those repenting of their sins. Yet Jesus is without sin. Despite John's objection, Jesus insists: "Let it be this time, for in that way it is suitable for us to carry out all that is righteous."—Matthew 3:15.

Why is it suitable for Jesus to be baptized? Jesus is not being baptized in symbol of repentance for sins. His baptism shows that he is presenting himself to do the will of his Father. (Hebrews 10:5-7) Jesus has been a carpenter, but now it is time for him to begin the ministry that his heavenly Father sent him to earth to perform. Do you think that John expects anything unusual to happen when he baptizes Jesus?

Well, John later reports: "The very One who sent me to baptize in water said to me: 'Whoever it is upon whom you see the spirit coming down and remaining, this is the one who baptizes in holy spirit.'" (John 1:33) So John is expecting God's spirit to come upon someone he baptizes. Accordingly, once Jesus comes up from the water, John may not be surprised to see "God's spirit descending like a dove and coming upon [Jesus]."—Matthew 3:16.

But more than that happens at Jesus' baptism. 'The heavens are opened up' to him. What

of J.C. 1 time

does this mean? Likely it means that at the time of Jesus' baptism, the memory of his prehuman life in heaven returns to him. Thus, Jesus now recalls his life as a spirit son of Jehovah, including truths that God taught him in heaven before he came to earth.

In addition, at Jesus' baptism a voice from heaven proclaims: "This is my Son, the beloved, whom I have approved." (Matthew 3:17) Whose voice is that? It cannot be Jesus' own voice; he is right there with John. That voice is God's. Clearly, Jesus is God's Son. He is not God himself.

It is noteworthy that Jesus is a human son of God, even as was the first man, Adam. The disciple Luke, after describing Jesus' baptism, writes: "When Jesus began his work, he was about 30 years old, being the son, as the opinion was, of Joseph, son of Heli, . . . son of David, . . . son of Abraham, . . . son of Noah, . . . son of Adam, son of God."—Luke 3:23-38.

Just as Adam was a human "son of God," so is Jesus. At his baptism, Jesus enters into a new relationship with God, becoming God's spiritual Son. Thus, Jesus is in a position to teach divine truth and to show the way to life. Jesus is starting on a course that will in time lead to his laying down his human life in sacrifice in behalf of sinful humankind.

God does not have a literal wife — expression is a word picture — relationship of Father & Son

◇ Why is Jesus no stranger to John?

◇ Jesus has committed no sins, so why is he baptized by John?

◇ Why might John not be surprised that God's spirit comes upon Jesus?

Beginning of ministry

LEARN FROM THE WAY JESUS FACED TEMPTATIONS

MATTHEW 4:1-11   MARK 1:12, 13   LUKE 4:1-13   *not put Jehovah to test as did at Massah*

Right after Jesus is baptized by John, God's spirit leads Jesus into the Judean wilderness. He has a lot to think about. At Jesus' baptism, "the heavens were opened up." (Matthew 3:16) He thus can recall things he learned and did in heaven. Indeed, there is much for him to meditate on!   *∅ by read Deut P.3*

Jesus spends 40 days and 40 nights in the wilderness. During that time, he eats nothing. Then, when Jesus is very hungry, Satan the Devil approaches to tempt him, saying: "If you are a son of God, tell these stones to become loaves of bread." (Matthew 4:3) Knowing that it is wrong to use his miraculous powers to satisfy his personal desires, Jesus rejects that temptation.   *means slander*

The Devil does not stop there. He tries another approach. He challenges Jesus to throw himself off the temple battlement. But Jesus is not tempted to make such a spectacular display. Quoting from the Scriptures, Jesus shows that it is wrong to put God to the test in such a way. Then, in a third temptation, the Devil in some way shows Jesus "all the kingdoms of the world and their glory" and says: "All these things I will give you if you fall down and do an act of worship to me." Again Jesus flatly refuses, saying:

"Go away, Satan!" (Matthew 4:8-10) He does not yield to temptation to do wrong, knowing that sacred service must be rendered only to Jehovah. Yes, he chooses to remain faithful to God.

We can learn from these temptations and from Jesus' response to them. The temptations were real, which shows that the Devil is not a mere quality of evil as some people claim. He is a real, invisible person. This account also shows that the world's governments actually are the Devil's property; he controls them. How else could his offering them to Christ have been a real temptation?

Furthermore, the Devil said that he was willing to reward Jesus for one act of worship, to the extent of giving Jesus *all the kingdoms of the world.* The Devil may well try to tempt us in a similar way, perhaps placing before us tantalizing opportunities to obtain worldly wealth, power, or position. How wise we prove to be when we follow Jesus' example by remaining faithful to God whatever the temptation is! But recall that the Devil left Jesus only "until another convenient time." (Luke 4:13) It may be similar with us, so we must not let our guard down.

◇ What things might Jesus meditate on during his 40 days in the wilderness?

◇ In what ways does the Devil try to tempt Jesus?

◇ What can we learn from the temptations and from Jesus' response to them?

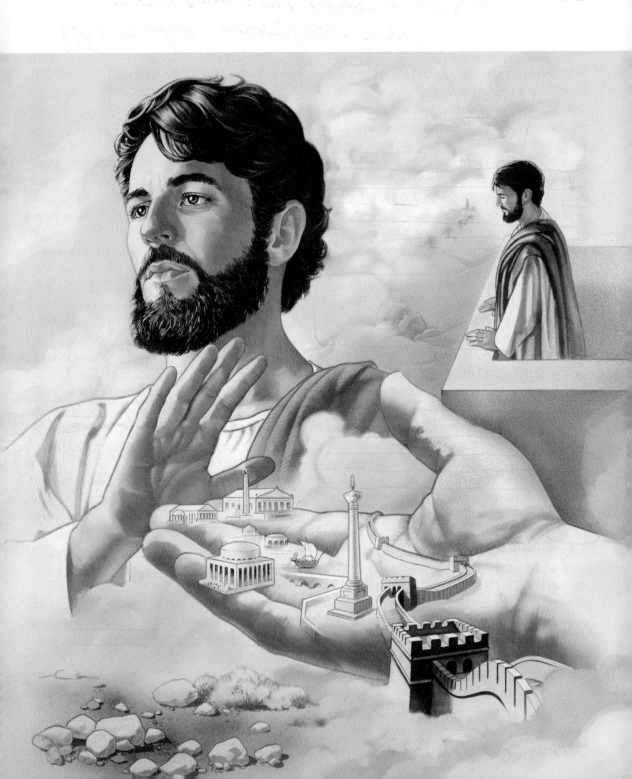

[Handwritten top margin: Lamb of God - throughout, both sheep played a role in remission of sin / however none of these sacrifices could bring perm. release from sin & death. Paul uses pictorial sign at 1 COR 5:7]

JESUS BEGINS TO MAKE DISCIPLES

JOHN 1:29-51

After 40 days in the wilderness and before heading back to Galilee, Jesus returns to John, who had baptized him. As Jesus approaches, John points him out and exclaims to those present: "See, the Lamb of God who takes away the sin of the world! This is the one about whom I said: 'Behind me there comes a man who has advanced in front of me, for he existed before me.'" (John 1:29, 30) Though John is a bit older than Jesus, he is aware that Jesus existed before him as a spirit person in heaven.

A few weeks earlier, when Jesus came to be baptized, John did not seem certain that Jesus was to be the Messiah. "Even I did not know him," John acknowledges, "but the reason why I came baptizing in water was so that he might be made manifest to Israel."—John 1:31.

John goes on to relate to his listeners what happened when he baptized Jesus: "I viewed the spirit coming down as a dove out of heaven, and it remained upon him. Even I did not know him, but the very One who sent me to baptize in water said to me: 'Whoever it is upon whom you see the spirit coming down and remaining, this is the one who baptizes in holy spirit.' And I have seen it, and I have given witness that this one is the Son of God."—John 1:32-34.

John is with two of his disciples the next day when Jesus again approaches. John says: "See, the Lamb of God!" (John 1:36) At this, these two disciples of John the Baptist follow Jesus. One of the two is named Andrew. Likely the other is the very person who recorded this event, who is also named John. It seems that this John is a cousin of Jesus, being a son of Salome. She is probably Mary's sister, and her husband is Zebedee.

Turning and seeing Andrew and John following him, Jesus asks: "What are you looking for?" *Checking their motive*

"Rabbi," they ask him, "where are you staying?"

"Come, and you will see," answers Jesus. —John 1:37-39.

It is about four o'clock in the afternoon, and Andrew and John stay with Jesus the rest of the day. Andrew is so excited that at one point he finds his brother Simon, also called Peter, and tells him: "We have found the Messiah." (John 1:41) Andrew takes Peter to Jesus. Later events suggest that John similarly finds his brother James and brings him to Jesus; yet, John does not include this personal detail in his record of events.

The next day, Jesus finds Philip, who is from Bethsaida. It is near the north shore of the Sea

[Handwritten bottom margin: 10 hour = 4 PM]

— "Christ our Passover has been sacrificed"

of Galilee and is the home city of Andrew and Peter. Jesus invites Philip: "Be my follower." —John 1:43.

Philip then finds <u>Nathanael, also called Bartholomew,</u> and says: "We have found the one of whom Moses, in the Law, and the Prophets wrote: Jesus, the son of Joseph, from Nazareth." Nathanael is doubtful and says to Philip: "Can anything good come out of Nazareth?"

"Come and see," Philip urges him. Jesus notices Nathanael approaching and says: "See, truly an Israelite in whom there is no deceit."

"How do you know me?" Nathanael asks.

Jesus answers: "Before Philip called you, while you were under the fig tree, I saw you."

Nathanael replies in amazement: "Rabbi, you are the Son of God, you are King of Israel."

"Do you believe because I told you I saw you under the fig tree?" Jesus asks. "You will see things greater than these." Then Jesus promises: "Most truly I say to you men, you will see heaven opened up and the angels of God ascending and descending to the Son of man." —John 1:45-51.

Very soon after this, Jesus, along with his newly acquired disciples, leaves the Jordan Valley and travels to Galilee.

◇ Who are the first of Jesus' disciples?

◇ How is Peter, as well as perhaps James, introduced to Jesus?

◇ What helps to convince Nathanael that Jesus is the Son of God?

It is now the third day since Nathanael has become one of Jesus' earliest disciples. Jesus and at least some of those early disciples head north to the district of Galilee, their home area. Their destination is the town of Cana, the hometown of Nathanael. Cana is located in the hills north of Nazareth, where Jesus himself grew up. They have been invited to a wedding feast in Cana.

Jesus' mother has also come to the wedding. As a friend of the family of those getting married, Mary seems to have been involved in helping to care for the many guests. So she is quick to note a shortage, which she reports to Jesus: "They have no wine."—John 2:3.

In effect, Mary is suggesting that Jesus do something about the lack of wine. Using an idiom that indicates his objection, Jesus replies: "Woman, why is that of concern to me and to you?" (John 2:4) As God's appointed King, Jesus is to have his activities directed by his heavenly Father, not by family or friends. Mary wisely leaves the matter in her son's hands, simply saying to those ministering: "Do whatever he tells you."—John 2:5.

There are six stone water jars, each of which can hold more than ten gallons. Jesus instructs the attendants: "Fill the jars with water." Then Jesus says: "Now draw some out and take it to the director of the feast."—John 2:7, 8.

The director is impressed by the fine quality of the wine but is unaware that it has been miraculously produced. Calling the bridegroom, he says: "Everyone else puts out the fine wine first, and when people are intoxicated, the inferior. You have saved the fine wine until now."—John 2:10.

This is the first miracle that Jesus performs. When his new disciples see this miracle, their faith in him is strengthened. Afterward, Jesus, his mother, and his half brothers travel to the city of Capernaum on the northwest shore of the Sea of Galilee.

◇ When during Jesus' ministry does the wedding in Cana occur?

◇ How does Jesus respond to his mother's suggestion about the wine?

◇ Jesus performs what miracle, and how does that affect others?

After the wedding in Cana, Jesus heads to Capernaum. Jesus' mother and his half brothers —James, Joseph, Simon, and Judas—are traveling with him.

But why does Jesus go to Capernaum? This city is more prominently situated than Nazareth or Cana and is evidently larger. Also, many of Jesus' newly acquired disciples live in or near Capernaum. So Jesus can provide them with some training in their home area.

During his stay in Capernaum, Jesus also performs marvelous works. Thus many people of the city and in the surrounding area hear about the things he does there. But Jesus and his companions, who are devoted Jewish men, must soon be on their way to Jerusalem to attend the Passover of 30 C.E.

While at the temple in Jerusalem, Jesus' disciples see something about Jesus that is most impressive, different from what they have seen before.

God's Law calls upon Israelites to make animal sacrifices at the temple, and visitors need food provisions during their stay. So the Law allows for those traveling to Jerusalem from a distant location to bring money to spend on "cattle, sheep, goats," and other things useful during their stay in the city. (Deuteronomy 14: 24-26) As a result, merchants in Jerusalem sell animals or birds right inside a large courtyard of the temple. And some of them are cheating the people by charging too much.

Filled with indignation, Jesus pours out the coins of the money changers, overturns their tables, and drives the men out. Jesus then says: "Take these things away from here! Stop making the house of my Father a house of commerce!"—John 2:16.

When Jesus' disciples see this, they remember the prophecy about God's Son: "The zeal for your house will consume me." But the Jews ask: "What sign can you show us, since you are doing these things?" Jesus answers: "Tear down this temple, and in three days I will raise it up." —John 2:17-19; Psalm 69:9.

The Jews assume that Jesus means the literal temple there in Jerusalem, so they ask: "This temple was built in 46 years, and will you raise it up in three days?" (John 2:20) However, Jesus is referring to his body as a temple. Three years later, his disciples remember these words when he is resurrected.

◇ After the wedding in Cana, Jesus travels to what places?
◇ Why is Jesus angry over what he sees at the temple, and what does he do?
◇ To what does Jesus refer as "this temple," and what does he mean?

HE TEACHES NICODEMUS AT NIGHT

JOHN 2:23–3:21

While he is in Jerusalem for the Passover of 30 C.E., Jesus performs remarkable signs, or miracles. As a result, many people put faith in him. Nicodemus, a Pharisee and a member of the Jewish high court called the Sanhedrin, is impressed. Wanting to learn more, he visits Jesus after dark, probably because he fears that his reputation with the other Jewish leaders will be damaged if he is seen.

"Rabbi," Nicodemus says, "we know that you have come from God as a teacher, for no one can perform these signs that you perform unless God is with him." In reply, Jesus tells Nicodemus that in order to enter the Kingdom of God, a person must be "born again."—John 3: 2, 3.

How, though, can a person be born again? "He cannot enter into the womb of his mother a second time and be born, can he?" Nicodemus asks.—John 3:4.

No, that is not what being born again means. Jesus explains: "Unless anyone is born from water and spirit, he cannot enter into the Kingdom of God." (John 3:5) When Jesus was baptized and holy spirit descended upon him, he was thus born "from water and spirit." At that time, there was an accompanying declaration from heaven: "This is my Son, the beloved, whom I have approved." (Matthew 3:16, 17) In this way, God announced that he had brought forth Jesus as a spiritual son having the prospect of entering into the heavenly Kingdom. Later, at Pentecost 33 C.E., holy spirit will be poured out on other baptized ones, and they will thus be born again as spiritual sons of God. —Acts 2:1-4.

It is difficult for Nicodemus to understand what Jesus is teaching him about the King-

dom. So Jesus gives further information regarding his special role as God's human Son. Jesus says: "Just as Moses lifted up the serpent in the wilderness, so the Son of man must be lifted up, so that everyone believing in him may have everlasting life."—John 3:14, 15.

Long ago those Israelites who were bitten by poisonous snakes had to look at the copper serpent to be saved. (Numbers 21:9) Similarly, all humans need to exercise faith in God's Son to be saved from their dying condition and to gain everlasting life. Stressing Jehovah's loving role in this, Jesus next tells Nicodemus: "God loved the world so much that he gave his only-begotten Son, so that everyone exercising faith in him might not be destroyed but have everlasting life." (John 3:16) Hence, here in Jerusalem some six months after beginning his ministry, Jesus makes clear that he is the way to salvation for mankind.

Jesus tells Nicodemus: "God did not send his Son into the world for him to judge the world." This means that he was not sent to judge it adversely, condemning all humans to destruction. Rather, as Jesus says, he was sent "for the world to be saved through him."—John 3:17.

Nicodemus has fearfully come to Jesus under cover of darkness. So it is interesting that Jesus closes his conversation with him by saying: "Now this is the basis for judgment: that the light [which Jesus is by his life and teachings] has come into the world, but men have loved the darkness rather than the light, for their works

were wicked. For whoever practices vile things hates the light and does not come to the light, so that his works may not be reproved. But whoever does what is true comes to the light, so that his works may be made manifest as having been done in harmony with God."—John 3: 19-21.

Now it is up to this Pharisee and teacher of Israel, Nicodemus, to reflect on what he has just heard about Jesus' role in God's purpose.

◊ What prompts Nicodemus to visit Jesus, and why at night?

◊ What does it mean to be "born again"?

◊ In what sense has Jesus not come "to judge the world"?

JESUS INCREASES AS JOHN DECREASES

MATTHEW 4:12 MARK 6:17-20 LUKE 3:19, 20 JOHN 3:22–4:3

After celebrating the Passover in the spring of 30 C.E., Jesus and his disciples leave Jerusalem. However, they do not directly return to their homes in Galilee. They go into the country of Judea, where they baptize many. John the Baptist has been doing a similar work for about a year, and some of his disciples are still with him, perhaps in the Jordan River valley.

Jesus himself does not baptize anyone—his disciples do so under his direction. At this point in Jesus' ministry, both Jesus and John are teaching Jews who are repentant over their sins against God's Law covenant.—Acts 19:4.

But John's disciples are jealous, complaining to him about Jesus: "The man [Jesus] who was with you . . . is baptizing, and all are going to him." (John 3:26) Yet, John is not jealous. He rejoices in Jesus' success and wants his disciples to rejoice too. John reminds them: "You yourselves bear me witness that I said, 'I am not the Christ, but I have been sent ahead of that one.'" He illustrates this point in a way that all can understand: "Whoever has the bride is the bridegroom. But the friend of the bridegroom, when he stands and hears him, has a great deal of joy on account of the voice of the bridegroom. So my joy has been made complete."—John 3:28, 29.

John, like the friend of the bridegroom, rejoiced months earlier upon introducing his disciples to Jesus. Some of them followed Jesus and would in time be anointed with holy spirit. John also wants his present disciples to follow Jesus. In fact, John's purpose is to prepare the way for Christ's ministry. John explains: "That one must keep on increasing, but I must keep on decreasing."—John 3:30.

A different John, who had earlier begun to follow Jesus, later writes concerning Jesus' origin and key role in human salvation: "The one who comes from above is over all others. . . . The Father loves the Son and has given all things into his hand. The one who exercises faith in the Son has everlasting life; the one who disobeys the Son will not see life, but the wrath of God remains upon him." (John 3:31, 35, 36) What an important truth for people to know!

Not long after John the Baptist discusses that his role and work must decrease, he is arrested by King Herod. Herod has taken Herodias, the wife of his half brother Philip, and married her. When John publicly exposes his adulterous deed, Herod has him put in prison. Upon hearing about John's being arrested, Jesus leaves Judea with his disciples and 'withdraws into Galilee.'—Matthew 4:12; Mark 1:14.

◊ What is the meaning of the baptism done by John? the baptism done under Jesus' direction prior to his resurrection?

◊ How does John show that his disciples should not be jealous of Jesus' activity?

◊ Why is John put in prison?

TEACHING A SAMARITAN WOMAN

JOHN 4:3-43

On their way from Judea to Galilee, Jesus and his disciples travel north through the district of Samaria. They are tired from the journey. About noon they stop near the city of Sychar to rest by a well that Jacob likely dug or paid to have dug centuries earlier. Down to our time, such a well can be found near the modern-day city of Nablus.

While Jesus rests near the well, his disciples go into the nearby city to buy some food. In their absence, a Samaritan woman comes to draw water. Jesus says to her: "Give me a drink."—John 4:7.

Jews and Samaritans generally have no dealings with one another because of deep-seated prejudices. So the woman is astonished and asks: "How is it that you, despite being a Jew, ask me for a drink even though I am a Samaritan woman?" Jesus answers: "If you had known of the free gift of God and who it is who says to you, 'Give me a drink,' you would have asked him, and he would have given you living water." "Sir," she replies, "you do not even have a bucket for drawing water, and the well is deep. From what source, then, do you have this living water? You are not greater than our forefather Jacob, who gave us the well and who together with his sons and his cattle drank out of it, are you?" —John 4:9-12.

"Everyone drinking from this water will get thirsty again," Jesus declares. "Whoever drinks from the water that I will give him will never get thirsty at all, but the water that I will give him will become in him a spring of water bubbling up to impart everlasting life." (John 4:13, 14) Yes, though tired, Jesus is willing to share life-giving words of truth with the Samaritan woman.

The woman then says: "Sir, give me this water, so that I may neither thirst nor keep coming over to this place to draw water." Jesus now seems to change the subject and says to her: "Go, call your husband and come to this place." She replies: "I do not have a husband." But how shocked she must be at what Jesus knows when he tells her: "You are right in saying, 'I do not have a husband.' For you have had five husbands, and the man you now have is not your husband."—John 4:15-18.

The significance of his statement is clear to her, and she says in amazement: "Sir, I see that you are a prophet." She then shows that she has an interest in spiritual things. How? She continues: "Our forefathers [the Samaritans] worshipped on this mountain [Mt. Gerizim, which is close by], but you people [the Jews] say that in Jerusalem is the place where people must worship."—John 4:19, 20.

However, Jesus explains that the place of worship is not important. He says: "The hour is coming when neither on this mountain nor in Jerusalem will you worship the Father." Then he tells her: "The hour is coming, and it is now, when the true worshippers will worship the

◇ Why is the Samaritan woman surprised that Jesus speaks to her?

◇ What does Jesus teach the woman about living water and where to worship God?

◇ How does Jesus reveal to the Samaritan woman who he is, and what kind of worship does he encourage?

WHO WERE THE SAMARITANS? The region called Samaria lay between Judea to the south and Galilee to the north. After King Solomon's death, the ten northern tribes of Israel broke away from the tribes of Judah and Benjamin.

The people of those ten tribes turned to calf worship. So in 740 B.C.E., Jehovah allowed the Assyrians to overrun Samaria. The invaders carried off much of the population, replacing them with people from elsewhere in the Assyrian Empire. These worshippers of foreign gods intermarried with Israelites who remained in the land. Over time, people of this area developed a form of worship that incorporated some of the beliefs and practices set out in God's Law, such as circumcision. Still, their religious practices could not be called true worship.—2 Kings 17:9-33; Isaiah 9:9.

In Jesus' day, the Samaritans accepted the books of Moses but did not worship at the temple in Jerusalem. For years they had used a temple built on Mount Gerizim, not far from Sychar, and they continued worshipping on that mountain even after that temple was destroyed. The animosity between the Samaritans and the Jews was evident during Jesus' ministry.—John 8:48.

you are a S. + have a demon — *sins of Jeroboam*

Father with spirit and truth, for indeed, the Father is looking for ones like these to worship him."—John 4:21, 23, 24.

What the Father looks for in true worshippers is not where they worship but how they worship. The woman is impressed. "I know that Messiah is coming, who is called Christ," she says. "Whenever that one comes, he will declare all things to us openly."—John 4:25.

Then Jesus reveals an important truth: "I am he, the one speaking to you." (John 4:26) Think of that! Here is a woman who comes at midday to draw water. Yet, Jesus favors her in a wonderful way. He tells her pointedly what he has apparently not yet confessed openly to others —that he is the Messiah.

MANY SAMARITANS BELIEVE

Jesus' disciples return from Sychar with food. They find him at Jacob's well where they left him, but now he is talking with a Samaritan woman. As the disciples arrive, she leaves her water jar and heads for the city.

Once in Sychar, the woman recounts to the people the things that Jesus told her. With conviction, she tells them: "Come and see a man who told me everything I did." Then, perhaps to arouse curiosity, she asks: "Could this not perhaps be the Christ?" (John 4:29) That is a question on a vital subject—one that has been of interest since Moses' day. (Deuteronomy 18:18) It moves the people of the city to come out to see Jesus for themselves.

Meanwhile, the disciples urge Jesus to eat the food they have brought. But he replies: "I have food to eat that you do not know about." The disciples wonder at that, saying to one another: "No one brought him anything to eat, did he?" Jesus kindly explains with words that hold meaning for all of his followers: "My food is to do the will of him who sent me and to finish his work."—John 4:32-34.

The work Jesus is talking about is not that of the grain harvest, which is some four months away. Rather, Jesus is referring to a spiritual harvest, as he goes on to show: "Lift up your eyes and view the fields, that they are white for harvesting. Already the reaper is receiving wages and gathering fruit for everlasting life, so that the sower and the reaper may rejoice together."—John 4:35, 36.

Jesus may already realize the effect of his encounter with the Samaritan woman. Many from Sychar are putting faith in him on account of her testimony, for she is telling the people: "He told me all the things I did." (John 4:39) Therefore, when they come from Sychar to the well, they ask Jesus to stay and talk to them some more. Jesus accepts the invitation and remains in Samaria for two days.

As the Samaritans listen to Jesus, many more believe in him. They tell the woman: "We no longer believe just because of what you said; for we have heard for ourselves, and we know that this man really is the savior of the world." (John 4:42) Surely the Samaritan woman provides a fine example of how we can witness about Christ, arousing curiosity so that our listeners will welcome more information.

Recall that it is four months before the harvest—evidently the barley harvest, which in this region occurs in the spring. So it is now probably November or December. This means that following the Passover of 30 C.E., Jesus and his disciples have spent eight months or so in Judea, teaching and baptizing. They now head north to their home territory of Galilee. What awaits them there?

◇ What conclusion about Jesus does the Samaritan woman reach, and what does she then do?
◇ What have Jesus and his disciples been doing following the Passover of 30 C.E.?

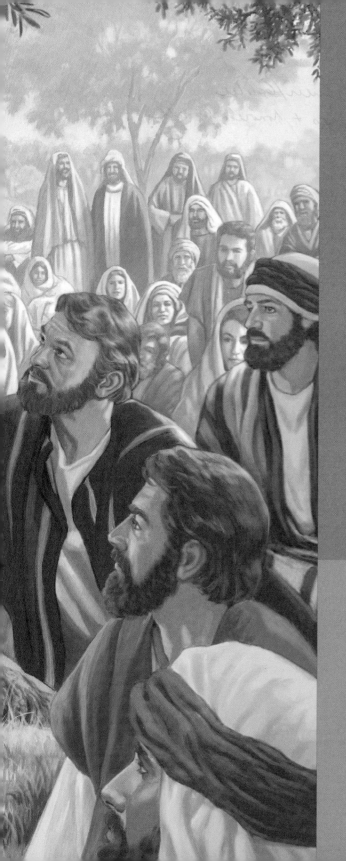

JESUS' GREAT MINISTRY IN GALILEE

'JESUS BEGAN
PREACHING:
"THE KINGDOM HAS
DRAWN NEAR."'
—MATTHEW 4:17

SECOND MIRACLE WHILE IN CANA

MARK 1:(14, 15) LUKE 4:(14, 15) JOHN 4:(43-54) *Kuen/Galilee*

post *Johns arrest* *Teach in synagogues + honored by all*

After some two days in Samaria, Jesus moves on to his home territory. He has had an extended preaching campaign in Judea, but he is not returning to Galilee to rest. Rather, he begins an even greater ministry in the land where he grew up. He might not expect to be well-received there, because as Jesus stated, "a prophet has no honor in his own homeland." (John 4:44) Instead of staying with him, his disciples return home to their families and their former occupations.

✓What message does Jesus begin preaching? It is this: "The Kingdom of God has drawn near. Repent, and have faith in the good news." (Mark 1:15) And what is the response? Actually, many Galileans receive Jesus well, giving him honor. This is not just because of his message. Some from Galilee were at the Passover in Jerusalem months before and saw the remarkable signs Jesus performed.—John 2:23.

✓Where does Jesus begin his great Galilean ministry? Apparently in Cana, where he had once turned water into wine at a wedding feast. While there on this second occasion, Jesus learns of a lad who is very sick, at the point of death. He is the son of a government official of Herod Antipas, the king who later has John the Baptist beheaded. This official hears that Jesus has come out of Judea to Cana. So the man travels from his home in Capernaum to Cana to find Jesus. The grief-stricken official urges him: "Lord, come down before my young child dies." —John 4:49.

✓ Jesus responds with a statement that must astonish the man: "Go your way; your son lives." (John 4:50) Herod's official believes Jesus and starts his return trip home. On the way he is met by his slaves, who have hurried to tell him good news. Yes, his son is alive and well! 'When did he get better?' he asks, trying to put the pieces together.

"The fever left him yesterday at the seventh hour," they answer.—John 4:52.

The official realizes that this is exactly when Jesus said, "Your son lives." After that, both this man, who is wealthy enough to have slaves, and his entire household become disciples of Christ.

Cana is thus a place where Jesus twice performs miracles, turning water into wine and later curing the young boy from a distance of some 16 miles. These, of course, are not his only miracles. But this cure is significant because it marks his return to Galilee. He is clearly a prophet approved by God, yet to what extent will this 'prophet be honored in his own homeland'?

That will become evident as Jesus heads home to Nazareth. What awaits him there?

◇ When Jesus returns to Galilee, what message does he begin to preach and what response does he encounter?

◇ Jesus performs what miracle while again in Cana, and how does it affect those involved?

◇ What is noteworthy about the way Jesus cured a lad in Capernaum?

Deut 6:4-9 ♥ Jehovah lord whole ♥ soul & st
Shema - Jewish declaration of faith

home of worship

There is no doubt a stir of excitement in Nazareth. Before he left to be baptized by John a little over a year ago, Jesus was a carpenter here. But now he is known as a man who performs powerful works. The local residents are eager to see him do some of these works among them.

Their anticipation rises as Jesus, according to his custom, goes to the local synagogue. The service there includes prayer and a reading from the books of Moses, as is done "in the synagogues on every sabbath." (Acts 15:21) Portions of the prophetic books are also read. When Jesus stands up to read, he likely recognizes many faces from his years of attending this synagogue. The scroll of the prophet Isaiah is handed to him. He finds the place where it tells of the One anointed by Jehovah's spirit, which passage is found today at Isaiah 61:1, 2.

dead sea scroll

Jesus reads about how this foretold One would preach a release to the captives, a recovery of sight to the blind, and the coming of Jehovah's acceptable year. Jesus hands the scroll to the attendant and sits down. All eyes are intently fixed upon him. Then he speaks, probably at some length, and his comments include the significant statement: "Today this scripture that you just heard is fulfilled."—Luke 4:21.

once again shows A.H. ✝

Isa 61:1 - divine name

The people marvel at "the gracious words coming out of his mouth," and they say to one another: "This is a son of Joseph, is it not?"

But realizing that they want to see him perform powerful works like the ones they had heard about, Jesus continues: "No doubt you will apply this saying to me, 'Physician, cure yourself. Do also here in your home territory the things we have heard were done in Capernaum.'" (Luke 4:22, 23) Jesus' former neighbors likely feel that healing should begin at home, for the benefit of his own people first. So they may think that Jesus has slighted them.

Realizing their thinking, Jesus mentions some events in Israel's history. There were many widows in Israel during the days of Elijah, he notes, but Elijah was not sent to any of them. Rather, he went to a non-Israelite widow in Zarephath, a town near Sidon, where Elijah performed a lifesaving miracle. (1 Kings 17:8-16) And in Elisha's day, there were many lepers in Israel, but the prophet cleansed only Naaman the Syrian.—2 Kings 5:1, 8-14.

How do these people from Jesus' hometown react to what they might see as unfavorable historical comparisons that expose their selfishness and lack of faith? Those in the synagogue get angry, rise up, and rush Jesus outside the city. They take him to the brow of the mountain upon which Nazareth is built, and they try to throw him over the edge. But Jesus escapes from their grasp and gets away safely. Jesus now heads down to Capernaum, on the northwest shore of the Sea of Galilee.

of Isa 17 parchment strips 24 ft in length find it.
54 columns ↳ roughly same ✝ scripture

◇ Why is there a stir of excitement in Nazareth, Jesus' hometown?

◇ How do the people react to Jesus' speech, but what makes them angry?

◇ What do the people of Nazareth attempt to do to Jesus?

Jehovah anointed

FOUR DISCIPLES WILL BE FISHERS OF MEN

MATTHEW 4:13-22 MARK 1:16-20 LUKE 5:1-11

Handwritten annotations:

for they were fishermen

astonished at catch they had taken

began publicly preaching – usually on open pub. ⌐ declaration vs a sermon to a group

proclaiming – Gk word = make proclamation as a public minister

SIMON (PETER) & ANDREW

After the people of Nazareth try to take Jesus' life, he moves to the city of Capernaum, near the Sea of Galilee, also called "the lake of Gennesaret." (Luke 5:1) This fulfills the prophecy in the book of Isaiah that people of Galilee dwelling by the sea would see a great light.—Isaiah 9:1, 2.

Yes, here in Galilee, Jesus continues to announce that "the Kingdom of the heavens has drawn near." (Matthew 4:17) Jesus finds four of his disciples. They had traveled with him earlier, but upon returning with Jesus from Judea, they resumed their fishing business. (John 1:35-42) Now, though, it is time to be with Jesus constantly so that he can train them to carry on the ministry after he is gone.

As Jesus walks along the seashore, he sees Simon Peter, his brother Andrew, and some of their companions tending to their nets. Jesus goes over, climbs into Peter's boat, and asks him to pull away from land. When they get out a little distance, Jesus sits down and begins teaching the crowds who had gathered on the shore truths about the Kingdom.

Afterward, Jesus says to Peter: "Pull out to where it is deep, and let down your nets for a catch." Peter responds: "Instructor, we toiled all night and caught nothing, but at your word I will lower the nets."—Luke 5:4, 5.

They lower the nets and catch such a great number of fish that the nets begin to rip! Urgently, the men motion to their partners in a boat nearby to come and help. Soon both boats are filled with so many fish that the heavily laden vessels begin to sink. Seeing this, Peter falls down before Jesus and says: "Depart from me, Lord, because I am a sinful man." Jesus responds: "Stop being afraid. From now on you will be catching men alive."—Luke 5:8, 10.

Jesus tells Peter and Andrew: "Come after me, and I will make you fishers of men." (Matthew 4:19) He includes two other fishermen, James and John, the sons of Zebedee. They too respond without hesitation. So these four abandon their fishing business and become the first full-time disciples of Jesus.

◇ What sort of men does Jesus call to be full-time disciples, and who are they?
◇ What miracle frightens Peter?
◇ The four disciples will now be doing what type of fishing?

JESUS PERFORMS GREAT WORKS IN CAPERNAUM

MATTHEW 8:14-17   MARK 1:21-34   LUKE 4:31-41

Jesus has invited four disciples—Peter, Andrew, James, and John—to be fishers of men. Now, on the Sabbath, they all go to a local synagogue in Capernaum. Jesus teaches in the synagogue, and again the people are astounded at his manner of teaching. He does so as one having authority and not as the scribes.

On this Sabbath a demonized man is present. Right there in the synagogue, the man shouts in a loud voice: "What have we to do with you, Jesus the Nazarene? Did you come to destroy us? I know exactly who you are, the Holy One of God!" Rebuking the demon who is controlling the man, Jesus says: "Be silent, and come out of him!"—Mark 1:24, 25.

At that, the wicked spirit throws the man to the ground in a convulsion and yells at the top of its voice. But the demon comes out of

DEMON POSSESSION When a demon or demons gained possession of someone, they could cause much suffering. (Matthew 17:14-18) But upon being freed of the demons, the person returned to a normal state of mind and body. Repeatedly, Jesus displayed his power to expel demons by means of God's holy spirit. —Luke 8:39; 11:20.

the man "without hurting him." (Luke 4:35) The people around him in the synagogue are simply astonished! "What is this?" they ask. "He authoritatively orders even the unclean spirits, and they obey him." (Mark 1:27) Understandably, the news about this impressive event spreads throughout all Galilee.

Leaving the synagogue, Jesus and his disciples go to the home of Simon, or Peter. There Peter's mother-in-law is very sick with a high fever. They beg Jesus to help her. So Jesus goes over, takes her by the hand, and raises her up. Right away she is cured and begins to wait on Jesus and the disciples there with him, perhaps preparing a meal for them.

About sunset, people from all over come to Peter's house with their sick ones. Soon it seems that the whole city is gathered at the door. Why? They are seeking a cure. In fact, 'all those who had people sick with various diseases bring them to him. And laying his hands on each one of them, he cures them.' (Luke 4:40) Yes, no matter what their diseases are, Jesus helps them, just as was foretold. (Isaiah 53:4) He even frees those who are demon-possessed. As the wicked spirits come out, they shout: "You are the Son of God." (Luke 4:41) But Jesus rebukes them and does not allow them to speak anymore. They know that Jesus is the Christ, and he does not want them to put on the appearance of serving the true God.

◇ What happens in a synagogue in Capernaum on the Sabbath?
◇ When leaving the synagogue, where does Jesus go, and what does he do there?
◇ How do the people of the city react to what Jesus has done there?

EXPANDING HIS MINISTRY IN GALILEE

MATTHEW 4:23-25 MARK 1:35-39 LUKE 4:42, 43

Jesus' day in Capernaum with his four disciples has been a busy one. In the evening, the people of Capernaum bring him their sick ones to be cured. Jesus has had little time for privacy.

Now, early the following morning while it is still dark, Jesus gets up and goes outside by himself. He finds a lonely place where he can pray to his Father in private. But Jesus' privacy is short-lived. When they realize that he is missing, "Simon and those with him" hunt for Jesus. Peter may be taking the lead because Jesus had been at his home.—Mark 1:36; Luke 4:38.

When they find Jesus, Peter says: "Everyone is looking for you." (Mark 1:37) Understandably, the people of Capernaum want Jesus to stay. They truly appreciate what he has done, so they try "to keep him from going away from them." (Luke 4:42) However, did Jesus come to earth primarily to perform such miraculous healings? And is he to limit his activities just to this locality? What does he say about this?

Jesus answers his disciples: "Let us go somewhere else, into the towns nearby, so that I may preach there also, for this is why I have come." In fact, Jesus even tells the people who want him to stay: "I must also declare the good news of the Kingdom of God to other cities, because for this I was sent."—Mark 1:38; Luke 4:43.

Yes, a major reason why Jesus has come to earth is to preach about God's Kingdom. That Kingdom will sanctify his Father's name and permanently solve all human ills. Jesus gives evidence that he is sent by God by performing miraculous healings. In a similar way, centuries earlier, Moses performed outstanding works to establish his credentials as one sent by God. —Exodus 4:1-9, 30, 31.

So Jesus leaves Capernaum to preach in other cities, and his four disciples go with him. These four are Peter and his brother Andrew as well as John and his brother James. The week before, they had been invited to be Jesus' first traveling coworkers.

Jesus' preaching tour of Galilee with these four disciples is a wonderful success! In fact, word about Jesus reaches far and wide. "The report about him spread throughout all Syria," into the region of the ten cities called the Decapolis, and over to the other side of the Jordan River. (Matthew 4:24, 25) Great crowds from those areas, as well as from Judea, follow Jesus and his disciples. Many bring to him those seeking a cure. Jesus does not disappoint them—he cures the sick and expels wicked spirits from those who are demon-possessed.

◇ What happens early in the morning after Jesus' busy day in Capernaum?

◇ Why was Jesus sent to earth, and what purpose do his miracles serve?

◇ Who go with Jesus on his preaching tour of Galilee, and what is the response to his activities?

As Jesus and his four disciples go preaching in the "synagogues throughout the whole of Galilee," news about the wonderful things Jesus is doing spreads widely. (Mark 1:39) Word of his deeds reaches one city where there is a man sick with leprosy. The physician Luke describes him as being "full of leprosy." (Luke 5:12) In its advanced stages, this dreadful disease slowly disfigures various parts of the body.

So this leper is in a grievous condition and is required to live away from others. Moreover, he is supposed to call out "Unclean, unclean!" when people are nearby and thus protect them from coming too close and risking infection. (Leviticus 13:45, 46) But what does this leper now do? He approaches Jesus and falls upon his face, begging: "Lord, if you just want to, you can make me clean."—Matthew 8:2.

What faith the man has in Jesus! And how pitiful his disease must make him appear! How will Jesus respond? What would you have done if you were there? Moved with compassion, Jesus stretches out his hand and actually touches the man. Jesus says to him: "I want to! Be made clean." (Matthew 8:3) Hard as it might be for some to believe, the leprosy immediately vanishes from the sick man.

How would you like to have a king who is as compassionate and capable as Jesus? The way he treats this leper assures us that when Jesus is King over the whole earth, this Bible prophecy will be fulfilled: "He will have pity on the lowly and the poor, and the lives of the poor he will save." (Psalm 72:13) Yes, Jesus will then fulfill his heart's desire to help *all* afflicted ones.

Recall that even prior to the healing of this leper, Jesus' ministry has been creating great excitement among the people. Now people will hear about this wonderful thing that he has done. Jesus, though, does not want people to put faith in him merely on the basis of oral reports. He knows the prophecy that says he would "not make his voice heard in the street," that is, in some sensational way. (Isaiah 42:1, 2) Accordingly, Jesus gives the healed leper the order: "See that you tell no one, but go, show yourself to the priest, and offer the gift that Moses appointed."—Matthew 8:4.

As you can imagine, however, the man is so happy over being healed that he cannot keep to himself what has just happened. He goes off and spreads the news everywhere. This rouses increased interest and curiosity among the people. It gets to the point that Jesus cannot openly go into a city, so for a while he stays in lonely places where nobody lives. Still, people from all over come to be taught by him and to be cured.

◇ What effect can leprosy have on a person, and what was a leper required to do?

◇ How does a leper appeal to Jesus, and what can we conclude from Jesus' response?

◇ How does the healed man react to what Jesus did, and with what effect on others?

People from far and wide have now heard of Jesus. Many travel even to out-of-the-way places to hear him teach and to see his powerful works. However, after some days he returns to Capernaum, his center of activity. News of his return spreads quickly through this city alongside the Sea of Galilee. As a result, many come to the house where he is. Some are Pharisees and teachers of the Law who have come from all over Galilee and Judea, including Jerusalem.

'So many gather that there is no more room, not even around the door, and he begins to speak the word to them.' (Mark 2:2) The stage is now set for something truly remarkable. It is an event that can help us to appreciate that Jesus has the power to remove the cause of human suffering and restore health to all whom he chooses.

While Jesus is teaching in the crowded room, four men bring a paralyzed man on a stretcher. They want Jesus to heal their friend. Yet, because of the crowd, they cannot "bring him right to Jesus." (Mark 2:4) Imagine how disappointing that is. They climb up onto the flat roof of the house and make an opening through the tiles. Then they lower the stretcher holding the paralyzed man down into the house.

Does Jesus get angry at the interruption? No, indeed! He is deeply impressed by their faith and says to the paralyzed man: "Your sins are forgiven." (Matthew 9:2) But can Jesus actually forgive sins? The scribes and the Pharisees take issue with this, reasoning: "Why is this man talking this way? He is blaspheming. Who can forgive sins except one, God?"—Mark 2:7.

Knowing their thoughts, Jesus says to them: "Why are you reasoning these things in your hearts? Which is easier, to say to the paralytic, 'Your sins are forgiven,' or to say, 'Get up and pick up your stretcher and walk'?" (Mark 2:8, 9) Yes, based on the sacrifice that Jesus will in time offer, he can forgive the man's sins.

Then, Jesus shows the crowd, including his critics, that he has authority to forgive sins on earth. He turns to the paralytic and gives the command: "I say to you, Get up, pick up your stretcher, and go to your home." And the man immediately does that, walking out carrying his stretcher before the eyes of all those present. The people are amazed! They glorify God and exclaim: "We have never seen anything like this"!—Mark 2:11, 12.

It is worthy of note that Jesus mentions sins in connection with sickness and that forgiveness of sins can be linked to physical health. The Bible teaches that our first parent, Adam, sinned and that all of us have inherited the consequences of sin, namely, sickness and death. But under the rule of God's Kingdom, Jesus will forgive the sins of all who love and serve God. Then sickness will be removed forever.—Romans 5:12, 18, 19.

◊ What leads Jesus to heal a paralyzed man in Capernaum?
◊ How does the man reach Jesus?
◊ What can we learn from this event about the link between sin and sickness, and what hope does this offer us?

MATTHEW IS CALLED

MATTHEW 9:9-13 MARK 2:13-17 LUKE 5:27-32

For a short time after healing the paralytic, Jesus remains in the area of Capernaum by the Sea of Galilee. Again crowds come to him, and he begins teaching them. As he walks on, he sees Matthew, who is also called Levi, sitting at the tax office. Jesus extends a wonderful invitation to him: "Be my follower."—Matthew 9:9.

Likely, Matthew is already somewhat familiar with Jesus' teachings and the works he has performed in the area, as were Peter, Andrew, James, and John. Like them, Matthew responds immediately. Matthew describes this in his Gospel, saying: "At that he [Matthew himself] rose up and followed" Jesus. (Matthew 9:9) Hence, Matthew leaves his responsibilities as a tax collector behind and becomes a disciple of Jesus.

At some later point, perhaps to express appreciation for this special call from Jesus, Matthew holds a large feast at his house. Who are invited in addition to Jesus and his disciples? Well, a number of Matthew's former associates, other tax collectors, are present. They collect taxes for the hated Roman authorities, including taxes on ships coming into the harbor, taxes on caravan traffic on the main roads, and duties on imported goods. How do the Jews in general view those tax collectors? The people despise them because they often dishonestly exact more money than the regular tax rate. There are also 'sinners' at the feast, individuals who have a reputation for practicing wrongdoing.—Luke 7:37-39.

Observing Jesus at the feast with such people, the self-righteous Pharisees who are present ask his disciples: "Why does your teacher eat with tax collectors and sinners?" (Matthew 9:11) Overhearing them, Jesus answers: "Healthy people do not need a physician, but those who are ill do. Go, then, and learn what this means: 'I want mercy, and not sacrifice.' For I came to call, not righteous people, but sinners." (Matthew 9:12, 13; Hosea 6:6) The Pharisees are not sincere when they refer to Jesus as "teacher," but they can learn something from him about what is right.

Apparently, Matthew has invited tax collectors and sinners to his home so that they can listen to Jesus and receive spiritual healing, "for there were many of them who were following him." (Mark 2:15) Jesus wants to help them to attain a healthy relationship with God. Unlike the self-righteous Pharisees, Jesus does not despise such ones. He is moved with compassion and mercy; he can serve as a spiritual physician to all who are spiritually ill.

Jesus shows mercy toward tax collectors and sinners, not to condone their sins, but to show tender feelings similar to those that he displayed toward the physically ill. Recall, for example, when he compassionately touched the leper, saying: "I want to! Be made clean." (Matthew 8:3) Should we not cultivate the same merciful view and help those in need, especially by assisting them in a spiritual way?

◇ What is Matthew doing when Jesus sees him?
◇ Why do other Jews despise tax collectors?
◇ Why does Jesus associate with sinners?

WHY DO JESUS' DISCIPLES NOT FAST?

MATTHEW 9:14-17   MARK 2:18-22   LUKE 5:33-39

John the Baptist has been in prison since some time after Jesus attended the Passover of 30 C.E. John wanted his disciples to become followers of Jesus, but not all of them have done so in the months following John's imprisonment.

Now, as the Passover of 31 C.E. approaches, some of John's disciples come to Jesus and ask: "Why do we and the Pharisees practice fasting but your disciples do not fast?" (Matthew 9:14) The Pharisees practice fasting as a religious ritual. Later, Jesus even uses an illustration in which one Pharisee self-righteously prays: "O God, I thank you that I am not like everyone else . . . I fast twice a week." (Luke 18: 11, 12) John's disciples may similarly have been fasting as a custom. Or they may have been

ILLUSTRATIONS ABOUT FASTING Jesus used an illustration that many listeners could easily picture—sewing. If someone sewed a piece of new, unshrunk cloth onto a used garment or old cloth, what would happen? When the garment is washed, the new patch would shrink some and pull away from the old cloth, ripping it.

Similarly, wine was sometimes stored in bottles made from animal skins. Over time, the skin would harden and lose its elasticity. To put new wine into such a bottle was risky. New wine might continue to ferment, creating pressure. That could burst the old, hardened skin.

fasting to mourn John's imprisonment. Observers also wonder why Jesus' disciples do not fast, perhaps joining in an expression of grief over what has been done to John.

Jesus answers using an example: "The friends of the bridegroom have no reason to mourn as long as the bridegroom is with them, do they? But days will come when the bridegroom will be taken away from them, and then they will fast."—Matthew 9:15.

John himself spoke of Jesus as a bridegroom. (John 3:28, 29) Accordingly, while Jesus is present, Jesus' disciples do not fast. Later, when Jesus dies, his disciples will mourn and have no desire to eat. What a change, though, when he is resurrected! Then they will have no further cause for mournful fasting.

Next, Jesus gives these two illustrations: "Nobody sews a patch of unshrunk cloth on an old outer garment, for the new piece pulls away from the garment and the tear becomes worse. Nor do people put new wine into old wineskins. If they do, then the wineskins burst and the wine spills out and the wineskins are ruined. But people put new wine into new wineskins." (Matthew 9:16, 17) What is Jesus' point?

Jesus is helping the disciples of John the Baptist to appreciate that no one should expect Jesus' followers to conform to the old practices of Judaism, such as ritual fasting. He did not come to patch up and prolong an old, worn-out way of worship, a whole system of worship that was ready to be discarded. The worship that Jesus is encouraging is not one that conforms to the Judaism of the day with its traditions of men. No, he is not trying to put a new patch on an old garment or new wine into a stiff, old wineskin.

◇ Who in Jesus' day practice fasting, and why?

◇ Why do Jesus' disciples not fast while he is with them, but what might later be a cause for fasting?

◇ What is the meaning of the illustrations that Jesus relates about a new patch and new wine?

CAN ONE DO GOOD WORKS ON THE SABBATH?

JOHN 5:1-16

not to note the heavenly urging to do such a miracle

Jesus has accomplished a lot during his great ministry in Galilee. However, in saying, "I must also declare the good news of the Kingdom of God to other cities," Jesus has in mind more than just Galilee. Thus, he goes "preaching in the synagogues of Judea." (Luke 4:43, 44) This is logical because it is now spring and a festival in Jerusalem is approaching.

Compared with what we read of Jesus' Galilean ministry, we find little in the Gospels about his activity in Judea. Even if the general reaction in Judea is apathetic, it does not stop Jesus from preaching actively and doing good works wherever he is.

Soon Jesus is heading to Judea's principal city, Jerusalem, for the Passover of 31 C.E. In the busy area near the Sheep Gate, there is a large colonnaded pool called Bethzatha. Many sick, blind, and lame come to this pool. Why? Because it is commonly believed that people can be healed by getting into the pool when the water is agitated.

It is now the Sabbath, and Jesus sees a man at this pool who has been sick for 38 years. Jesus asks: "Do you want to get well?" The man answers: "Sir, I do not have anyone to put me into the pool when the water is stirred up, but while I am on my way, another steps down ahead of me."—John 5:6, 7.

Jesus says something that must surprise the man and anyone else who hears it: "Get up! Pick up your mat and walk." (John 5:8) And that is exactly what he does. Immediately healed, the man picks up his mat and begins to walk!

Rather than rejoice over the wonderful thing that has happened, the Jews see the man and say judgmentally: "It is the Sabbath, and it is not lawful for you to carry the mat." The man answers them: "The same one who made me well said to me, 'Pick up your mat and walk.'" (John 5:10, 11) Those Jews are critical of someone who is healing on the Sabbath.

"Who is the man who told you, 'Pick it up and walk'?" they want to know. Why do they ask the man that? Because Jesus has "slipped away into the crowd," and the healed man does not know Jesus' name. (John 5:12, 13) But this man is to have another encounter with Jesus. Later, in the temple, the man meets Jesus and learns the identity of the one who healed him at the pool.

The man who was healed finds the Jews who had asked him about his being made well. He tells them that it was Jesus. On learning this, the Jews go to Jesus. Do they go to learn by what means Jesus is able to do such wonderful things? No. It is, rather, to find fault with Jesus for doing good things on the Sabbath. And they even begin persecuting him!

◇ Why does Jesus head into Judea, and what is he still doing?

◇ For what reason do many go to the pool that is called Bethzatha?

◇ What miracle does Jesus perform at the pool, and how do some of the Jews react to what happened?

JESUS' RELATIONSHIP WITH HIS FATHER

JOHN 5:17-47

When some Jews accuse Jesus of breaking the Sabbath by healing a man, Jesus replies: "My Father has kept working until now, and I keep working."—John 5:17.

No, what Jesus is doing is not forbidden by God's law regarding the Sabbath. His work of preaching and healing is in imitation of God's good works. So Jesus keeps on doing good every day. His reply to his accusers, however, makes them even angrier than they were before, and they seek to kill Jesus. Why this reaction?

In addition to their having the mistaken view that Jesus is breaking the Sabbath by healing people, they take great offense at his saying that he is God's Son. They consider it blasphemy for him to view God as his Father, as if Jesus' saying that Jehovah is his Father amounts to making himself equal to God. However, Jesus is unafraid and answers them further regarding his special relationship with God. "The Father has affection for the Son," he says, "and shows him all the things he himself does."—John 5:20.

The Father is the Life-Giver, and he has shown this in the past by empowering men to resurrect individuals. Jesus continues: "Just as the Father raises the dead up and makes them alive, so the Son also makes alive whomever he wants to." (John 5:21) What a meaningful statement, giving hope for the future! Even now, the Son is raising the dead in a spiritual sense. Hence, Jesus says: "Whoever hears my word and believes the One who sent me has everlasting life, and he does not come into judgment but has passed over from death to life."—John 5:24.

There is no record that Jesus has as yet raised anyone who was actually dead back to life, but he tells his accusers that such literal resurrections will occur. "The hour is coming," he says, "in which all those in the memorial tombs will hear his voice and come out." —John 5:28, 29.

As extraordinary as Jesus' role is, he makes it clear that he is subordinate to God, stating: "I cannot do a single thing of my own initiative. . . . I seek, not my own will, but the will of him who sent me." (John 5:30) However, Jesus describes his own vital role in God's purpose, which he has not up to this time done in such a public way. But those accusing Jesus have more than his witness about these things. "You have sent men to John [the Baptist]," Jesus reminds them, "and he has borne witness to the truth."—John 5:33.

Jesus' accusers might well have heard that about two years earlier, John had told Jewish religious leaders about the One coming after him—who was termed "the Prophet" and "the Christ." (John 1:20-25) Reminding his accusers of their once high regard for the now imprisoned John, Jesus says: "For a short time you were willing to rejoice greatly in his light." (John 5:35) Yet he provides an even greater witness than John the Baptist.

"These works that I am doing [including the healing that he had just performed] bear witness that the Father sent me." Besides that, Jesus continues: "The Father who sent me has himself borne witness about me." (John 5:36, 37) For example, God bore witness about Jesus at his baptism.—Matthew 3:17.

Really, those accusing Jesus have no excuse for rejecting him. The Scriptures that they claim to be searching testify about him. "If you believed Moses, you would believe me," Jesus concludes, "for he wrote about me. But if you do not believe his writings, how will you believe what I say?"—John 5:46, 47.

◇ Why is it not a violation of the Sabbath for Jesus to do good works on that day?

◇ How does Jesus describe his vital role in God's purpose?

◇ What witnesses provide proof that Jesus is God's Son?

PLUCKING GRAIN ON THE SABBATH

MATTHEW 12:1-8   MARK 2:23-28   LUKE 6:1-5

Jesus and his disciples now travel northward toward Galilee. It is springtime, and in the fields there is grain on the stalks. Being hungry, the disciples pluck some heads of grain and eat. But the day is a Sabbath, and the Pharisees observe what they are doing.

Recall that recently certain Jews in Jerusalem wanted to kill Jesus, accusing him of violating the Sabbath. Now the Pharisees bring an accusation based on the disciples' actions. "Look! Your disciples are doing what is not lawful to do on the Sabbath."—Matthew 12:2.

The Pharisees claim that picking grain and rubbing it in the hands to eat is harvesting and threshing. (Exodus 34:21) Their strict interpretation of what constitutes work makes the Sabbath burdensome, whereas it was originally meant to be a joyous, spiritually upbuilding day. Jesus counters their wrong view with examples to show that Jehovah God never meant for His Sabbath law to be applied that way.

One example Jesus gives is that of David and his men. When they were hungry, they stopped at the tabernacle and ate the loaves of presentation. Those loaves, which had already been removed from before Jehovah and replaced by fresh ones, were ordinarily reserved for the priests to eat. Yet, under the circumstances, David and his men were not condemned for eating them.—Leviticus 24:5-9; 1 Samuel 21:1-6.

As a second example, Jesus says: "Have you not read in the Law that on the Sabbaths the

priests in the temple violate the Sabbath and continue guiltless?" What he means is that even on the Sabbath, the priests slaughter animals for sacrifice and do other work at the temple. "But I tell you," Jesus says, "that something greater than the temple is here."—Matthew 12: 5, 6; Numbers 28:9.

Jesus again draws on the Scriptures to make his point: "If you had understood what this means, 'I want mercy and not sacrifice,' you would not have condemned the guiltless ones." He concludes: "For the Son of man is Lord of the Sabbath." Jesus is referring to his coming peaceful Kingdom rule of a thousand years. —Matthew 12:7, 8; Hosea 6:6.

Humankind has long been suffering laborious enslavement by Satan, with violence and war abounding. What a contrast it will be under the great Sabbath rule of Christ, who will provide the time of rest we long for and need!

◇ The Pharisees make what charge against Jesus' disciples, and why?

◇ How does Jesus correct the Pharisees' view?

◇ In what way is Jesus "Lord of the Sabbath"?

WHAT IS LAWFUL ON THE SABBATH?

senseless rage

MATTHEW 12:9-14   MARK 3:1-6   LUKE 6:6-11

men in pit ∴

On another Sabbath, Jesus visits a synagogue, likely in Galilee. There he finds a man whose right hand is withered. (Luke 6:6) The scribes and the Pharisees are watching Jesus closely. Why? They reveal what their real intent is when they ask: "Is it lawful to cure on the Sabbath?" —Matthew 12:10. *or paralyzed*

The Jewish religious leaders believe that healing is lawful on the Sabbath *only* if life is in danger. Thus, for example, on the Sabbath it is unlawful to set a bone or bandage a sprain, *to do a fine deed* conditions that are not life threatening. Clearly the scribes and the Pharisees are not questioning Jesus because they feel genuine concern for this poor man's suffering. They are trying to find a pretext for condemning Jesus.

Jesus, however, knows their twisted reasoning. He realizes that they have adopted an extreme, unscriptural view of what constitutes a violation of the prohibition against doing work on the Sabbath. (Exodus 20:8-10) He has already faced such misplaced criticism of his good works. Now Jesus sets the stage for a dramatic confrontation by telling the man with the withered hand: "Get up and come to the center." —Mark 3:3.

Turning to the scribes and the Pharisees, Jesus says: "If you have one sheep and that sheep falls into a pit on the Sabbath, is there a man among you who will not grab hold of it and lift it out?" (Matthew 12:11) A sheep represents a financial investment, so they would not leave it in the pit until the next day; it might die in the meantime and thus cause them loss. Besides, the Scriptures say: "The righteous one takes care of his domestic animals."—Proverbs 12:10.

Drawing a reasonable parallel, Jesus contin-

ues: "How much more valuable is a man than a sheep! So it is lawful to do a fine thing on the Sabbath." (Matthew 12:12) Accordingly, Jesus would not be violating the Sabbath by healing the man. The religious leaders are unable to refute such logical, compassionate reasoning. They just remain silent.

With indignation, as well as grief at their misguided thinking, Jesus looks around. Then he says to the man: "Stretch out your hand." (Matthew 12:13) As the man stretches out his withered hand, it is restored. That is a cause for joy for the man, but how does it affect those trying to trap Jesus?

Instead of being happy that the man's hand is restored, the Pharisees go out and immediately conspire "with the party followers of Herod against [Jesus], in order to kill him." (Mark 3:6) This political party evidently includes members of the religious group called the Sadducees. Ordinarily, the Sadducees and the Pharisees are opposed to each other, but now they are solidly united in their opposition to Jesus.

◇ What is the setting for a confrontation between Jesus and Jewish religious leaders?

◇ The Jewish religious leaders have what wrong view of the Sabbath law?

◇ How does Jesus wisely refute wrong views about the Sabbath?

FULFILLING ISAIAH'S PROPHECY

MATTHEW 12:15-21   MARK 3:7-12

Upon learning that the Pharisees and the party followers of Herod plan to kill him, Jesus and his disciples withdraw to the Sea of Galilee. Great crowds flock to him from all over—from Galilee, the coastal cities of Tyre and Sidon, the eastern side of the Jordan River, Jerusalem, and Idumea farther south. Jesus cures many. As a result, those with serious diseases press forward. Not waiting for him to touch them, they eagerly reach out to touch him.—Mark 3: 9, 10.

The crowds are so large that Jesus tells his disciples to get a small boat ready for him so that he can pull away from shore and keep the crowds from pressing in on him. Also, he can teach them from the boat or move to another area along the shore to help more people.

The disciple Matthew notes that Jesus' activity fulfills "what was spoken through Isaiah the prophet." (Matthew 12:17) What prophecy is Jesus here fulfilling?

"Look! My servant whom I chose, my beloved, whom I have approved! I will put my spirit upon him, and what justice is he will make clear to the nations. He will not quarrel nor cry aloud, nor will anyone hear his voice in the main streets. No bruised reed will he crush, and no smoldering wick will he extinguish, until he brings justice with success. Indeed, in his name nations will hope."—Matthew 12:18-21; Isaiah 42:1-4.

Jesus, of course, is the beloved servant whom God approves. Jesus makes clear what is true justice, which is being obscured by false religious traditions. Unjustly applying God's Law in their own way, the Pharisees will not even come to a sick person's aid on the Sabbath! Making evident God's justice and showing that God's spirit is upon him, Jesus relieves people of the burden of unjust traditions. For that the religious leaders want to kill him. How deplorable!

What does it mean that "he will not quarrel nor cry aloud, nor will anyone hear his voice in the main streets"? When curing people, Jesus does not allow them—or the demons—"to make him known." (Mark 3:12) He does not want people to learn about him through noisy advertising in the streets or through distorted reports that are excitedly passed from mouth to mouth.

Also, Jesus carries his comforting message

X ref Isa 11:10 they will of Jesse will stand up for the peoples

to those who are figuratively like a bruised reed, bent over and knocked down. They are like a smoldering wick, whose last spark of life has nearly flickered out. Jesus does not crush the bruised reed or quench the flickering, smoking flax. Rather, with tenderness and love, he skillfully lifts up the meek. Truly, Jesus is the one in whom the nations can hope!

◇ How does Jesus make justice clear without quarreling or crying aloud in the main streets?
◇ Who are like bruised reeds and smoldering wicks, and how does Jesus treat them?

JESUS CHOOSES TWELVE APOSTLES

MARK 3:13-19   LUKE 6:12-16

[handwritten: one sent forth / most used in regard to those / disciples Jesus personally chose / selected as a group / of 12 appointed repre- / sentatives]

It has been about a year and a half since John the Baptist introduced Jesus as the Lamb of God. As Jesus began his public ministry, a number of sincere men became his disciples, such as Andrew, Simon Peter, John, perhaps James (John's brother), Philip, and Bartholomew (also called Nathanael). In time, many others joined in following Christ.—John 1:45-47. *[handwritten: ? good man Nath.]*

Now Jesus is ready to select his apostles. These will be his close associates and will receive special training. But before selecting them, Jesus goes out to a mountain, perhaps

one near the Sea of Galilee not far from Capernaum. He spends a whole night in prayer, likely asking for wisdom and God's blessing. The next day he calls his disciples to him and chooses 12 of his disciples as apostles.

Jesus selects the six named at the outset, as well as Matthew, whom Jesus called from the tax office. The other five chosen are Judas (also called Thaddaeus and "the son of James"),

Simon the Cananaean, Thomas, James the son of Alphaeus, and Judas Iscariot.—Matthew 10: 2-4; Luke 6:16. *[handwritten: who turned traitor]*

By now these 12 have traveled with Jesus, and he knows them well. A number of them are his relatives. The brothers James and John are evidently Jesus' first cousins. And if, as some think, Alphaeus was the brother of Joseph, Jesus' adoptive father, then Alphaeus' son, the apostle James, would be a cousin of Jesus.

Jesus, of course, has no problem remembering his apostles' names. But can you remember them? One help is to remember that there are two named Simon, two named James, and two named Judas. Simon (Peter) has a brother Andrew, and James (son of Zebedee) has a brother John. That is a key to remembering the names of eight apostles. The other four include a tax collector (Matthew), one who later doubts (Thomas), one called from under a tree (Nathanael), and Nathanael's friend (Philip).

Eleven of the apostles are from Galilee, Jesus' home territory. Nathanael is from Cana. Philip, Peter, and Andrew are originally from Bethsaida. Peter and Andrew in time move to Capernaum, where Matthew apparently lived. James and John also live in or close to Capernaum, and they had a fishing business nearby. Judas Iscariot, who later betrays Jesus, seems to be the only apostle from Judea.

◇ What serious decision does Jesus make after spending all night in prayer?

◇ Who are Jesus' apostles, and how may you be able to remember their names?

1 Jesus must be tired after spending the whole night in prayer and then choosing 12 disciples to be apostles. It is now day, but he still has the strength and desire to help people. He does so on a mountainside in Galilee, perhaps not far from his center of activity in Capernaum.

2 Crowds have come to him from distant locations. Some are from down south, from Jerusalem and places in Judea. Others are from the coastal cities of Tyre and Sidon to the northwest. Why have they come looking for Jesus? "To hear him and to be healed of their sicknesses." And that is just what happens—Jesus is "healing them all." Think of that! *All* the sick ones are healed. Jesus also ministers to "those troubled with unclean spirits," people who are afflicted by the wicked angels of Satan.—Luke 6:17-19.

3 Jesus next finds a level place on the mountainside and the crowd gathers around. His disciples, especially the 12 apostles, are probably nearest to him. All are eager to hear from this teacher who is able to perform such powerful works. Jesus delivers a sermon that clearly benefits his listeners. Since then, countless others have also benefited from it. We can too because of its depth of spiritual content presented with simplicity and clarity. Jesus draws on ordinary experiences and things familiar to people. This makes his ideas understandable to all who are seeking a better life in God's way. What key aspects of Jesus' sermon make it so valuable?

WHO ARE TRULY HAPPY?

4 Everyone wants to be happy. Knowing this, Jesus begins by describing those who are truly happy. Imagine how this captures the attention of his listeners. But some things must puzzle them.

5 He says: "Happy are those conscious of their spiritual need, since the Kingdom of the heavens belongs to them. Happy are those who mourn, since they will be comforted. . . . Happy are those hungering and thirsting for righteousness, since they will be filled. . . . Happy are those who have been persecuted for righteousness' sake, since the Kingdom of the heavens belongs to them. Happy are you when people reproach you and persecute you . . . for my sake. Rejoice and be overjoyed."—Matthew 5:3-12.

6 What does Jesus mean by saying "happy"? He is not referring to being jovial or mirthful, as when one is having a good time. Genuine happiness is deeper. It involves real contentment, a sense of satisfaction and fulfillment in life.

7 Jesus says that people who recognize their spiritual need, who are saddened by their sinful condition, and who come to know and serve God are the truly happy ones. Even if they are hated or persecuted for doing God's will, they are happy because they know that they are pleasing him and that he will reward them with everlasting life.

8 Many people, though, think that being prosperous and pursuing pleasures are what makes one happy. Jesus says otherwise. Drawing a

---

◇ Where does Jesus give his most memorable sermon, and who are present for it?

◇ What makes Jesus' sermon so valuable?

◇ Who are truly happy, and why?

contrast that must make many of his listeners think, he says: "Woe to you who are rich, for you are having your consolation in full. Woe to you who are filled up now, for you will go hungry. Woe, you who are laughing now, for you will mourn and weep. Woe whenever all men speak well of you, for this is what their forefathers did to the false prophets."—Luke 6:24-26.

9 Why do having riches, laughing in delight, and enjoying praise from others bring woe? Because when someone has and cherishes these

things, serving God may be neglected at the cost of true happiness. Jesus is not saying that simply being poor or hungry makes one happy. However, it is often the disadvantaged person who responds to Jesus' teachings and who gains the blessing of true happiness.

10 With his disciples in mind, Jesus says: "You are the salt of the earth." (Matthew 5:13) Of course, they are not literal salt. Rather, salt is a preservative. A large amount of it is kept near the altar at God's temple and is used to salt offerings. It also represents freedom from corruption or decay. (Leviticus 2:13; Ezekiel 43:23, 24) Jesus' disciples are "the salt of the earth" in that their influence on people has a preserving effect, helping them to avoid spiritual and moral decay. Yes, their message can preserve the lives of all who respond to it.

11 Jesus also tells the disciples: "You are the

light of the world." A lamp is not put under a basket but is set on a lampstand, where it can shed light. So Jesus urges: "Let your light shine before men, so that they may see your fine works and give glory to your Father who is in the heavens."—Matthew 5:14-16.

A HIGH STANDARD FOR HIS FOLLOWERS

12 The Jewish religious leaders view Jesus as a transgressor of God's Law and recently conspired to kill him. So Jesus says openly: "Do not think I came to destroy the Law or the Prophets. I came, not to destroy, but to fulfill."—Matthew 5:17.

13 Yes, Jesus has the highest regard for God's Law and urges others to have the same. In

fact, he says: "Whoever, therefore, breaks one of these least commandments and teaches others to do so will be called least in relation to the Kingdom of the heavens." He means that such a person will not get into the Kingdom at all. "But," he continues, "whoever does them and teaches them will be called great in relation to the Kingdom of the heavens."—Matthew 5:19.

14 Jesus condemns even attitudes that contribute to a person's breaking God's Law. After noting that the Law says "You must not murder," Jesus adds: "Everyone who continues wrathful with his brother will be accountable to the court of justice." (Matthew 5:21, 22) To continue wrathful with an associate is serious, perhaps even leading to murder. Hence, Jesus explains the extent to which one should go to achieve peace: "If, then, you are bringing your gift to the altar and there you remember that your brother has something against you, leave your gift there in front of the altar, and go away. First make your peace with your brother, and then come back and offer your gift."—Matthew 5:23, 24.

15 Another commandment of the Law is against adultery. Jesus comments: "You heard that it was said: 'You must not commit adultery.' But I say to you that everyone who keeps on looking at a woman so as to have a passion for her has already committed adultery with her in his heart." (Matthew 5:27, 28) Jesus is not speaking merely about a passing immoral thought; rather, he is stressing the seriousness of the matter when one "keeps on looking." Continued looking often arouses passionate desire. Then, if an opportunity arises, it can result in adultery. How can a person prevent this from happening? Extreme measures may be necessary. Jesus

says: "If, now, your right eye is making you stumble, tear it out and throw it away from you. . . . If your right hand is making you stumble, cut it off and throw it away from you." —Matthew 5:29, 30.

16 To save their life, some people have willingly sacrificed a severely diseased limb. Understandably, Jesus says that it is more important to 'throw away' anything, even something as precious as an eye or a hand, to avoid immoral thinking and its resulting actions. "Better for you to lose one of your members," Jesus explains, "than for your whole body to land in Gehenna" (a burning rubbish heap outside Jerusalem's walls), which implies permanent destruction.

17 Jesus also offers counsel on dealing with people who cause injury and offense. "Do not resist the one who is wicked," he says, "but whoever slaps you on your right cheek, turn the other also to him." (Matthew 5:39) That is not to say that a person cannot defend himself or his

◇ In contrast to those who are truly happy, who have woe, and why?

◇ How are Jesus' disciples "the salt of the earth" and "the light of the world"?

◇ Does Jesus show high regard for God's Law? Explain.

◇ How does Jesus provide help to root out the causes of murder and adultery?

family if attacked. Jesus mentions a slap, which is not given to hurt severely or to kill another; rather, it is an insult. He is saying that if someone tries to provoke a fight or an argument, either by giving an openhanded slap or by using insulting words, do not retaliate.

18 That advice is in line with God's law to love one's neighbor. So Jesus advises his listeners: "Continue to love your enemies and to pray for those who persecute you." He gives a powerful reason why: "So that you may prove yourselves sons of your Father who is in the heavens, since he makes his sun rise on both the wicked and the good."—Matthew 5:44, 45.

● Jesus sums up this portion of his sermon, saying: "You must accordingly be perfect, as your heavenly Father is perfect." (Matthew 5: 48) Obviously, he does not mean that people can be fully perfect. However, by imitating God, we can expand our love to embrace even our enemies. Put another way: "Continue being merciful, just as your Father is merciful."—Luke 6:36.

PRAYER AND TRUST IN GOD

19 As Jesus continues his sermon, he urges his listeners: "Take care not to practice your righteousness in front of men to be noticed by them." Jesus condemns a hypocritical show of godliness, adding: "When you make gifts of mercy, do not blow a trumpet ahead of you, as the hypocrites do." (Matthew 6:1, 2) It is better to give gifts of mercy in private.

20 Jesus next says: "When you pray, do not act like the hypocrites, for they like to pray standing in the synagogues and on the corners of the main streets to be seen by men." Rather, he says: "When you pray, go into your private room and, after shutting your door, pray to your Father who is in secret." (Matthew 6:5, 6) Jesus is not against all public prayers, for he himself offered such prayers. He is denouncing prayers said in a way to impress listeners and draw admiring compliments.

21 He counsels the crowd: "When praying, do not say the same things over and over again as the people of the nations do." (Matthew 6:7) Jesus does not mean that repeatedly praying about the same subject is wrong. He is expressing disapproval of using memorized phrases "over and over again," praying by rote. He then provides a model prayer that includes seven petitions. The first three recognize God's right to rule and his purposes—that his name be sanctified, that his Kingdom come, and that his will be done. Only after such matters should we make personal requests for our daily food and for forgiveness of sins, as well as requests not to be tempted beyond one's endurance and to be delivered from the wicked one.

◊ What does Jesus mean when he says to turn the other cheek?

◊ How can we be perfect as God is perfect?

◊ What instructions on prayer does Jesus provide?

On occasion, Jesus repeated key teachings. For example, in the Sermon on the Mount, he taught his listeners how to pray and helped them to have a proper view of material things.—Matthew 6:9-13, 25-34.

About a year and a half later, Jesus restated those teachings. (Luke 11:1-4; 12:22-31) This repetition, in addition to benefiting those who were not present on the first occasion, helped his disciples to fix in mind the main points.

How important should our possessions be to us? Jesus urges the crowd: "Stop storing up for yourselves treasures on the earth, where moth and rust consume and where thieves break in and steal." How reasonable! Material treasures can and do perish, and our having them builds up no merit with God. Accordingly, Jesus next says: "Store up for yourselves treasures in heaven." We can do this by putting God's service first in life. Nobody can take away our good standing with God or its reward of everlasting life. So true are Jesus' words: "Where your treasure is, there your heart will be also."—Matthew 6: 19-21.

Emphasizing this point, Jesus gives an illustration: "The lamp of the body is the eye. If, then, your eye is focused, your whole body will be bright. But if your eye is envious, your whole body will be dark." (Matthew 6:22, 23) When our eye functions properly, it is like a lighted lamp to our body. But to be such, our eye must be focused on one thing; otherwise, we could develop a mistaken esti-mate of life. Focusing on material possessions instead of on serving God would mean that our "whole body will be dark," perhaps drawn to what is shady or dark.

Jesus then gives a powerful example: "No one can slave for two masters; for either he will hate the one and love the other, or he will stick to the one and despise the other. You cannot slave for God and for Riches."—Matthew 6:24.

Some hearing Jesus might be concerned about how they should view their material needs. So he assures them that they do not need to be anxious if they put God's service first. "Observe intently the birds of heaven; they do not sow seed or reap or gather into storehouses, yet your heavenly Father feeds them."—Matthew 6:26.

24 And what about the lilies of the field there on the mountain? Jesus notes that "not even Solomon in all his glory was arrayed as one of these." What does this show? "If this is how God clothes the vegetation of the field that is here today and tomorrow is thrown into the oven, will he not much rather clothe you?" (Matthew 6:29, 30) Jesus wisely urges: "Never be anxious and say, 'What are we to eat?' or, 'What are we to drink?' or, 'What are we to wear?' . . . Your heavenly Father knows that you need all these things. Keep on, then, seeking first the Kingdom and his righteousness, and all these other things will be added to you."—Matthew 6:31-33.

HOW TO GAIN LIFE

25 The apostles and other sincere ones want to live in a way that pleases God, but that is not easy in their circumstances. Many Pharisees, for example, are critical, harshly judging others. So Jesus admonishes his listeners: "Stop judging that you may not be judged; for with the judgment you are judging, you will be judged." —Matthew 7:1, 2.

26 It is dangerous to follow the lead of the overly critical Pharisees, as Jesus illustrates: "A blind man cannot guide a blind man, can he? Both will fall into a pit, will they not?" Then how should Jesus' listeners view others? Not with a critical eye, because that would be a serious offense. He asks: "How can you say to your brother, 'Brother, allow me to remove the straw that is in your eye,' while you yourself do not see the rafter in your own eye? Hypocrite! First remove the rafter from your own eye, and then you will see clearly how to remove the straw that is in your brother's eye."—Luke 6:39-42.

27 This does not mean that the disciples are not to make any judgments at all. "Do not give what is holy to dogs nor throw your pearls before swine," Jesus urges them. (Matthew 7:6) Truths from God's Word are precious, like figurative pearls. If some people act like animals, showing no appreciation for these precious truths, the disciples should leave them and seek ones who are receptive.

28 Returning to the subject of prayer, Jesus stresses the need to persist in it. "Keep on asking, and it will be given you." God is ready to

answer prayers, as Jesus emphasizes by asking: "Which one of you, if his son asks for bread, will hand him a stone? . . . Therefore, if you, although being wicked, know how to give good gifts to your children, how much more so will your Father who is in the heavens give good things to those asking him!"—Matthew 7:7-11.

29 Jesus then sets out what has become a famous rule of conduct: "All things, therefore, that you want men to do to you, you also must do to them." Should not all of us take to heart and apply that positive exhortation in our dealings with others? Doing so, however, may be challenging, as revealed by Jesus' instruction: "Go in through the narrow gate, because broad

90

trees can be recognized by their fruits, Jesus notes. It is similar with people. Thus, we can recognize false prophets by their teachings and actions. Yes, Jesus explains, it is not simply what a person *says* that makes him his disciple but also what he *does*. Some people claim that Jesus is their Lord, but what if they are not doing God's will? Jesus says: "I will declare to them: 'I never knew you! Get away from me, you workers of lawlessness!'"—Matthew 7:23.

Concluding his sermon, Jesus declares: "Everyone who hears these sayings of mine and does them will be like a discreet man who built his house on the rock. And the rain poured down and the floods came and the winds blew and lashed against that house, but it did not cave in, for it had been founded on the rock." (Matthew 7:24, 25) Why did the house stand? Because the man "dug and went down deep and laid a foundation on the rock." (Luke 6:48) So more is involved than just hearing Jesus' words. We must exert ourselves to 'do them.'

What, though, about the one "hearing these sayings" but "not doing them"? He is "like a foolish man who built his house on the sand." (Matthew 7:26) Rain, floods, and winds would cause such a house to collapse.

The crowds are astounded at Jesus' way of teaching in this sermon. He does so as a person having authority and not as the religious leaders. Probably many of those who listened to him become his disciples.

in fact

is the gate and spacious is the road leading off into destruction, and many are going in through it; whereas narrow is the gate and cramped the road leading off into life, and few are finding it." —Matthew 7:12-14.

There are those who would try to divert the disciples from the way leading to life, so Jesus warns: "Be on the watch for the false prophets who come to you in sheep's covering, but inside they are ravenous wolves." (Matthew 7: 15) Good trees and bad

obeys

◇ Why are spiritual treasures superior, and how are they obtained?

◇ Why do Jesus' followers have no need to be anxious?

✔◇ What does Jesus say about judging others, yet why do we need to make some judgments at times?

◇ What does Jesus further say about prayer, and what rule of conduct does he give?

◇ How does Jesus show that being his disciple is not easy and that being misled is a danger?

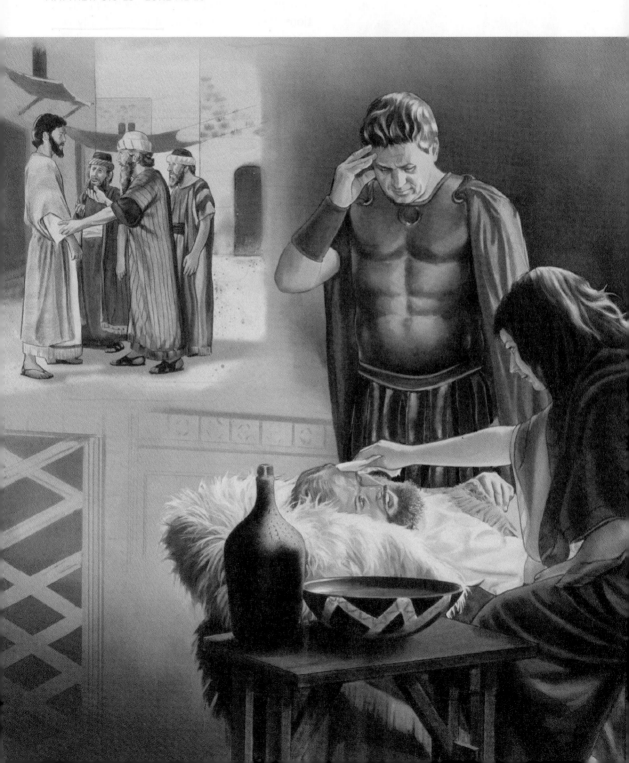

After giving his Sermon on the Mount, Jesus goes to the city of Capernaum. Here some elders of the Jews approach him. They have been sent by a man of a different background—a Roman army officer, a centurion.

The army officer's beloved servant is seriously ill and about to die. Though the centurion is a Gentile, he is seeking Jesus' help. The Jews tell Jesus that the man's servant "is laid up in the house with paralysis, and he is suffering terribly," perhaps being in great pain. (Matthew 8:6) The Jewish elders assure Jesus that this centurion is worthy of being granted this help, explaining: "He loves our nation and he himself built our synagogue."—Luke 7:4, 5.

Soon, Jesus leaves with the elders for the army officer's house. As they near it, the officer sends out friends to say: "Sir, do not bother, for I am not worthy to have you come under my roof. That is why I did not consider myself worthy to come to you." (Luke 7:6, 7) What a humble expression from someone used to giving orders! And it shows how different this man is from Romans who treat slaves harshly.—Matthew 8:9.

The centurion no doubt is aware that Jews avoid fellowshipping with non-Jews. (Acts 10:28) Perhaps with this in mind, the officer has his friends urge Jesus: "Say the word, and let my servant be healed."—Luke 7:7.

Jesus is amazed to hear this and comments:

"I tell you, not even in Israel have I found so great a faith." (Luke 7:9) On returning to the centurion's house, his friends discover that the slave who was so ill is now in good health.

Once Jesus has performed that healing, he uses the occasion to confirm that non-Jews of faith will be favored with blessings, saying: "Many from east and west will come and recline at the table with Abraham and Isaac and Jacob in the Kingdom of the heavens." What about faithless Jews? Jesus says that they "will be thrown into the darkness outside. There is where their weeping and the gnashing of their teeth will be."—Matthew 8:11, 12.

Hence, natural Jews who do not accept the opportunity offered first to them to be part of the Kingdom with Christ will be rejected. But Gentiles will be welcomed to recline at his table, as it were, "in the Kingdom of the heavens."

◇ Why do Jews plead on behalf of a Gentile army officer?

◇ What may explain why the centurion has not asked Jesus to enter his house?

◇ What prospect for Gentiles does Jesus highlight?

JESUS RESURRECTS A WIDOW'S SON

LUKE 7:11-17

site of Jesus' 1st ress.
900 years earlier nearby City of
Shunem Elijah ress. the son of Shun. woman

Soon after healing the army officer's servant, Jesus leaves Capernaum for Nain, a city over 20 miles to the southwest. He is not alone. His disciples and a great crowd travel with him. It is likely toward evening when they approach the outskirts of Nain. There they encounter a considerable number of Jews in a funeral procession. The dead body of a young man is being carried out of the city for burial.

The most grief-stricken among them is the mother of the young man. She is a widow, and now her only child has died. When her husband died, at least she still had her beloved son with her. Imagine how close she must have felt to him, for her hopes and her security for the future were tied up with him. Now he too has died. Who is there left to provide her with company and support?

When Jesus sees this woman, his heart is touched by her extreme grief and the sad-ness of her situation. Tenderly and yet with as-surance that imparts confidence, he tells her: "Stop weeping." Yet, he does more. He ap-proaches and touches the bier on which the body is being carried. (Luke 7:13, 14) His man-ner and actions are such that the mourning townspeople stop in their tracks. 'What does he mean, and what is he going to do?' many must wonder.   *funeral stretcher*

And what of those traveling with Jesus who have seen him perform powerful works, heal-ing many diseases? They apparently have nev-er seen Jesus resurrect anyone from the dead. Although resurrections did occur in the distant past, can Jesus do such a thing? (1 Kings 17:17-23; 2 Kings 4:32-37) Jesus gives the command: "Young man, I say to you, get up!" (Luke 7:14) And that happens. The man sits up and starts to speak! Jesus gives him to his shocked yet overjoyed mother. She is no longer alone.

parallel account

blessed with a son
one day in field has an
aneurism - dies - she lies
him in bed of Elijah
ress - sneeze 7 time

When the people see that the young man truly is alive, they praise the Life-Giver, Jehovah, saying: "A great prophet has been raised up among us." Others grasp the significance of Jesus' wonderful deed, saying: "God has turned his attention to his people." (Luke 7:16) The news of this amazing thing quickly spreads into the surrounding country and likely to Jesus' hometown, Nazareth, some six miles away. The report even spreads down south into Judea.

John the Baptist is still in prison, and he is very interested in the works that Jesus is able to perform. John's disciples tell him about these miracles. How does he respond?

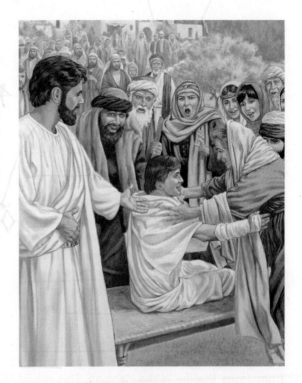

◇ What is happening as Jesus approaches Nain?

◇ How is Jesus affected by what he sees, and how does he respond?

◇ What is the reaction of the people to what Jesus does?

JOHN WANTS TO HEAR FROM JESUS

MATTHEW 11:2-15   LUKE 7:18-30

For about a year, John the Baptist has been in prison. Still, he hears of Jesus' marvelous works. Imagine how John feels when his disciples tell him that Jesus has resurrected the widow's son at Nain. However, John wants to hear directly from Jesus about what this all means. So John summons two of his disciples. To do what? They are to ask Jesus: "Are you the Coming One, or are we to expect a different one?" —Luke 7:19.

Does that seem to be a strange question? John is a devoted man who, when baptizing Jesus nearly two years before, saw God's spirit descend upon Jesus and heard God's voice of approval. We have no reason to think that John's faith has grown weak. Otherwise, Jesus would not speak so highly of John, as he does on this occasion. But if John is not having doubts, why does he ask this question of Jesus?

John may simply want verification directly from Jesus that he is the Messiah. This would strengthen John as he languishes in prison. And John's question apparently has an added sense. He is acquainted with the Bible prophecies that show that the Anointed One of God is to be a king and a deliverer. Yet, many months after Jesus was baptized, John is in prison. So John is asking if there is to be another one coming, a successor to Jesus, as it were, who will complete the fulfillment of all that the Messiah was foretold to accomplish.

Rather than simply tell John's disciples, 'Of course I am the One who is to come,' Jesus gives evidence that he has God's backing by healing many people of all kinds of diseases and ailments. Then he tells the disciples: "Go and report to John what you are hearing and seeing: The blind are now seeing and the lame

are walking, the lepers are being cleansed and the deaf are hearing, the dead are being raised up and the poor are being told the good news." —Matthew 11:4, 5.

John's question might imply an expectation that Jesus will do more than he is now doing and will perhaps free John from prison. Jesus, however, is telling John not to expect more than the miracles he is actually performing.

When John's disciples leave, Jesus assures the crowd that John is more than a prophet. He is "the messenger" of Jehovah prophesied about at Malachi 3:1. He is also the prophet Elijah, as foretold at Malachi 4:5, 6. Jesus explains: "Truly I say to you, among those born of women, there has not been raised up anyone greater than John the Baptist, but a lesser person in the Kingdom of the heavens is greater than he is."—Matthew 11:11.

By saying that a lesser one in the Kingdom of the heavens is greater than John, Jesus is showing that John will not be in the heavenly Kingdom. John prepared the way for Jesus but dies before Christ opens the way to heaven. (Hebrews 10:19, 20) John is, though, a faithful prophet of God and will be an earthly subject of God's Kingdom.

◇ Why does John ask whether Jesus is the Coming One or whether to expect a different one?

◇ Jesus says that John the Baptist fulfilled what prophecies?

◇ Why will John the Baptist not be in heaven with Jesus?

Tues October 23rd
By Faith Moses, when grown up refused to be called son of
Pharaoh's daughter—
HEB 11:24

WOE TO AN UNRESPONSIVE GENERATION

MATTHEW 11:16-30   LUKE 7:31-35

Jesus has high regard for John the Baptist, but how do most people regard John? "This generation," Jesus declares, "is like young children sitting in the marketplaces who call out to their playmates, saying: 'We played the flute for you, but you did not dance; we wailed, but you did not beat yourselves in grief.'"—Matthew 11: 16, 17.

What does Jesus mean? He clarifies the thought: "John came neither eating nor drinking, but people say, 'He has a demon.' The Son of man did come eating and drinking, but people say, 'Look! A man who is a glutton and is given to drinking wine, a friend of tax collectors and sinners.'" (Matthew 11:18, 19) On the one hand, John has lived a simple life as a Nazirite, even abstaining from wine, yet this generation says he is demonized. (Numbers 6:2, 3; Luke 1: 15) On the other hand, Jesus lives like other men. He eats and drinks in a balanced way, but he is accused of going to excess. It seems impossible to satisfy the people.

Jesus likens the generation to young children in the marketplaces who refuse to respond by dancing when other children play the flute or by grieving when others wail. "All the same," he says, "wisdom is proved righteous by its works." (Matthew 11:16, 19) Yes, the "works" —that is, the evidence produced by John and Jesus—prove that the accusations against them are false.

After Jesus characterizes the generation as unresponsive, he singles out for reproach the cities of Chorazin, Bethsaida, and Capernaum, where he has done powerful works. Jesus says that if he had performed such works in the Phoenician cities of Tyre and Sidon, those cities would have repented. He also mentions Capernaum, which has been his home base for some time. Even there, most did not respond. Jesus says of that city: "It will be more endurable for the land of Sodom on Judgment Day than for you."—Matthew 11:24.

Jesus then praises his Father, who hides precious spiritual truths "from the wise and intellectual ones" but reveals these things to lowly ones, who are like young children. (Matthew 11: 25) He extends an appealing invitation to such ones: "Come to me, all you who are toiling and loaded down, and I will refresh you. Take my yoke upon you and learn from me, for I am mild-tempered and lowly in heart, and you will find refreshment for yourselves. For my yoke is kindly, and my load is light."—Matthew 11:28-30.

How does Jesus offer refreshment? The religious leaders have burdened the people with enslaving traditions, such as overly restrictive Sabbath regulations. But Jesus refreshes them by teaching the truth of God, free from the taint of those traditions. He also shows the way of relief to ones who feel crushed by the domination of political authorities and to those who feel weighed down by sin. Yes, Jesus reveals to them how their sins can be forgiven and how they can be at peace with God.

All of those accepting Jesus' kindly yoke can dedicate themselves to God and serve our compassionate, merciful heavenly Father. Doing so does not involve a heavy load, for God's requirements are not at all burdensome.—1 John 5:3.

c/o visit

◇ How are the people of Jesus' generation like children?

◇ What moves Jesus to praise his heavenly Father?

◇ In what ways are many people burdened, but what relief does Jesus offer?

A LESSON IN FORGIVENESS

LUKE 7:36-50 *only Luke records account of prostitute*

Depending on their heart condition, people respond differently to what Jesus says and does. That becomes clear at a house in Galilee. A Pharisee named Simon invites Jesus to a meal, perhaps to get a closer look at the one performing such remarkable works. Likely viewing this as an opportunity to minister to those present, Jesus accepts, even as he has on other occasions accepted invitations to eat with tax collectors and sinners.

However, Jesus does not receive the cordial attention usually given to guests. On dusty roads in Palestine, sandal-clad feet become hot and dirty, so it is a customary act of hospitality to wash a guest's feet with cool water. That is not done for Jesus. Neither does he receive a welcoming kiss, as is common. Another custom is to pour some oil on a guest's hair out of kindness and hospitality. This too is not done for Jesus. So how welcome is he really?

The meal begins, with the guests reclining at the table. As they eat, a woman quietly enters the room uninvited. She is "known in the city to be a sinner." (Luke 7:37) All imperfect humans are sinners, yet this woman seems to be living an immoral life, perhaps as a prostitute. She may have heard Jesus' teachings, including his invitation for 'all those who are loaded down to come to him for refreshment.' (Matthew 11: 28, 29) Apparently moved by Jesus' words and deeds, she has now sought him out.

SE. Rom 3:23 all have sin

She comes up behind Jesus at the table and kneels at his feet. Tears fall from her eyes onto his feet, and she wipes them with her hair. She tenderly kisses his feet and pours on them some fragrant oil that she has brought. Simon watches with disapproval, saying to himself: "If this man were really a prophet, he would know who and what kind of woman it is who is touching him, that she is a sinner."—Luke 7:39.

Perceiving Simon's thinking, Jesus says: "Simon, I have something to say to you." He replies: "Teacher, say it!" Jesus continues: "Two men were debtors to a certain lender; the one was in debt for 500 denarii, but the other for 50. When they did not have anything to pay him back with, he freely forgave them both. Therefore, which one of them will love him more?" Perhaps with an air of indifference, Simon answers: "I suppose it is the one whom he forgave more."—Luke 7:40-43.

Jesus agrees. Then looking at the woman, he says to Simon: "Do you see this woman? I entered your house; you gave me no water for my feet. But this woman wet my feet with her tears and wiped them off with her hair. You gave me no kiss, but this woman, from the hour that I came in, did not stop tenderly kissing my feet. You did not pour oil on my head, but this woman poured perfumed oil on my feet." Jesus could see that this woman was giving evidence of heartfelt repentance for her immoral life. So he concludes: "I tell you, her sins, many though they are, are forgiven, because she loved much. But the one who is forgiven little, loves little."—Luke 7:44-47.

Jesus is not excusing immorality. Rather, he is manifesting compassionate understanding of people who commit serious sins but who then show that they are sorry and turn to Christ for relief. And what relief this woman feels when Jesus says: "Your sins are forgiven. . . . Your faith has saved you; go in peace."—Luke 7: 48, 50.

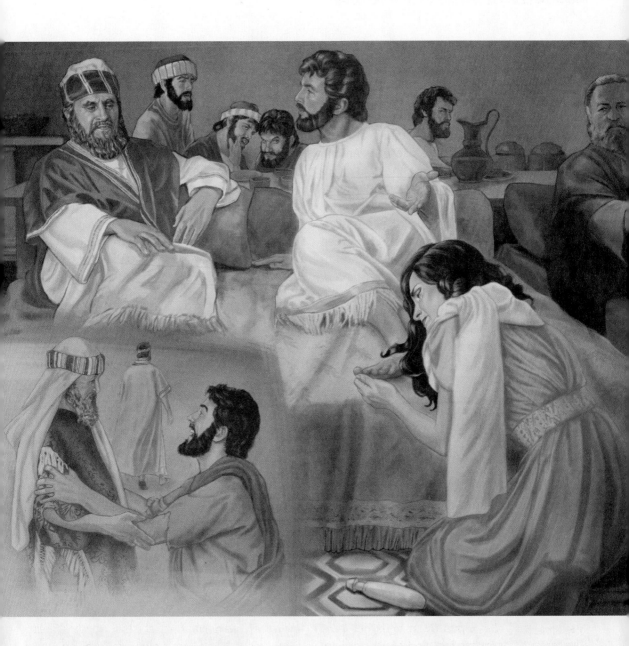

◇ How is Jesus received by his host, Simon?

◇ Why does a local woman seek Jesus out?

◇ What illustration does Jesus use, and how does he apply it?

MIRACLES—BY WHOSE POWER?

MATTHEW 12:22-32 MARK 3:19-30 LUKE 8:1-3

Soon after speaking about forgiveness at the home of the Pharisee Simon, Jesus begins another preaching tour of Galilee. He is in the second year of his ministry, and he is not traveling alone. The 12 apostles are with him, as well as certain women whom he had "cured of wicked spirits and sicknesses." (Luke 8:2) Among them are Mary Magdalene, Susanna, and Joanna, whose husband is an officer of King Herod Antipas.

As more people learn of Jesus, the controversy over his activity intensifies. That is clear when a demon-possessed man, who is blind and unable to speak, is brought to Jesus and is cured. Now the man is free of demon control and can both see and speak. The people are simply carried away, saying: "May this not perhaps be the Son of David?"—Matthew 12:23.

The crowds gathered around the house where Jesus is staying are so large that he and his disciples cannot even eat a meal. Not all, though, think that Jesus is the promised "Son of David." Some scribes and Pharisees have come all the way from Jerusalem—but not to learn from Jesus or to support him. They are telling people: "He has Beelzebub" and thus is in league with "the ruler of the demons." (Mark 3: 22) When Jesus' relatives hear about the commotion, they come to lay hold of Jesus. For what reason?

Well, at this point, Jesus' own brothers do not believe that he is God's Son. (John 7:5) The Jesus who seems to be creating this public uproar is not like the Jesus they knew while they were growing up together in Nazareth. Concluding that something must be mentally wrong with

bro of half faith

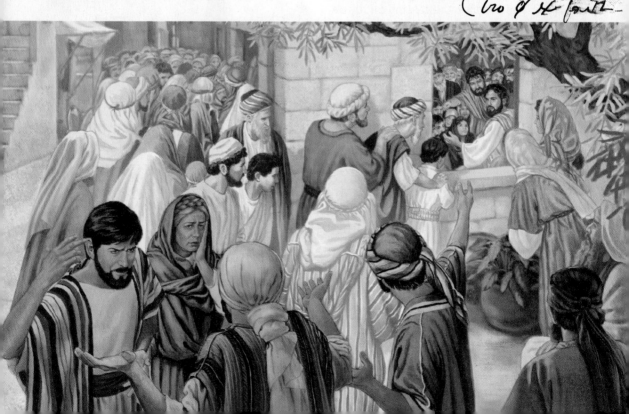

him, they say: "He has gone out of his mind." —Mark 3:21.

What does the evidence prove, though? Jesus just healed a demonized man, who can now see and speak. No one can deny this. So the scribes and Pharisees try to discredit Jesus with a false charge. They say: "This fellow does not expel the demons except by means of Beelzebub, the ruler of the demons."—Matthew 12:24.

Jesus knows what the scribes and Pharisees are thinking, so he points out: "Every kingdom divided against itself comes to ruin, and every city or house divided against itself will not stand. In the same way, if Satan expels Satan, he has become divided against himself; how, then, will his kingdom stand?"—Matthew 12:25, 26.

What impressive logic! The Pharisees know that some Jews practice the casting out of demons. (Acts 19:13) So Jesus asks: "If I expel the demons by means of Beelzebub, by whom do your sons expel them?" In other words, their charge should just as well be applied to them. Jesus then extends the reasoning: "But if it is by means of God's spirit that I expel the demons, the Kingdom of God has really overtaken you."—Matthew 12:27, 28.

To illustrate that his expelling demons is evidence of his power over Satan, Jesus says: "How can anyone invade the house of a strong man and seize his possessions unless he first ties up the strong man? Only then can he plunder his house. Whoever is not on my side is against me, and whoever does not gather with me scatters." (Matthew 12:29, 30) The scribes and Pharisees surely are against Jesus, thus giving evidence that they are Satan's agents. They are scattering people away from the Son of God, who is acting with Jehovah's backing.

Jesus warns these satanic opposers: "All things will be forgiven the sons of men, no matter what sins they commit and what blasphemies they speak. But whoever blasphemes against the holy spirit has no forgiveness forever but is guilty of everlasting sin." (Mark 3:28, 29) Think of the implications of that for those who are attributing to Satan what is plainly being done by God's spirit!

◇ Who are with Jesus on his second tour of Galilee?
◇ Why do Jesus' relatives attempt to lay hold of him?
◇ How do the scribes and Pharisees attempt to discredit Jesus' miracles, and how does Jesus refute them?

103

JESUS REBUKES THE PHARISEES

MATTHEW 12:33-50   MARK 3:31-35   LUKE 8:19-21

*x men will render an account for every improfitable
x or worthless
v3 36*

By denying that Jesus expels demons with God's power, the scribes and Pharisees are at risk of blaspheming the holy spirit. Hence, whose side will they take—God's or Satan's? Jesus says: "Either you make the tree fine and its fruit fine or make the tree rotten and its fruit rotten, for by its fruit the tree is known."—Matthew 12:33.

It is foolish to charge that the good fruit of casting out demons results from Jesus' serving Satan. As Jesus made plain in his Sermon on the Mount, if the fruit is fine, the tree is fine, not rotten. So, what does the Pharisees' fruit, their absurd accusations against Jesus, prove? That they are rotten. Jesus tells them: "Offspring of vipers, how can you speak good things when you are wicked? For out of the abundance of the heart the mouth speaks."—Matthew 7:16, 17; 12:34.

Yes, our words reflect the condition of our hearts and provide a basis for judgment. Hence, Jesus says: "I tell you that men will render an account on Judgment Day for every unprofitable saying that they speak; for by your words you will be declared righteous, and by your words you will be condemned."—Matthew 12:36, 37.

Despite the powerful works Jesus is doing, the scribes and Pharisees demand more: "Teacher, we want to see a sign from you." Whether they have personally seen him perform miracles or not, there is ample eyewitness testimony of what he is doing. Jesus can thus tell those Jewish leaders: "A wicked and adulterous generation keeps on seeking a sign, but no sign will be given it except the sign of Jonah the prophet."—Matthew 12:38, 39.

Jesus does not leave them to wonder about what he means: "Just as Jonah was in the belly of the huge fish for three days and three nights, so the Son of man will be in the heart of the earth for three days and three nights." Jonah was swallowed by some sort of huge fish but then came out as if resurrected. Jesus thus foretells that he himself will die and on the third day be raised. When that later occurs, the Jewish leaders reject "the sign of Jonah," refusing to repent and change. (Matthew 27:63-66; 28:12-15) In contrast, the "men of Nineveh" did repent after Jonah preached to them. So they will condemn this generation. Jesus also says that by her example, the queen of Sheba will likewise denounce them. She desired to hear Solomon's wisdom and marveled at it. Now, Je-

*called him
an impostor
asked Pilate
to stand*

sus notes, "something more than Solomon is here."—Matthew 12:40-42.

Jesus likens the situation of this wicked generation to a man from whom an unclean spirit comes out. (Matthew 12:45) Because the man does not fill the void with good things, the wicked spirit returns with seven spirits more wicked than himself and they possess him. Comparably, the Israelite nation had been cleansed and had reformed—much like the man from whom the unclean spirit came out. But the nation rejected God's prophets, culminating in its opposing this one who clearly has God's spirit, Jesus. This shows the nation's condition to be worse than at its start.

While Jesus is speaking, his mother and his brothers arrive and stand at the edge of the crowd. Some sitting near him say: "Your mother and your brothers are standing outside, wanting to see you." Jesus then shows how close he feels to his disciples, who are like real brothers, sisters, and mothers to him. Extending his hand toward his disciples, he says: "My mother and my brothers are these who hear the word of God and do it." (Luke 8:20, 21) He thus shows that regardless of how precious the ties are that bind him to his relatives, his relationship with his disciples is even more precious. How refreshing it is for us to have such closeness with our spiritual brothers, especially when others doubt us or reproach us and our good works!

◇ In what way are the Pharisees like a rotten tree?
◇ What is "the sign of Jonah," and how is it later rejected?
◇ How is the first-century Israelite nation like the man from whom an unclean spirit came out?
◇ How does Jesus emphasize his close relationship with his disciples?

ILLUSTRATIONS ABOUT THE KINGDOM

MATTHEW 13:1-53 MARK 4:1-34 LUKE 8:4-18

Jesus is apparently in Capernaum when he rebukes the Pharisees. Later that day, he leaves the house and walks to the nearby Sea of Galilee, where crowds gather. Jesus boards a boat, pulls out from the shore, and begins teaching the people about the Kingdom of the heavens. He does so by means of a number of illustrations, or parables. His listeners are familiar with many of the settings or features that Jesus mentions, making it easier for them to grasp various aspects of the Kingdom.

First, Jesus tells of a sower who is sowing seed. Some seeds fall alongside the road and are eaten by birds. Other seeds fall on rocky ground where there is not much soil. The roots that develop cannot reach down far, and the new plants are scorched by the sun and wither. Still other seeds fall among thorns, which choke the young plants when they come up. Finally, some seeds fall on fine soil. These seeds produce fruit, "this one 100 times more, that one 60, the other 30."—Matthew 13:8.

In another illustration, Jesus likens the Kingdom to when a man sows seeds. In this case, whether the man sleeps or is awake, the seeds grow. Just how, "he does not know." (Mark 4:27) They grow by themselves and produce grain, which he can harvest.

Jesus then tells a third illustration about sowing. A man sows the right kind of seed, but "while men were sleeping," an enemy sows weeds in among the wheat. The man's slaves ask if they should pull out the weeds. He replies: "No, for fear that while collecting the weeds,

---

◇ When and where does Jesus speak with illustrations to the crowds?

you uproot the wheat with them. Let both grow together until the harvest, and in the harvest season, I will tell the reapers: First collect the weeds and bind them in bundles to burn them up; then gather the wheat into my storehouse." —Matthew 13:24-30.

5 Many who are listening to Jesus know about farming. He also mentions something else commonly known, the tiny mustard seed. It grows into a tree so large that birds can lodge in its branches. About this seed, he says: "The Kingdom of the heavens is like a mustard grain that a man took and planted in his field." (Matthew 13:31) Jesus, however, is not giving a botany lesson. He is illustrating spectacular growth, how something very small can grow or expand into something very large.

6 Then Jesus draws on a process that is familiar to many of his listeners. He likens the Kingdom of the heavens to "leaven that a woman took and mixed with three large measures of flour." (Matthew 13:33) Although such leaven is hidden from view, it permeates every part of the dough and makes it rise. It produces considerable growth and changes that are not readily discernible.

7 After giving these illustrations, Jesus dismisses the crowds and returns to the house where he is staying. Soon his disciples come to him, wanting to understand what he meant.

BENEFITING FROM JESUS' ILLUSTRATIONS

8 The disciples have heard Jesus use illustrations before, but never to this extent. They put to him the question: "Why do you speak to them by the use of illustrations?"—Matthew 13:10.

9 One reason he does so is to fulfill Bible proph-ecy. Matthew's account states: "Without an illustration he would not speak to them, in order to fulfill what was spoken through the prophet who said: 'I will open my mouth with illustrations; I will proclaim things hidden since the founding.'"—Matthew 13:34, 35; Psalm 78:2.

10 But there is more to Jesus' use of illustrations. It serves to reveal the attitude of people. Many of them are interested in Jesus simply as a masterful storyteller and miracle worker. They do not see him as someone to be obeyed as Lord and to be unselfishly followed. (Luke 6:46, 47) They do not want to be disturbed in their view of things or their way of life. No, they do not want the message to penetrate that deeply.

11 In answer to the disciples' question, Jesus says: "That is why I speak to them by the use of illustrations; for looking, they look in vain, and hearing, they hear in vain, nor do they get the sense of it. And the prophecy of Isaiah is being fulfilled in their case. It says: '. . .The heart of this people has grown unreceptive.'"—Matthew 13:13-15; Isaiah 6:9, 10.

12 That does not, though, apply to all who are hearing Jesus. He explains: "Happy are your eyes because they see and your ears because they hear. For truly I say to you, many prophets and righteous men desired to see the things you are observing but did not see them, and to hear the things you are hearing but did not hear them."—Matthew 13:16, 17.

13 Yes, the 12 apostles and other loyal disciples have receptive hearts. Accordingly, Jesus says: "To you it is granted to understand the sacred secrets of the Kingdom of the heavens, but to them it is not granted." (Matthew 13:11) Be-

---

◇ What five illustrations does Jesus first present?
◇ Why does Jesus speak in illustrations?
◇ How do Jesus' disciples show themselves to be different from the crowds?
◇ How does Jesus explain the illustration of the sower?

(handwritten margin notes)

ISH is not blunt or tastless the fault lies c the people

I understand that we are living in last days can be truly happy B/c we lift our heads up

cause of their sincere desire to understand, Jesus provides his disciples with an explanation of the illustration of the sower.

14 "The seed is the word of God," Jesus says. (Luke 8:11) And the soil is the heart. That is a key to getting the sense of his illustration.

15 Of the seed sown on the trampled-down soil alongside the road, he explains: "The Devil comes and takes the word away from their hearts so that they may not believe and be saved." (Luke 8:12) In speaking of the seed sown on rocky ground, Jesus means the hearts of people who receive the word with joy but the word does not take root deep in their hearts. "After tribulation or persecution has arisen on account of the word," they are stumbled. Yes, when "a season of testing" comes, perhaps opposition from family members or others, they fall away.—Matthew 13:21; Luke 8:13.

because of anx. + not in this current system *no. root*

16 What of the seed that falls among the thorns? Jesus tells his disciples that this refers to people who have heard the word. These, however, are overcome by "the anxiety of this system of things and the deceptive power of riches." (Matthew 13:22) They had the word in their heart, but now it is choked and becomes unfruitful.

17 The last type of soil that Jesus comments on is the fine soil. This refers to those who hear the word and accept it into their heart, getting the real sense of it. With what result? They "bear fruit." Because of their circumstances, such as age or health, not all can do the same; one produces 100 times more, another 60 times more, and another 30 times more. Yes, blessings in serving God come to "ones who, after hearing the word with a fine and good heart, retain it and bear fruit with endurance."—Luke 8:15.

all of these + factors

109

18 These words must be particularly impressive to the disciples who have sought out Jesus to get an explanation of his teachings! They now have more than a surface grasp of the illustrations. Jesus wants them to understand his illustrations so that they, in turn, can impart truth to others. "A lamp is not brought out to be put under a basket or under a bed, is it?" he asks. "Is it not brought out to be put on a lampstand?" Thus, Jesus advises: "Whoever has ears to listen, let him listen."—Mark 4:21-23.

BLESSED WITH MORE INSTRUCTION

After receiving Jesus' explanation of the illustration of the sower, the disciples want to learn more. "Explain to us," they request, "the illustration of the weeds in the field."—Matthew 13:36.

In asking that, they display quite a different attitude from that of the rest of the crowd on the beach. Evidently, those people hear but lack the desire to learn the meaning behind the illustrations and their application. They are satisfied with merely the outline of things set out in the illustrations. Jesus contrasts that seaside audience with his inquisitive disciples who have come to him for more instruction, saying:

"Pay attention to what you are hearing. With the measure that you are measuring out, you will have it measured out to you, yes, you will

have more added to you." (Mark 4:24) The disciples are paying attention to what they are hearing from him. They are measuring out to Jesus earnest interest and attention, and they are blessed with more instruction, more enlightenment. Thus, in answer to his disciples' inquiry about the illustration of the wheat and the weeds, Jesus explains:

"The sower of the fine seed is the Son of man; the field is the world. As for the fine seed, these are the sons of the Kingdom, but the weeds are the sons of the wicked one, and the enemy who sowed them is the Devil. The harvest is a conclusion of a system of things, and the reapers are angels."—Matthew 13:37-39.

After identifying each feature of his illustration, Jesus describes the outcome. He says that at the conclusion of the system of things, the reapers, or angels, will separate weedlike imitation Christians from the true "sons of the Kingdom." "The righteous ones" will be gathered and will eventually shine brightly "in the Kingdom of their Father." And what about "the sons of the wicked one"? The outcome for them will be destruction, a just cause for "their weeping and the gnashing of their teeth."—Matthew 13: 41-43.

Jesus next blesses his disciples with three more illustrations. First, he says: "The Kingdom

[Handwritten note at top: "Come after me & I will make you fishers of men. At once they abandone nets & go"]

of the heavens is like a treasure, hidden in the field, that a man found and hid; and because of his joy, he goes and sells everything he has and buys that field."—Matthew 13:44.

2 He continues: "The Kingdom of the heavens is like a traveling merchant seeking fine pearls. Upon finding one pearl of high value, he went away and promptly sold all the things he had and bought it."—Matthew 13:45, 46.

With both illustrations, Jesus highlights a person's willingness to make sacrifices for what is truly valuable. The merchant promptly sells "all the things he had" to obtain the one pearl of high value. Jesus' disciples can understand that example regarding a precious pearl. And the man who finds treasure hidden in a field "sells everything" to possess it. In both cases, something valuable is available,

something to be obtained and treasured. This can be compared to the sacrifices a person makes to satisfy his spiritual need. (Matthew 5:3) Some of those hearing Jesus give these illustrations have already shown a willingness to go to great lengths to satisfy their spiritual need and to be his true followers.—Matthew 4: 19, 20; 19:27.) *[Handwritten: "— left all things behind"]*

3 Finally, Jesus likens the Kingdom of the heavens to a dragnet that gathers up fish of every kind. (Matthew 13:47) *[Handwritten: "what of us?"]* When the fish are separated, the good ones are kept in containers but the unsuitable ones are thrown away. Jesus says that it will be the same in the conclusion of the system of things—the angels will separate the wicked from the righteous.

Jesus himself was doing a type of spiritual fishing when he called his first disciples to be "fishers of men." (Mark 1:17) However, he says that his illustration about the dragnet applies in the future, "in the conclusion of the system of things." (Matthew 13:49) So the apostles and other disciples hearing Jesus can sense that very interesting things are yet to develop.

Those who heard the illustrations given from the boat are further enriched. Jesus is showing his willingness to "explain all things privately to his disciples." (Mark 4:34) He is "like a man, the master of the house, who brings out of his treasure store things both new and old." (Matthew 13:52) In giving these illustrations, Jesus is not showing off his teaching ability. Rather, he is sharing with his disciples truths that are like a priceless treasure. He truly is a "public instructor" beyond compare.

[Handwritten: "when recreation or new world is here — lawless will bring to earth perfect cord."]

◊ In the illustration of the wheat and the weeds, who or what is represented by the sower, the field, the fine seed, the weeds, the enemy, the harvest, and the reapers?

◊ What three additional illustrations does Jesus provide, and what can we learn from them?

covered by waves ↓

Jesus has had a long, tiring day. When evening comes, he says to the disciples: "Let us cross to the other shore," which is across from the area of Capernaum.—Mark 4:35.

Over on the eastern shore of the Sea of Galilee is the region of the Gerasenes. This area is also known as the Decapolis. The cities of the Decapolis are a center of Greek culture, though many Jews live there too.

Jesus' departure from Capernaum does not go unnoticed. There are other boats that at least start to cross the sea. (Mark 4:36) Actually, it is not that far across. The Sea of Galilee is like a large freshwater lake, being about 13 miles long and having a maximum width of about 7 miles. But it is not shallow.

Though Jesus is a perfect man, he is understandably tired from his active ministry. So after they set sail, he lies down in the back of the boat, puts his head on a pillow, and falls asleep.

Several of the apostles are well-qualified to sail the boat, but this is not going to be an easy trip. There are surrounding mountains, and the surface of the Sea of Galilee is often quite warm. At times, colder air in the mountains rushes down and meets the warm surface water, creating sudden, violent windstorms on the sea. This is what now occurs. Soon the waves are dashing against the boat. It begins "to fill up with water and to be in danger." (Luke 8:23) Still, Jesus remains asleep!

The seamen work frantically to steer the boat, drawing on their past experience at maneuvering through storms. But this time is different. Fearing for their lives, they wake Jesus up and exclaim: "Lord, save us, we are about to perish!" (Matthew 8:25) The disciples are now afraid that they are going to drown!

When Jesus wakes up, he says to the apostles: "Why are you so afraid, you with little faith?" (Matthew 8:26) Then Jesus commands the wind and the sea: "Hush! Be quiet!" (Mark 4: 39) The raging wind stops and the sea becomes calm. (Mark and Luke tell of this impressive episode, first emphasizing that Jesus miraculously calms the storm, and then they mention the disciples' lack of faith.)

Imagine the effect this has on the disciples! They have just seen the sea go from a raging storm to complete calm. An unusual fear grips them. They say to one another: "Who really is this? Even the wind and the sea obey him." And they come to the other side of the sea safely. (Mark 4:41–5:1) Perhaps the other boats that put to sea have been able to return to the western shore.

How reassuring it is to know that God's Son has power over the elements! When his full attention is directed toward our earth during his Kingdom rule, all people will dwell in security, for there will be no terrifying natural calamities!

power of Jehovah

◇ What natural features may contribute to the violent storm that occurs on the Sea of Galilee?
◇ In desperation, what do the disciples do?
◇ Why can we be reassured by this event?

POWER OVER MANY DEMONS

MATTHEW 8:28-34   MARK 5:1-20   LUKE 8:26-39

As the disciples return to shore after their harrowing ordeal at sea, they experience quite a shock. Two very fierce men, both demon-possessed, come out from a nearby cemetery and run toward Jesus! One of the men becomes the focus of attention, possibly being more violent and having been controlled longer by the demons.

This pitiful man has been going about naked. Night and day, he is "crying out in the tombs and in the mountains and slashing himself with stones." (Mark 5:5) He is so wild that people are afraid to pass along that stretch of road. Some have tried to bind him, but he tears the chains apart and breaks the fetters off his feet. Nobody has the strength to subdue him.

As the man approaches Jesus and falls at his feet, the demons controlling him make him scream: "What have I to do with you, Jesus, Son of the Most High God? I put you under oath by God not to torment me." Jesus shows that he has authority over the demons, commanding: "Come out of the man, you unclean spirit." —Mark 5:7, 8.

In reality, many demons are possessing the man. When Jesus asks, "What is your name?" the reply is: "My name is Legion, because there are many of us." (Mark 5:9) A Roman legion is made up of thousands of soldiers; hence, many demons are ganging up on this man, reveling in his sufferings. They beg Jesus "not to order them to go away into the abyss." They apparently realize what is ahead for both them and their leader, Satan.—Luke 8:31.

Grazing nearby is a herd of about 2,000 swine, animals that are unclean according to the Law and that Jews should not even own. The demons say: "Send us into the swine, so that we may enter into them." (Mark 5:12) Jesus tells them to go, and they enter the swine. At that, all 2,000 of them stampede over the cliff and drown in the sea below.

"Go home to your relatives, and report to them all the things Jehovah has done for you and the mercy he has shown you."—Mark 5:19.

Jesus usually instructs those whom he heals not to tell anyone because he does not want people to reach conclusions about him on the basis of sensational reports. In this case, the formerly demonized man is living proof of Jesus' power and can witness to people whom Jesus may not reach personally. His testimony may also counteract any unfavorable report about the loss of the swine. So the man goes and starts proclaiming throughout the Decapolis what Jesus did for him.

When those taking care of the swine see this, they rush to report the news in the city and in the countryside. The people come out to see what has happened. As they arrive, they observe that the man from whom the demons came out is now well and acting sanely. Why, he is clothed and sitting at Jesus' feet!

People who hear of this or see the man are gripped with fear, not understanding what this may mean for them. They urge Jesus to leave their territory. While Jesus is boarding the boat to leave, the formerly demonized man begs him to let him come along. But Jesus tells the man:

◇ Why is attention focused on one of the two demon-possessed men?
◇ What do the demons know about their own future?
◇ For what reasons does Jesus have the formerly demonized man tell others about what Jesus did?

HEALED BY TOUCHING JESUS' GARMENT

MATTHEW 9:18-22 MARK 5:21-34 LUKE 8:40-48

News of Jesus' return from the Decapolis spreads among Jews living on the northwest shore of the Sea of Galilee. Likely many have heard that during the recent storm, Jesus calmed the wind and the waters, and some may know that he cured the demon-possessed men. Hence, "a large crowd" gather by the sea, likely in the area of Capernaum, to welcome Jesus back. (Mark 5:21) As he steps ashore, they are eager and expectant.

One of those anxious to see Jesus is Jairus, a presiding officer of the synagogue, perhaps the one in Capernaum. He falls at Jesus' feet and begs again and again: "My little daughter is extremely ill. Please come and put your hands on her so that she may get well and live." (Mark 5:23) How will Jesus respond to Jairus' fervent plea to help his only daughter, who is just 12 years old and very precious to him?—Luke 8:42.

On his way to Jairus' house, Jesus is confronted with another emotion-filled situation. Many of the people accompanying Jesus are excited, wondering whether they will be able to see him perform another miracle. However, one woman in the crowd is focused on her own severe health problem.

For 12 long years, this Jewish woman has been suffering from a flow of blood. She has sought help from one doctor after another, using up all her money on treatments they have recommended. But she has not been helped. In fact, her problem has "become worse."—Mark 5:26.

You can likely appreciate that her ailment, besides weakening her, is embarrassing and humiliating. One generally does not speak openly about such a condition. Moreover, under the Mosaic Law, a discharge of blood makes a woman ceremonially unclean. Anyone touching her or her blood-stained garments needs to wash and is unclean until the evening.—Leviticus 15:25-27.

This woman has "heard the reports about Jesus," and she now seeks him out. Because of her uncleanness, she makes her way through the crowd as inconspicuously as possible, saying to herself: "If I touch just his outer garments, I will get well." When she does touch the fringe of his garment, she immediately senses that her flow of blood has stopped! She has "been healed of the grievous sickness."—Mark 5:27-29.

Jesus then says: "Who touched me?" How do you think the woman feels at hearing those words? Peter protests with an implied reproof of Jesus: "The crowds are hemming you in and pressing against you." So why did Jesus ask, "Who touched me?" Jesus explains: "Someone touched me, for I know that power went out of me." (Luke 8:45, 46) Yes, the healing that occurred has drawn on Jesus' vitality.

Realizing that she has not escaped notice, the woman falls down before Jesus, frightened and trembling. In front of all, she tells the truth about her illness and that she has just been cured. Jesus kindly comforts her: "Daughter, your faith has made you well. Go in peace, and be healed from your grievous sickness."—Mark 5:34.

Clearly, the One whom God has chosen to rule the earth is a warm, compassionate person who not only cares for people but also has the power to help them!

◇ Why do the people gather to greet Jesus as he returns to the area of Capernaum?

◇ What problem does one woman have, and why is she seeking help from Jesus?

◇ How is the woman healed, and what comfort does Jesus give her?

A YOUNG GIRL LIVES AGAIN!

MATTHEW 9:18, 23-26   MARK 5:22-24, 35-43   LUKE 8:40-42, 49-56

Jairus pleads only da. sick (scornfully) laugh

J.C. asked those singing dirges to leave

Jairus sees that the woman with the flow of blood was healed by Jesus. Surely, Jesus can help his daughter too, though he feels that 'by now his daughter must be dead.' (Matthew 9:18) Could it be that she can still be helped?

just lay your hand on

While Jesus is still speaking with the woman he has healed, some men arrive from Jairus' home and tell him: "Your daughter died!" They add: "Why bother the Teacher any longer?" —Mark 5:35.

What devastating news! This man, so highly respected in the community, is now completely helpless. His only daughter has died. Jesus, however, overhears the report, and turning to Jairus, he says encouragingly: "Have no fear, only exercise faith."—Mark 5:36.

Jesus then accompanies Jairus back to his home. On arriving, they find a great commotion.

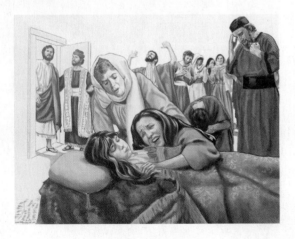

Those who have gathered there are weeping, wailing, and beating themselves in grief. Jesus steps inside and makes the startling statement: "The child has not died but is sleeping." (Mark 5:39) On hearing this, the people laugh at Jesus. They know that the girl really is dead. Yet, using his God-given powers, Jesus will show that it is possible for people to be brought back from death just as they can be awakened from a deep sleep. *time?*

Jesus now sends everyone outside except for Peter, James, John, and the dead girl's parents. Jesus takes these five with him and goes to where the girl is lying. Taking her by the hand, he says: "'Tal'i·tha cu'mi,' which, when translated, means: 'Little girl, I say to you, "Get up!"'" (Mark 5:41) Immediately, she rises and begins walking. Imagine the ecstasy that Jairus and his wife feel on seeing this! Providing further evidence that the girl really is alive, Jesus directs that she be given something to eat.

On earlier occasions, Jesus ordered those whom he healed not to publicize what he had done for them, and he does so again with these parents. Nevertheless, the delighted parents and others spread the news "into all that region." (Matthew 9:26) Would you not talk about it excitedly if you had seen one of your loved ones raised from the dead? This is the second recorded resurrection Jesus performs.

7/15/92 NT → uncleanness of dead body but J.C. makes clean

◇ What report does Jairus receive, and how does Jesus encourage him?
◇ When Jesus and Jairus arrive at the home, what is the situation there?
◇ Why does Jesus say that the dead child is only sleeping?

Show they acknowledge J.C. is heir to throne of David is messiah & covenant to be fulfilled by someone in D. line

It has been a full day for Jesus. After a voyage from the region of the Decapolis, he healed the woman with the flow of blood and he resurrected Jairus' daughter. But the day is not over. As Jesus leaves Jairus' home, two blind men follow him, shouting: "Have mercy on us, Son of David."—Matthew 9:27.

By calling Jesus "Son of David," these men express their belief that Jesus is heir to the throne of David and thus the Messiah. Jesus seems to ignore their cries, perhaps to see whether they will be persistent, and they are. When Jesus enters a house, the two men follow him inside. Jesus asks them: "Do you have faith that I can do this?" They answer confidently: "Yes, Lord." At that, Jesus touches their eyes and says: "According to your faith let it happen to you."—Matthew 9:28, 29.

Suddenly they can see! As he has earlier instructed others, Jesus directs them not to publicize what he did. But filled with gladness, they later talk about him far and wide.

As these two men are leaving, people bring in a man who cannot speak because he is demon-possessed. Jesus expels the demon, and instantly the man begins to talk. The crowds marvel at this, saying: "Never has anything like this been seen in Israel." Pharisees are also present. They cannot deny the miracles, so they repeat their charge as to the source of Jesus' works: "It is by the ruler of the demons that he expels the demons."—Matthew 9:33, 34.

Shortly thereafter, Jesus heads back to his hometown, Nazareth, now accompanied by his disciples. About a year earlier, he taught in the synagogue there. The people initially marveled at what he said, but they later took offense at his teaching and tried to kill him. Now Jesus again tries to help his former neighbors.

On the Sabbath, he returns to the synagogue to teach. Many are astounded, even asking: "Where did this man get this wisdom and these powerful works?" They say: "Is this not the carpenter's son? Is not his mother called Mary, and his brothers James and Joseph and Simon and Judas? And his sisters, are they not all with us? Where, then, did he get all of this?"—Matthew 13:54-56.

The people feel that Jesus is just a local man. 'We saw him grow up,' they think, 'so how can he be the Messiah?' Consequently, despite all the evidence—including Jesus' great wisdom and powerful works—they reject him. Because of their familiarity with Jesus, even his relatives stumble at him, causing him to observe: "A prophet is not without honor except in his home territory and in his own house."—Matthew 13:57.

Indeed, Jesus is amazed at their lack of faith. So he does not perform any miracles there "except to lay his hands on a few sick people and cure them."—Mark 6:5, 6.

had a positive attitude & believed

training young ones to serve in D. capacity

◇ By addressing Jesus as "Son of David," what do the blind men show they believe?
◇ The Pharisees fall back on what explanation for Jesus' miracles?
◇ What reception does Jesus receive in Nazareth, and why?

PREACHING IN GALILEE AND TRAINING THE APOSTLES

MATTHEW 9:35–10:15 MARK 6:6-11 LUKE 9:1-5

Jesus has been preaching intensively for some two years. Is it now time to let up and take it easy? On the contrary, Jesus expands his preaching activity by setting out "on a tour of all the cities and villages [of Galilee], teaching in their synagogues and preaching the good news of the Kingdom and curing every sort of disease and every sort of infirmity." (Matthew 9:35) What he sees convinces him of the need to expand the preaching work. But how will he accomplish this?

As he travels, Jesus sees people in need of spiritual healing and comfort. They are like sheep without a shepherd, skinned and thrown about. He feels pity for them and tells his disciples: "Yes, the harvest is great, but the workers are few. Therefore, beg the Master of the harvest to send out workers into his harvest." —Matthew 9:37, 38.

Jesus knows what will help. He summons the 12 apostles and divides them into pairs, making six teams of preachers. He then gives them clear instructions: "Do not go off into the road of the nations, and do not enter any Samaritan city; but instead, go continually to the lost sheep of the house of Israel. As you go, preach, saying: 'The Kingdom of the heavens has drawn near.'"—Matthew 10:5-7.

The Kingdom they are to preach about is the one Jesus spoke of in the model prayer. 'The Kingdom has drawn near' in the sense that God's designated King, Jesus Christ, is present.

What, though, will prove that his disciples truly represent this Kingdom government? Jesus empowers them to cure the sick and even raise the dead, all of this at no charge. How, then, will the apostles care for their own needs, such as their daily food?

Jesus tells his disciples not to make their own material preparations for this preaching tour. They are not to get gold, silver, or copper for their purses. They do not even need a food pouch for the trip nor extra undergarments or sandals. Why not? Jesus assures them: "The worker deserves his food." (Matthew 10:10) The people they find who appreciate their message will help care for the disciples' basic needs. Jesus says: "Wherever you enter into a home, stay there until you leave that place."—Mark 6:10.

Jesus also gives instructions on how to approach householders with the Kingdom message, saying: "When you enter the house, greet the household. If the house is deserving, let the peace you wish it come upon it; but if it is not deserving, let the peace from you return upon you. Wherever anyone does not receive you or listen to your words, on going out of that house or that city, shake the dust off your feet."—Matthew 10:12-14.

It could even be that an entire city or village rejects their message. What does that mean for such a place? Jesus reveals that severe adverse

judgment will result. He explains: "Truly I say to you, it will be more endurable for the land of Sodom and Gomorrah on Judgment Day than for that city."—Matthew 10:15.

◇ When does Jesus begin another preaching tour of Galilee, and what does he note about the people?
◇ How does Jesus send out the 12 apostles, and with what instructions?
◇ In what sense has 'the Kingdom drawn near'?

PREPARED TO PREACH DESPITE PERSECUTION

MATTHEW 10:16–11:1   MARK 6:12, 13   LUKE 9:6

Jesus provides his apostles with excellent instructions on how to carry out the preaching work as they go forth in pairs. He does not stop there, however. He kindly warns them about opposers: "Look! I am sending you out as sheep among wolves . . . Be on your guard against men, for they will hand you over to local courts and they will scourge you in their synagogues. And you will be brought before governors and kings for my sake."—Matthew 10:16-18.

Yes, Jesus' followers may encounter severe persecution, yet he reassuringly promises them: "When they hand you over, do not become anxious about how or what you are to speak, for what you are to speak will be given you in that hour; for the ones speaking are not just you, but it is the spirit of your Father that speaks by you." Jesus continues: "Brother will hand brother over to death, and a father his child, and children will rise up against parents and will have them put to death. And you will be hated by all people on account of my name, but the one who has endured to the end will be saved."—Matthew 10:19-22.

Because the preaching is of primary importance, Jesus emphasizes the need for his followers to be discreet so as to remain free to car-ry out this work. He says: "When they persecute you in one city, flee to another; for truly I say to you, you will by no means complete the circuit of the cities of Israel until the Son of man arrives."—Matthew 10:23.

What outstanding instructions, warnings, and encouragement Jesus gives to his 12 apostles! You can appreciate, though, that these words are also meant for those who will share in the preaching work after Jesus' death and resurrection. This is shown by his saying that his disciples will be "hated by *all* people," not just by those to whom the apostles are being sent to preach. Furthermore, we do not read of the apostles' being brought before governors and kings during this short preaching campaign in Galilee nor of their being delivered up to death by family members.

Clearly, Jesus has the future in mind in saying these things to the apostles. Consider his statement that his disciples will not complete their circuit of preaching "until the Son of man arrives." Jesus is indicating that his disciples will not complete the preaching about God's Kingdom before the glorified King Jesus Christ arrives as God's judge.

While carrying out the preaching work, the

apostles should not be surprised to face opposition, for Jesus says: "A disciple is not above his teacher, nor a slave above his master." Jesus' point is clear. He faces ill-treatment and persecution for preaching God's Kingdom, and so will they. Yet Jesus urges: "Do not become fearful of those who kill the body but cannot kill the soul; rather, fear him who can destroy both soul and body in Gehenna."—Matthew 10: 24, 28.

In this, Jesus set the example. He fearlessly endured death rather than compromise his loyalty to the one with all power, Jehovah. It is Almighty God who can destroy a person's "soul" (his future prospects for life) or who can resurrect him to enjoy everlasting life. How reassuring this must be to the apostles!

Jesus illustrates God's loving care for his followers in this way: "Two sparrows sell for a coin of small value, do they not? Yet not one of them will fall to the ground without your Father's knowledge. . . . So have no fear; you are worth more than many sparrows."—Matthew 10: 29, 31.

The message Jesus' disciples preach will divide households, some family members accepting it and others not. "Do not think I came to bring peace to the earth," Jesus explains. Yes, it takes courage for a family member to embrace Bible truth. "Whoever has greater affection for father or mother than for me is not worthy of me," Jesus observes, "and whoever has greater affection for son or daughter than for me is not worthy of me."—Matthew 10:34, 37.

Yet, some will receive his disciples favorably. He says: "Whoever gives one of these little ones only a cup of cold water to drink because he is a disciple, I tell you truly, he will by no means lose his reward."—Matthew 10:42.

Well-equipped with Jesus' instructions, warnings, and encouragement, the apostles head out "through the territory from village to village, declaring the good news and performing cures everywhere."—Luke 9:6.

◇ Jesus provides what warnings for his disciples?
◇ What encouragement and comfort does he give them?
◇ Why do Jesus' instructions also apply to us today?

MURDER DURING A BIRTHDAY PARTY

MATTHEW 14:1-12   MARK 6:14-29   LUKE 9:7-9

[handwritten annotations: HER 3RD HEROD AGRIPPA; 1ST MARRIAGE TO HEROD THE GREAT'S SON (THROUGH 3RD WIFE MARIANNE II) HEROD PHILIP; ENTITLED QUESTION]

While Jesus' apostles are carrying out their ministry in Galilee, the one who introduced Jesus has no such liberty. John the Baptist is still in prison after almost two years.

John had openly declared that it was wrong for King Herod Antipas to take Herodias, the wife of his half brother Philip, as his own. Herod had divorced his first wife to marry Herodias. According to the Mosaic Law, which Herod claims to follow, this marriage is adulterous and illegal. In response to John's reproof, Herod had John thrown into prison, perhaps at the urging of Herodias.

Herod is at a loss as to what to do with John, because the people 'take him for a prophet.' (Matthew 14:5) Herodias, though, feels no such indecision. She is "nursing a grudge against him," and in fact, she keeps seeking to have him put to death. (Mark 6:19) Finally, the opportunity arises.

Shortly before the Passover of 32 C.E., Herod arranges a large celebration for his birthday. All of Herod's top-ranking officials and army officers, as well as the leading citizens of Galilee, assemble for the party. During the festivities, Salome, the young daughter of Herodias by her former husband Philip, is sent in to dance for the guests. The men are enthralled by her performance.

Highly pleased with his stepdaughter, Herod says to her: "Ask me for whatever you want, and I will give it to you." He even swears: "Whatever you ask me for, I will give it to you, up to half my kingdom." Before answering, Salome goes out and says to her mother: "What should I ask for?"—Mark 6:22-24.

This is the opportunity that Herodias has been seeking! "The head of John the Baptizer," she promptly answers. Immediately, Salome comes back to Herod with her request: "I want you to give me right away on a platter the head of John the Baptist."—Mark 6:24, 25.

This greatly distresses Herod, but his guests have heard his oath to Salome. He is embarrassed not to grant it, even if this means murdering an innocent man. Hence, Herod sends a bodyguard to the prison with the grisly instructions. Soon the bodyguard returns with John's head on a platter. He gives it to Salome, who takes it to her mother.

When John's disciples hear what has happened, they come and remove his body and bury it. Then they report the matter to Jesus.

Later, when Herod hears of Jesus' healing people and casting out demons, he is disturbed. He wonders if the man doing these things—Jesus—is actually John the Baptist now "raised up from the dead." (Luke 9:7) So Herod Antipas greatly desires to see Jesus. This is certainly not to hear Jesus' preaching. Rather, Herod wants to see Jesus to confirm whether his concerns are well-founded or not.

◇ Why is John the Baptist in prison?

◇ How does Herodias finally manage to have John killed?

◇ After John's death, why does Herod Antipas want to see Jesus?

Herod Ag PA ~~~~~ He the Great
one of sons of → he slew son on suspicion of sedition
H. Agrippas good friend
was Caligula (Emperor was T. Tiberius

• HEROD HAS JOHN THE BAPTIST BEHEADED
51

FEEDING THOUSANDS WITH A FEW LOAVES AND FISH

MATTHEW 14:13-21   MARK 6:30-44   LUKE 9:10-17   JOHN 6:1-13

The 12 apostles have enjoyed a preaching tour throughout Galilee, and they relate to Jesus "all the things they had done and taught." Understandably, they are tired. Yet, they do not even have time to eat because so many people are coming and going. So Jesus says: "Come, you yourselves, privately into an isolated place and rest up a little."—Mark 6:30, 31.

They board a boat, probably near Capernaum, and head for an out-of-the-way place east of the Jordan River beyond Bethsaida. Many people, however, see them leave, and others learn about it. Together they run along the shore and are there when the boat lands.

Leaving the boat, Jesus sees the crowd and is moved with pity, for they are as sheep without a shepherd. So he starts "to teach them

many things" about the Kingdom. (Mark 6:34) He also heals "those needing a cure." (Luke 9:11) As time passes, the disciples say to him: "The place is isolated and the hour is already late; send the crowds away, so that they may go into the villages and buy themselves food." —Matthew 14:15.

Jesus replies: "They do not have to leave; you give them something to eat." (Matthew 14:16) Although Jesus already knows what he is going to do, he tests Philip with the question: "Where will we buy bread for these people to eat?" Philip is the one to ask, for he is from nearby Bethsaida. Still, buying bread is not the solution. There are about 5,000 men. And the total may be double that, counting women and children! Philip responds: "Two hundred denarii [a denarius is a day's wage] worth of bread is not enough for each of them to get even a little." —John 6:5-7.

Perhaps to show the impossibility of feeding them all, Andrew comments: "Here is a little boy who has five barley loaves and two small fish. But what are these among so many?" —John 6:9.

It is springtime, just before the Passover of 32 C.E., and green grass covers the hillside. Jesus has his disciples tell the people to recline on the grass in groups of 50 and of 100. He takes the five loaves and two fish and gives thanks to God. Then he breaks the loaves and divides up the fish. Jesus gives these to the disciples to distribute to the people. Amazingly, all the people eat until they are satisfied!

Later, Jesus tells his disciples: "Gather together the fragments left over, so that nothing is wasted." (John 6:12) They are able to fill 12 baskets with the leftovers gathered!

◇ Why does Jesus seek a place of privacy for his apostles?

◇ Where do Jesus and the disciples go, and what do they encounter there?

◇ What do the disciples urge Jesus to do, but how does he care for the people?

Jesus' miraculous ability to feed thousands has a strong impact on the people. They conclude that "this really is the Prophet who was to come into the world," the Messiah, and that he certainly would make a desirable ruler. (John 6:14; Deuteronomy 18:18) So the people plan to seize Jesus and make him king.

Jesus, however, realizes what the people are planning. He dismisses the crowds and instructs his disciples to get back in their boat. Their route and destination? They are to head toward Bethsaida and then on to Capernaum. As for Jesus himself, he withdraws to the mountain to pray alone that night.

In the light of the moon shortly before dawn, Jesus observes the boat from a distance. The waves of the sea are being whipped up by a strong wind, and the apostles are 'struggling to row, for the wind is against them.' (Mark 6: 48) Jesus descends from the mountain and begins walking over the waves toward them. By now "they had rowed about three or four miles." (John 6:19) The disciples observe Jesus seeming to pass by them, and they cry out in fear: "It is an apparition!"—Mark 6:49.

Jesus comfortingly responds: "Take courage! It is I; do not be afraid." But Peter says: "Lord, if it is you, command me to come to you over the waters." Jesus answers: "Come!" At that, Peter gets out of the boat and actually walks on water toward Jesus. But when he looks at the windstorm, Peter becomes afraid and starts to sink. He cries out: "Lord, save me!" Stretching out his hand, Jesus catches hold of Peter and says: "You with little faith, why did you give way to doubt?"—Matthew 14:27-31.

Peter and Jesus get into the boat, and the wind abates. The disciples are amazed, but should they be? If they had grasped "the meaning of the loaves," the miracle Jesus performed a few hours earlier when he fed thousands, it should not have been amazing that he could walk on water and calm the wind. Now they react by doing obeisance to him, saying: "You really are God's Son."—Mark 6:52; Matthew 14:33.

Soon they reach the beautiful, fruitful plain of Gennesaret, south of Capernaum. They anchor the boat and then come ashore. The people recognize Jesus, and together with others from the surrounding country, they bring the sick to him. When these just touch the fringe of Jesus' outer garment, they are made completely well.

Meanwhile, the crowd that had witnessed the miraculous feeding of the thousands discover that Jesus has left. So when little boats from Tiberias arrive, the people get aboard and sail to Capernaum to find Jesus. When they do, they ask: "Rabbi, when did you get here?" (John 6: 25) With good reason, Jesus rebukes them, as we will see.

◇ After Jesus feeds the thousands, what do the people want to do to him?

◇ Why should the disciples not be amazed that Jesus can walk on water and calm the wind?

◇ What happens after Jesus reaches the shore near Capernaum?

JESUS—"THE BREAD OF LIFE"

JOHN 6:25-48

Over on the eastern side of the Sea of Galilee, Jesus miraculously fed thousands and then escaped when they wanted to make him king. That night he walked on the stormy sea and rescued Peter, who also walked on water but began to sink when his faith wavered. Jesus also calmed the wind, perhaps saving his disciples from shipwreck.

Now Jesus is back on the western side of the sea, in the area of Capernaum. Those he miraculously fed find him and inquire: "When did you get here?" Rebuking them, Jesus says that they are looking for him in the hope of being fed again. He urges them to "work, not for the food that perishes, but for the food that remains for everlasting life." So they ask: "What must we do to carry out the works of God?"—John 6:25-28.

They may be thinking of works set out in the Law, but Jesus points to the work of highest value: "This is the work of God, that you exercise faith in the one whom he sent." The people, however, do not exercise such faith in Jesus, despite all that he has done. They demand that he perform a sign so that they may believe in him. "What work are you doing?" they ask. "Our forefathers ate the manna in the wilderness, just as it is written: 'He gave them bread from heaven to eat.'"—John 6:29-31; Psalm 78:24.

Regarding their request for a sign, Jesus directs the people to the real Source of miraculous provisions: "I say to you, Moses did not give you the bread from heaven, but my Father gives you the true bread from heaven. For the bread of God is the one who comes down from heaven and gives life to the world." Not grasping his point, they plead: "Lord, always give us this bread." (John 6:32-34) What "bread," though, does Jesus mean?

He explains: "I am the bread of life. Whoever comes to me will not get hungry at all, and whoever exercises faith in me will never get thirsty at all. But as I said to you, you have even seen me and yet do not believe. . . . I have come down from heaven to do, not my own will, but the will of him who sent me. This is the will of him who sent me, that I should lose none out of all those whom he has given me, but that I should resurrect them on the last day. For this is the will of my Father, that everyone who recognizes the Son and exercises faith in him should have everlasting life."—John 6:35-40.

This causes quite a stir, and the Jews begin murmuring about him. How can he claim that he is "the bread that came down from heaven"? (John 6:41) To them, he is just a son of human parents from the Galilean city of Nazareth. The people ask: "Is this not Jesus the son of Joseph, whose father and mother we know?" —John 6:42.

"Stop murmuring among yourselves," Jesus responds. "No man can come to me unless the Father, who sent me, draws him, and I will resurrect him on the last day. It is written in the Prophets: 'They will all be taught by Jehovah.' Everyone who has listened to the Father and has learned comes to me. Not that any man has seen the Father, except the one who is from God; this one has seen the Father. Most truly I say to you, whoever believes has everlasting life."—John 6:43-47; Isaiah 54:13.

When earlier he spoke with Nicodemus, Jesus mentioned everlasting life and linked that with faith in the Son of man, stating: "Everyone exercising faith in [God's only-begotten Son] might not be destroyed but have everlasting life." (John 3:15, 16) But now he is speak-

ing to a much larger audience, telling them that he has a role in their gaining everlasting life, which neither the manna nor the bread commonly available in Galilee can provide. So how can everlasting life be gained? Jesus re-peats his words: "I am the bread of life."—John 6:48.

This discussion regarding the bread from heaven continues, reaching a climax while Jesus teaches in a synagogue in Capernaum.

◇ Considering recent events, why is the request for Jesus to produce a sign inappropriate?

◇ How do the Jews react to Jesus' saying that he is the true "bread from heaven"?

◇ Why is the bread that Jesus speaks of superior to manna or literal bread?

JESUS' WORDS SHOCK MANY

JOHN 6:48-71

In a synagogue in Capernaum, Jesus is teaching about his being the true bread from heaven. His comments evidently add to what he said to the people who returned from the eastern side of the Sea of Galilee, those who ate from the loaves and fish provided there.

Jesus continues his discussion, saying: "Your forefathers ate the manna in the wilderness and yet they died." In contrast, he explains: "I am the living bread that came down from heaven. If anyone eats of this bread he will live forever; and for a fact, the bread that I will give is my flesh in behalf of the life of the world."—John 6: 48-51.

In the spring of 30 C.E., Jesus told Nicodemus that God loved the world so much that he provided his Son as a Savior. Jesus now stresses the need to eat of his flesh by exercising faith in the sacrifice he will make. That is the way to receive everlasting life.

However, the people take exception to Jesus' words. "How can this man give us his flesh to eat?" they ask. (John 6:52) Jesus wants them to understand that he means this figuratively, not literally. What he adds shows this to be his meaning.

"Unless you eat the flesh of the Son of man and drink his blood, you have no life in yourselves. Whoever feeds on my flesh and drinks my blood has everlasting life, . . . for my flesh is true food and my blood is true drink. Whoever feeds on my flesh and drinks my blood remains in union with me."—John 6:53-56.

Imagine how offensive that may sound to Jewish listeners! They might think that Jesus is suggesting cannibalism or a violation of God's law against consuming blood. (Genesis 9:4; Leviticus 17:10, 11) But Jesus is not referring to eating flesh or drinking blood literally. He is showing that all who want everlasting life must exercise faith in the sacrifice that he is to make when he offers up his perfect human body and pours out his lifeblood. Yet, even many of his disciples do not understand this teaching. Some react: "This speech is shocking; who can listen to it?"—John 6:60.

Because Jesus realizes that some of his disciples are murmuring, he asks: "Does this stumble you? What, therefore, if you should see the Son of man ascending to where he was before? . . . The sayings that I have spoken to you are spirit and are life. But there are some of you who do not believe." With that, many disciples leave and no longer follow him.—John 6: 61-64.

So Jesus addresses his 12 apostles with the question: "You do not want to go also, do you?" Peter responds: "Lord, whom shall we go away to? You have sayings of everlasting life. We have believed and have come to know that you are the Holy One of God." (John 6:67-69) What an expression of loyalty, even though at this point Peter and the other apostles do not fully understand what Jesus is teaching on this matter!

While pleased by Peter's response, Jesus observes: "I chose you twelve, did I not? Yet one of you is a slanderer." (John 6:70) Jesus is speaking about Judas Iscariot. It is possible that at this point Jesus detects that Judas is starting down a wrong course.

Still, it certainly brings Jesus satisfaction to know that Peter and the other apostles are not dissuaded from following him and from sharing in the lifesaving work that he is doing.

◇ How does Jesus give his flesh to people, and how can someone 'eat Jesus' flesh'?

◇ Why are people shocked at what Jesus says about his flesh and blood, but what is he emphasizing?

◇ When many quit following Jesus, what is Peter's reaction?

WHAT REALLY DEFILES A PERSON?

MATTHEW 15:1-20   MARK 7:1-23   JOHN 7:1

As the Passover of 32 C.E. approaches, Jesus is busy teaching in Galilee. Then he likely heads to Jerusalem for the Passover, as God's Law requires. However, Jesus does so cautiously because the Jews are seeking to kill him. (John 7:1) After that he returns to Galilee.

Jesus is probably in Capernaum when Pharisees and scribes come to him from Jerusalem. Why do they make this trip? They are looking for grounds on which to accuse Jesus of a religious offense. They ask: "Why do your disciples overstep the tradition of the men of former times? For example, they do not wash their hands when about to eat a meal." (Matthew 15:2) God never told his people to observe this ritual of 'washing their hands up to the elbow.' (Mark 7:3) Yet the Pharisees consider not doing so to be a serious offense.

Rather than answer their accusation directly, Jesus points to how they willfully break God's Law. "Why do you overstep the commandment of God because of your tradition?" he asks them. "For example, God said, 'Honor your father and your mother,' and, 'Let the one who speaks abusively of his father or mother be put to death.' But you say, 'Whoever says to his father or mother: "Whatever I have that could benefit you is a gift dedicated to God," he need not honor his father at all.'"—Matthew 15:3-6; Exodus 20:12; 21:17.

The Pharisees claim that money, property, or anything dedicated as a gift to God belongs to the temple, so it cannot be used for a different purpose. In reality, though, the person is still in possession of the dedicated gift. For example, a son might say that his money or property is "corban," a gift dedicated to God or to the temple, as if the temple now has prior claim to the gift. The money or property is still the son's to use, yet he claims that it cannot be used to help his aged and needy parents. He thereby evades his responsibility toward them.—Mark 7:11.

Jesus is rightly indignant at this twisting of God's Law and says: "You have made the word of God invalid because of your tradition. You hypocrites, Isaiah aptly prophesied about you when he said: 'This people honor me with their lips, but their hearts are far removed from me. It is in vain that they keep worshipping me, for they teach commands of men as doctrines.'" The Pharisees have no response to Jesus' strong criticism. So he calls the crowd to come near. "Listen and get the sense of it," he says. "It is not what enters into a man's mouth that defiles him, but it is what comes out of his mouth that defiles him."—Matthew 15:6-11; Isaiah 29:13.

Later when in a house, the disciples ask Jesus: "Do you know that the Pharisees were stumbled at hearing what you said?" He replies: "Every plant that my heavenly Father did not plant will be uprooted. Let them be. Blind guides is what they are. If, then, a blind man guides a blind man, both will fall into a pit."—Matthew 15:12-14.

Jesus seems surprised when, on behalf of the disciples, Peter asks for clarification about what defiles a man. Jesus responds: "Are you not aware that whatever enters into the mouth passes through the stomach and is discharged into the sewer? However, whatever comes out of the mouth comes from the heart, and those things defile a man. For example, out of the heart come wicked reasonings, murders, adulteries, sexual immorality, thefts, false testimo-

nies, blasphemies. These are the things that defile a man; but to take a meal with unwashed hands does not defile a man."—Matthew 15: 17-20.

Jesus is not discouraging normal hygiene, nor is he arguing that a person need not wash his hands before preparing food or eating a meal. Rather, he is condemning the hypocrisy of religious leaders who try to bypass God's righteous laws by resorting to human traditions. The fact is, wicked deeds originating in the heart are what defile a man.

◇ The Pharisees and scribes make what accusation?

◇ As Jesus points out, how do the Pharisees willfully overstep God's Law?

◇ What are the things that actually defile a man?

JESUS CURES A GIRL AND A DEAF MAN

MATTHEW 15:21-31   MARK 7:24-37

Having denounced the Pharisees for their self-serving traditions, Jesus leaves with his disciples. He heads for the regions of Tyre and Sidon in Phoenicia, many miles to the northwest.

Jesus finds a house to stay in but does not want people to know that he is there. Yet, even here he cannot escape notice. A woman of Greek descent who was born in this area finds Jesus and begins begging: "Have mercy on me, Lord, Son of David. My daughter is cruelly demon possessed."—Matthew 15:22; Mark 7:26.

After a while, Jesus' disciples urge him: "Send her away, because she keeps crying out after us." In response, Jesus explains his reason for ignoring her: "I was not sent to anyone except to the lost sheep of the house of Israel." The woman does not give up, though. She approaches and falls down before Jesus, pleading: "Lord, help me!"—Matthew 15:23-25.

Apparently to test her faith, Jesus alludes to the Jews' negative view of people of other nationalities: "It is not right to take the bread of the children and throw it to the little dogs." (Matthew 15:26) In speaking of *little* dogs," or puppies, Jesus reveals his tender feelings toward non-Jews. His facial expression and compassionate voice must also convey those feelings.

Rather than taking offense, the woman picks up on the reference to Jewish prejudices and humbly observes: "Yes, Lord, but really the little dogs do eat of the crumbs falling from the table of their masters." Jesus recognizes her good heart condition and says: "O woman, great is your faith; let it happen to you as you wish."

(Matthew 15:27, 28) And it does, even though the girl is not right there! When the woman returns home, she finds her daughter lying on the bed, completely healed—"the demon was gone"!—Mark 7:30.

From the region of Phoenicia, Jesus and his disciples head across the country toward the upper Jordan River. They apparently cross the Jordan somewhere north of the Sea of Galilee and go into the region of the Decapolis. There, they go up on a mountain, but the crowds find them. The people bring to Jesus their lame, maimed, blind, and speechless. They lay these sick ones at Jesus' feet, and he cures them. Amazed, the people glorify the God of Israel.

Jesus gives special attention to one man who is deaf and has a speech problem. You can understand how he must feel in a large crowd. Perhaps noting how nervous this man is, Jesus takes him away from the crowd. When they are alone, Jesus indicates what he is going to do for him. He puts his fingers into the man's ears and, after spitting, touches the man's tongue. Then looking toward heaven, Jesus utters a Semitic expression that means "Be opened." At that, the man's hearing is restored, and he is able to speak normally. Jesus does not want this publicized, preferring that people believe in him based on what they personally see and hear.—Mark 7:32-36.

Jesus' power to perform such cures has a deep effect on the observers, who are "astounded beyond measure." They say: "He has done all things well. He even makes the deaf hear and the speechless speak."—Mark 7:37.

◊ Why does Jesus not immediately heal the Phoenician woman's daughter?

◊ After leaving the region of Phoenicia, where do Jesus and his disciples go?

◊ How does Jesus show compassion when dealing with the man who is deaf and speechless?

HE MULTIPLIES LOAVES AND WARNS ABOUT LEAVEN

MATTHEW 15:32–16:12 MARK 8:1-21

Great crowds have flocked to Jesus in the region of the Decapolis, on the east side of the Sea of Galilee. They have come to hear him and to be healed, bringing along large baskets, or hampers, of provisions.

In time, however, Jesus tells his disciples: "I feel pity for the crowd, because they have already stayed with me for three days and they have nothing to eat. If I send them off to their homes hungry, they will give out on the road, and some of them are from far away." The disciples ask: "From where will anyone get enough bread in this isolated place to satisfy these people?"—Mark 8:2-4.

Jesus responds: "How many loaves do you have?" The disciples say: "Seven, and a few small fish." (Matthew 15:34) Then Jesus has the people recline on the ground. He takes the loaves and the fish, prays to God, and gives them to his disciples to distribute. Amazingly, all eat to satisfaction. The leftovers collected fill seven large provision baskets, even though

about 4,000 men, as well as women and children, have eaten!

After Jesus sends the crowds away, he and the disciples cross by boat to Magadan, on the western shore of the Sea of Galilee. Here, Pharisees accompanied by some of the sect of the Sadducees try to test Jesus, asking him to display a sign from heaven.

Realizing what their motives are, Jesus replies: "When evening falls, you say, 'It will be fair weather, for the sky is fire-red,' and in the morning, 'It will be wintry, rainy weather today, for the sky is fire-red but gloomy.' You know how to interpret the appearance of the sky, but the signs of the times you cannot interpret." (Matthew 16:2, 3) Then Jesus tells the Pharisees and Sadducees that no sign will be given them except the sign of Jonah.

Jesus and his disciples get in a boat and head toward Bethsaida on the northeast shore of the sea. En route, the disciples discover that they forgot to bring enough bread. They have just one loaf. Having in mind his recent encounter with the Pharisees and the Sadducean supporters of Herod, Jesus warns: "Keep your eyes open; look out for the leaven of the Pharisees and the leaven of Herod." The disciples mistakenly think that his mention of leaven refers to their forgetting to bring bread. Noting their mistake, Jesus says: "Why do you argue over your having no bread?"—Mark 8:15-17.

Jesus had recently provided bread for thousands of people. So the disciples should know that he is not concerned about a lack of literal loaves. "Do you not remember," he asks, "when I broke the five loaves for the 5,000 men, how many baskets full of fragments you collected?" They answer: "Twelve." Continuing, Jesus says:

"When I broke the seven loaves for the 4,000 men, how many large baskets full of fragments did you take up?" They reply: "Seven."—Mark 8: 18-20.

Jesus asks: "How is it you do not discern that I did not speak to you about bread?" He adds: "Watch out for the leaven of the Pharisees and Sadducees."—Matthew 16:11.

Finally, the disciples get the point. Leaven is used to cause fermentation and make bread rise. Jesus is here using leaven as a symbol of corruption. He is warning the disciples to be on guard against "the *teaching* of the Pharisees and Sadducees," which has a corrupting effect. —Matthew 16:12.

◇ Why do people flock to Jesus?

◇ When Jesus mentions leaven, what do the disciples mistakenly think?

◇ What does Jesus mean by the expression "the leaven of the Pharisees and Sadducees"?

WHO IS THE SON OF MAN?

MATTHEW 16:13-27   MARK 8:22-38   LUKE 9:18-26

Jesus and his disciples arrive at Bethsaida. The people then bring a blind man to him and beg Jesus to touch the man to heal him.

Taking the man by the hand, Jesus leads him outside the village. After spitting on the man's eyes, Jesus asks him: "Do you see anything?" The man replies: "I see people, but they look like trees walking about." (Mark 8:23, 24) Laying his hands on the man's eyes, Jesus restores his sight. He then sends home the man who can now see clearly, instructing him not to enter into the village.

Next, Jesus and his disciples travel northward to the region of Caesarea Philippi. It is a long ascent, covering about 25 miles. The village is at an elevation of 1,150 feet above sea level, with snowcapped Mount Hermon rising to the northeast. The trip probably takes a couple of days.

At one point along the way, Jesus goes off to pray alone. Only about nine or ten months remain before his death, and Jesus is concerned about his disciples. Many have recently left off following him, and others apparently are confused or disappointed. They may be wondering why he rejected the people's efforts to make him king or why he would not provide a sign to show unquestionably who he really is.

When the disciples come to where he is praying, Jesus asks: "Who are men saying the Son of man is?" They reply: "Some say John the Baptist, others Elijah, and still others Jeremiah or one of the prophets." Yes, people think that Jesus may actually be one of those men raised from the dead. To draw out their thinking, Jesus asks his disciples: "You, though, who do you say I am?" Peter quickly replies: "You are the Christ, the Son of the living God."—Matthew 16:13-16.

Jesus says that Peter can be happy that God revealed this to him, adding: "I say to you: You are Peter, and on this rock I will build my congregation, and the gates of the Grave will not overpower it." Jesus means that he himself will build a congregation and that even the Grave will not hold captive its members if they maintain a faithful course on earth. He promises Peter: "I will give you the keys of the Kingdom of the heavens."—Matthew 16:18, 19.

Jesus does not give Peter first place among the apostles, nor does Jesus make him the foundation of the congregation. Jesus himself is the Rock upon which his congregation will be built. (1 Corinthians 3:11; Ephesians 2:20) Peter, though, is to receive three keys. He will have the privilege of opening, as it were, the opportunity for groups of people to enter the Kingdom of the heavens.

Peter would use the first key at Pentecost 33 C.E., showing repentant Jews and proselytes what they must do to be saved. He would use the second to open to believing Samaritans the opportunity to enter God's Kingdom. Then, in 36 C.E., Peter would use the third to extend that opportunity to uncircumcised Gentiles, Cornelius and others.—Acts 2:37, 38; 8: 14-17; 10:44-48.

In this discussion, Jesus' apostles are troubled when he foretells the sufferings and death that he will soon face in Jerusalem. Not grasping that Jesus is to be resurrected to heavenly life, Peter takes him aside and rebukes him, saying: "Be kind to yourself, Lord; you will not have this happen to you at all." But Jesus turns his back and answers: "Get behind me, Satan! You are a stumbling block to me, because you think, not God's thoughts, but those of men." —Matthew 16:22, 23.

Jesus now calls others besides the apostles and explains that it will not be easy to be his follower. He says: "If anyone wants to come after me, let him disown himself and pick up his torture stake and keep following me. For whoever wants to save his life will lose it, but whoever loses his life for my sake and for the sake of the good news will save it."—Mark 8:34, 35.

Yes, to prove worthy of Jesus' favor, his followers must be courageous and self-sacrificing. Jesus states: "Whoever becomes ashamed

of me and my words in this adulterous and sinful generation, the Son of man will also be ashamed of him when he comes in the glory of his Father with the holy angels." (Mark 8:38) Yes, when Jesus thus comes, "he will repay each one according to his behavior."—Matthew 16:27.

◇ What views do some people have as to Jesus' identity? How do the apostles view him?

◇ Peter receives what keys, and how are they to be used?

◇ What correction does Peter receive, and why?

THE TRANSFIGURATION—A VIEW OF CHRIST IN GLORY

MATTHEW 16:28–17:13   MARK 9:1-13   LUKE 9:27-36

While Jesus is teaching the people in the region of Caesarea Philippi, which is about 15 miles from Mount Hermon, he makes a startling announcement to his apostles: "Truly I say to you that there are some of those standing here who will not taste death at all until first they see the Son of man coming in his Kingdom."—Matthew 16:28.

The disciples must wonder what Jesus means. About a week later, he takes three of the apostles—Peter, James, and John—with him up to a lofty mountain. It may well be nighttime, for the three men are sleepy. While Jesus is praying, he is transfigured before them. The apostles see his face shine as the sun and see his garments become brilliant as light, glitteringly white.

Then, two figures, identified as "Moses and Elijah," appear. They start talking to Jesus about his 'departure that is to occur at Jerusalem.' (Luke 9:30, 31) His departure evidently refers to Jesus' death and subsequent resurrection, which he recently spoke of. (Matthew 16:21) This conversation proves that contrary to what Peter urged, Jesus' humiliating death is not something to be avoided.

Fully awake now, the three apostles watch and listen in amazement. This is a vision, yet it appears so real that Peter begins to get personally involved in the scene, saying: "Rabbi, it is fine for us to be here. So let us erect three tents, one for you, one for Moses, and one for Elijah." (Mark 9:5) Does Peter want the tents set up so that the vision will be prolonged for some time?

While Peter is speaking, a bright cloud covers them and a voice from the cloud says: "This is my Son, the beloved, whom I have approved. Listen to him." At hearing God's voice, the frightened apostles fall on their faces, but Jesus urges them: "Get up. Have no fear." (Matthew 17:5-7) When they do, the three apostles see no one except Jesus. The vision has ended. When it is day and they are descending from the mountain, Jesus commands: "Tell the vision to no one until the Son of man is raised up from the dead."—Matthew 17:9.

Elijah's appearance in the vision raises a question. "Why," the apostles ask, "do the scribes say that Elijah must come first?" Jesus replies: "Elijah has already come, and they did not recognize him." (Matthew 17:10-12) Jesus is speaking about John the Baptist, who fulfilled a role similar to Elijah's. Elijah prepared the way for Elisha, and John did so for Christ.

How strengthening this vision is to Jesus and to the apostles! It is a preview of Christ's Kingdom glory. Thus the disciples saw "the Son of man coming in his Kingdom," as Jesus had promised. (Matthew 16:28) While on the mountain, they were "eyewitnesses of his magnificence." Though the Pharisees wanted a sign to prove that Jesus was to be God's chosen King, he would not give them one. But Jesus' close disciples were allowed to see Jesus' transfiguration, which confirms Kingdom prophecies. Thus, Peter could later write: "We have the prophetic word made more sure."—2 Peter 1:16-19.

◇ Before their death, how do some see Jesus coming in his Kingdom?

◇ In the vision, what do Moses and Elijah talk about with Jesus?

◇ Why is the transfiguration vision strengthening to Christ's followers?

JESUS HEALS A DEMON-POSSESSED BOY

MATTHEW 17:14-20 MARK 9:14-29 LUKE 9:37-43

When Jesus, Peter, James, and John descend from the mountain, they meet a large crowd. Something is wrong. Scribes are gathered around the disciples, arguing with them. The people are quite surprised to see Jesus, and they run to greet him. "What are you arguing about with them?" he asks.—Mark 9:16.

A man from the crowd kneels before Jesus and explains: "Teacher, I brought my son to you because he has a speechless spirit. Wherever it seizes him, it throws him to the ground, and he foams at the mouth and grinds his teeth and loses his strength. I asked your disciples to expel it, but they were not able to do so."—Mark 9:17, 18.

Apparently, the scribes are criticizing the disciples because of their failure to heal the boy, perhaps ridiculing their efforts. So instead of replying to the distraught father, Jesus addresses the crowd, saying: "O faithless and twisted generation, how long must I continue with you? How long must I put up with you?" These strong words certainly apply to the scribes who have been making trouble for his disciples in his absence. Turning to the distressed father, Jesus says: "Bring him here to me."—Matthew 17:17.

As the boy approaches Jesus, the demon that possesses him knocks him to the ground and throws him into a violent convulsion. The boy keeps rolling on the ground, foaming at the mouth. "How long has this been happening to him?" Jesus asks the father. He answers: "From childhood on, and often it would throw him into the fire and also into the water to destroy him." The man pleads: "If you can do any-

thing, have pity on us and help us."—Mark 9: 21, 22.

The father is desperate, because even Jesus' disciples have not been able to help. In response to the man's desperate appeal, Jesus gives the encouraging assurance: "That expression, 'If you can'! Why, all things are possible for the one who has faith." Immediately the father cries out: "I have faith! Help me out where I need faith!"—Mark 9:23, 24.

Jesus notices the crowd running toward him. With all of these looking on, Jesus rebukes the demon: "You speechless and deaf spirit, I order you, get out of him and do not enter into him again!" In departing, the demon causes the boy to scream and have many convulsions. Then the boy lies there motionless. Seeing this, many people say: "He is dead!" (Mark 9:25, 26) But when Jesus takes the boy's hand, he rises and is "cured from that hour." (Matthew 17:18) Understandably, the people are astonished at what Jesus is doing.

Earlier, when Jesus sent the disciples forth to preach, they were able to expel demons. So now, privately in a house, they ask him: "Why could we not expel it?" Jesus explains that it was because of their lack of faith, saying: "This kind can come out only by prayer." (Mark 9:28, 29) Strong faith along with prayer for God's empowering help was needed to expel the powerful demon.

Jesus concludes: "Truly I say to you, if you have faith the size of a mustard grain, you will say to this mountain, 'Move from here to there,' and it will move, and nothing will be impossible for you." (Matthew 17:20) How powerful faith can be!

Obstacles and difficulties that block progress in Jehovah's service may seem to be as insurmountable and irremovable as a literal mountain. Yet, if we cultivate faith, we can overcome such mountainlike obstacles and difficulties.

◇ What situation does Jesus find upon returning from the mountain?
◇ Why were the disciples unable to expel the demon from the boy?
◇ How powerful can our faith become?

AN IMPORTANT LESSON IN HUMILITY

MATTHEW 17:22–18:5   MARK 9:30-37   LUKE 9:43-48

After the transfiguration and the healing of a demon-possessed boy in the region of Caesarea Philippi, Jesus heads toward Capernaum. He travels privately, just with his disciples, so that the crowds do not "get to know about it." (Mark 9:30) This gives him further opportunity to prepare his disciples for his death and for the work they will then do. "The Son of man is going to be betrayed into men's hands," he explains, "and they will kill him, and on the third day he will be raised up."—Matthew 17: 22, 23.

That idea should not strike his disciples as new. Jesus spoke earlier about his being killed, though Peter refused to believe that this would happen. (Matthew 16:21, 22) And three apostles saw the transfiguration and heard the discussion about Jesus' "departure." (Luke 9:31) His followers now become "very much grieved" over what Jesus is saying, even though they do not understand the full impact of his words. (Matthew 17:23) Still, they are afraid to question him further about it.

In time they come into Capernaum, Jesus' base of activity and the hometown of a number of the apostles. There, men who collect the temple tax approach Peter. Perhaps attempting to accuse Jesus of failing to pay taxes, they ask: "Does your teacher not pay the two drachmas [temple] tax?"—Matthew 17:24.

"Yes," Peter replies. Back at the house, Jesus is already aware of what has occurred. So rather than wait for Peter to bring the matter up, Jesus asks: "What do you think, Simon? From whom do the kings of the earth receive duties or head tax? From their sons or from the strangers?" Peter answers: "From the strangers." Thereupon Jesus observes: "Real-

ly, then, the sons are tax-free."—Matthew 17: 25, 26.

Jesus' Father is the King of the universe and the One who is worshipped at the temple. Hence, God's Son is not legally required to pay the temple tax. "But that we do not cause them to stumble," Jesus says, "go to the sea, cast a fishhook, and take the first

fish that comes up, and when you open its mouth, you will find a silver coin [a stater, or tetradrachma]. Take that and give it to them for me and you."—Matthew 17:27.

Soon the disciples are together, and they have a question for Jesus about who would be greatest in the Kingdom. These same men were recently afraid to question Jesus about his coming death, yet now they are not afraid to approach him about their future. Jesus knows what they are thinking. It is something they had already been arguing about as they trailed behind him on their trip back to Capernaum. So he asks: "What were you arguing about on the road?" (Mark 9:33) Embarrassed, the disciples keep silent, because they were arguing among themselves about who is greatest. Finally, the apostles present to Jesus the question that they have been discussing: "Who really is greatest in the Kingdom of the heavens?"—Matthew 18:1.

It seems incredible that the disciples would have such an argument after nearly three years of observing and hearing Jesus. However, they are imperfect. And they have grown up in a religious climate where position and

• JESUS AGAIN FORETELLS HIS DEATH
• HE PAYS TAX WITH COIN FROM FISH'S MOUTH
• WHO IS TO BE GREATEST IN THE KINGDOM?

62

rank are stressed. Moreover, Peter had recently heard Jesus promise him certain "keys" of the Kingdom. Might he thus feel superior? James and John may feel similarly, having been eyewitnesses of Jesus' transfiguration.

Whatever the case, Jesus acts to correct their attitude. He calls a child, stands him in their midst, and tells the disciples: "Unless you turn around and become as young children, you will by no means enter into the Kingdom of the heavens. Therefore, whoever will humble himself like this young child is the one who is the greatest in the Kingdom of the heavens; and whoever receives one such young child on the basis of my name receives me also."—Matthew 18:3-5.

What a marvelous method of teaching! Jesus does not become angry with his disciples and call them greedy or ambitious. Rather, he uses an object lesson. Young children do not have high status or prominence at all. Jesus thus shows that his disciples need to develop this view of themselves. Then Jesus concludes the lesson for his followers, saying: "The one who conducts himself as a lesser one among all of you is the one who is great."—Luke 9:48.

◇ On returning to Capernaum, Jesus repeats what important fact, and how do his disciples receive this?

◇ Why is Jesus not under obligation to pay the temple tax, but why does he do so?

◇ What might contribute to the disciples' concern about position, and how does Jesus correct them?

JESUS OFFERS COUNSEL ABOUT STUMBLING AND SIN

MATTHEW 18:6-20 MARK 9:38-50 LUKE 9:49, 50

any impediment that would cause 1 to stumble - VERBS -

Jesus has just illustrated the attitude that his followers should have. They should view themselves as children, lowly and without status. The disciples should 'receive such young children on the basis of his name and thus receive Jesus also.'—Matthew 18:5.

The apostles had recently been arguing over who is the greatest, so they may take Jesus' words as a reproof. Now the apostle John brings up something else that has just happened: "We saw someone expelling demons by using your name, and we tried to prevent him, because he is not following with us."—Luke 9:49. *so diff to counsel*

Does John view the apostles as the only ones who are authorized to heal others or to expel demons? If so, how is it that this Jewish man is successful in casting out wicked spirits? John seems to feel that the man should not be performing powerful works because he is not accompanying Jesus and the apostles.

To John's surprise, Jesus says: "Do not try to prevent him, for there is no one who will do a powerful work on the basis of my name who will quickly be able to say anything bad about me. For whoever is not against us is for us. And whoever gives you a cup of water to drink because you belong to Christ, I tell you truly, he will by no means lose his reward."—Mark 9:39-41.

No, at this time the man does not need to accompany Christ in order to be on Jesus' side. The Christian congregation is yet to be formed, so the fact that the man is not traveling with Jesus does not mean that he is an opposer or promoting a false religion. The man obviously has faith in Jesus' name, and what Jesus says indicates that the man will not lose his reward.

but today it is well established

On the other hand, it would be serious if the man was stumbled by the words and actions of the apostles. Jesus observes: "Whoever stumbles one of these little ones who have faith, it would be better for him if a millstone that is turned by a donkey were put around his neck and he were pitched into the sea." (Mark 9:42) Jesus then says that his followers should

4-5 feet

remove even something as precious as a hand, a foot, or an eye if that causes them to stumble. It is better to be without such a cherished thing and enter into God's Kingdom than to hold on to it and end up in Gehenna (Valley of Hinnom). The apostles have likely seen this valley near Jerusalem where refuse is burned, so they can understand it as representing permanent destruction.

Jesus also warns: "See that you do not despise one of these little ones, for I tell you that their angels in heaven always look upon the face of my Father." How precious are such "lit-

hyperbole "deaden body members as resp sex im... Col 3:5

Stumbling - May = breaking Gods moral law *losing faith or accepting false teachings*
could also = "become a snare or; cause to sin"

tle ones" to his Father? Jesus tells of a man who has 100 sheep but loses one. The man leaves the 99 to search for that lost one, and on finding it he rejoices more over it than over the 99. Jesus adds: "It is not a desirable thing to my Father who is in heaven for even one of these little ones to perish."—Matthew 18:10, 14.

Perhaps thinking of his apostles' arguing about who would be greatest, Jesus urges them: "Have salt in yourselves, and keep peace with one another." (Mark 9:50) Salt makes foods more palatable. Figurative salt makes what one says easier to accept and thus can help to preserve peace, which arguing does not do.—Colossians 4:6.

At times, serious issues will arise, and Jesus tells how to handle them. "If your brother commits a sin," Jesus says, "go and reveal his fault between you and him alone. If he listens to you, you have gained your brother." What if he does not listen? "Take along with you one or two more," Jesus advises, "so that on the testimony of two or three witnesses every matter may be established." If that does not resolve the matter, they are to speak to "the congregation," that is, to responsible elders who can render a decision. What if the sinner still does not listen? "Let him be to you just as a man of the nations and as a tax collector," people with whom Jews would not fellowship.—Matthew 18:15-17.

Congregation overseers need to adhere to God's Word. If they find a sinner guilty and needing discipline, their judgment 'will already be bound in heaven.' But when they find one innocent, it will have been loosened in heaven." These guidelines will prove helpful once the Christian congregation is formed. In such serious deliberations, Jesus says: "Where there are two or three gathered together in my name, there I am in their midst."—Matthew 18:18-20.

men counseling women on immorality?

◇ Why is the man casting out demons not to be viewed as an opposer?
◇ How serious is the matter of stumbling a little one, and how does Jesus illustrate the importance of such little ones?
◇ What guidance does Jesus provide about the course to follow if a brother commits a sin?

greediness = idolatry

THE NEED TO FORGIVE

MATTHEW 18:21-35

Peter has heard Jesus' advice on how to handle a difficulty between brothers by trying to settle it one-on-one. Yet, Peter seems to want to quantify the number of times one should make such an effort.

Peter asks: "Lord, how many times is my brother to sin against me and am I to forgive him? Up to seven times?" Some religious leaders teach that one should grant forgiveness up to three times. So Peter may feel that he would be very generous if he forgave a brother "up to seven times."—Matthew 18:21.

However, the idea of keeping such a record of wrongs is not in the spirit of Jesus' teaching. So he corrects Peter: "I say to you, not up to seven times, but up to 77 times." (Matthew 18:22) That, in other words, means indefinitely. There should be no limit to the number of times Peter forgives his brother.

Jesus then tells Peter and the others an illustration to impress on them their obligation to be forgiving. It is about a slave who fails to imitate his merciful master. The king wants to settle accounts with his slaves. One slave who owes the enormous debt of 10,000 talents [60,000,000 denarii] is brought to him. There is no possible way he can pay that debt. So the king orders that the slave, his wife, and his children be sold and payment be made. At that, the slave falls down at his master's feet and begs: "Be patient with me, and I will pay back everything to you."—Matthew 18:26.

The king is moved with pity and mercifully cancels the slave's huge debt. Once the king has done so, this slave goes and finds a fellow slave who owes him 100 denarii. He grabs the other slave and begins choking him, saying: "Pay back whatever you owe." But that fellow slave

you in the same way if each of you does not forgive your brother from your heart."—Matthew 18:32-35.

What a lesson that should teach us about forgiveness! God has forgiven us a large debt of sin. Whatever transgression a Christian brother commits against us is small in comparison. And Jehovah forgives us not once but thousands of times. Can we not forgive our brother a number of times, even if we have a cause for complaint? As Jesus taught in the Sermon on the Mount, God will "forgive us our debts, as we also have forgiven our debtors."—Matthew 6:12.

falls at the feet of the slave to whom he is in debt, begging: "Be patient with me, and I will pay you back." (Matthew 18:28, 29) However, the slave whose debt the king forgave does not imitate his master. He has his fellow slave, who owes much less, thrown into prison until he can pay what he owes.

Jesus then relates that other slaves who see this unmerciful treatment go and tell the master, who angrily summons the slave and says: "Wicked slave, I canceled all that debt for you when you pleaded with me. Should you not also have shown mercy to your fellow slave as I showed mercy to you?" The angry king delivers the unmerciful slave over to the jailers until he repays all that he owes. Jesus concludes: "My heavenly Father will also deal with

◇ What prompts Peter to ask about forgiving his brother, and why may he consider it generous to forgive someone seven times?

◇ How does the king's response to his slave's plea for mercy differ from the way that slave deals with his fellow slave?

◇ What lesson should we learn from Jesus' illustration?

TEACHING WHILE TRAVELING TO JERUSALEM

MATTHEW 8:19-22 LUKE 9:51-62 JOHN 7:2-10

For some time, Jesus has confined his activity mainly to Galilee, where he has found a better response than in Judea. Besides, when he was in Jerusalem and healed a man on the Sabbath, "the Jews began seeking all the more to kill him."—John 5:18; 7:1.

It is now the autumn of 32 C.E., and the Festival of Tabernacles (or, Booths) is near. This festival is celebrated for seven days, followed by a solemn assembly on the eighth day. The festival marks the end of the agricultural year and is a time of great rejoicing and thanksgiving.

Jesus' half brothers—James, Simon, Joseph, and Judas—urge him: "Leave here and go into Judea." Jerusalem is the religious center of the country. During the three annual festivals, the city is crowded. Jesus' brothers reason: "No one does anything in secret when he seeks to be known publicly. If you are doing these things, show yourself to the world."—John 7:3, 4.

Actually, these four brothers are "not exercising faith in him" as the Messiah. Yet, they want those gathered at the festival to see him do some powerful works. Jesus, aware of the danger, tells them: "The world has no reason to hate you, but it hates me, because I bear witness about it that its works are wicked. You go up to the festival; I am not yet going up to this festival, because my time has not yet fully come."—John 7:5-8.

Some days after Jesus' brothers depart with the main body of travelers, Jesus and his disciples go secretly, out of the public eye. They take the more direct route through Samaria, rather than the common one near the Jordan River. Jesus and his disciples will need accommodations in Samaria, so he sends messengers ahead to make preparations. The people in one place re-

fuse to welcome them or show ordinary hospitality because Jesus is heading for Jerusalem for the Jewish festival. James and John angrily ask: "Lord, do you want us to call fire down from heaven and annihilate them?" (Luke 9:54) Jesus rebukes them for even suggesting that, and they travel on.

While on the road, a scribe says to Jesus: "Teacher, I will follow you wherever you go." Jesus responds: "Foxes have dens and birds of heaven have nests, but the Son of man has nowhere to lay down his head." (Matthew 8:19, 20) He is pointing out that the scribe will experience hardship if he becomes Jesus' follower. And it seems that the scribe is too proud to accept this

• HOW JESUS' BROTHERS VIEW HIM
• HOW IMPORTANT IS KINGDOM SERVICE?

65

mode of life. Each of us, thus, can ask, 'How willing am I to follow Jesus?'

To another man, Jesus says: "Be my follower." The man replies: "Lord, permit me first to go and bury my father." Knowing the man's circumstances, Jesus says: "Let the dead bury their dead, but you go and declare abroad the Kingdom of God." (Luke 9:59, 60) The father evidently has not yet died. If he had, it is unlikely that his son would be here talking with Jesus. The son is not prepared to put the Kingdom of God first in his life.

As they move down the road toward Jerusalem, another man tells Jesus: "I will follow you, Lord, but first permit me to say good-bye to those in my household." Jesus answers: "No man who has put his hand to a plow and looks at the things behind is well-suited for the Kingdom of God."—Luke 9:61, 62.

Those who want to be Jesus' true disciples must have their eyes focused on Kingdom service. If the plowman does not keep looking straight ahead, a furrow will likely become crooked. If he sets the plow down in order to see what is behind, the work in the field will fall behind. Similarly, anyone who looks behind at this old system of things may well stumble off the road leading to eternal life.

◊ How do Jesus' four half brothers feel about him?

◊ Why do the Samaritans turn Jesus away, and what do James and John want to do?

◊ What three conversations does Jesus have on the road, and what is he emphasizing about service to God?

JESUS' LATER MINISTRY IN JUDEA

"BEG THE MASTER OF THE HARVEST TO SEND OUT WORKERS."

—LUKE 10:2

IN JERUSALEM FOR THE FESTIVAL OF TABERNACLES

JOHN 7:11-32

Jesus has become well-known during the years since his baptism. Thousands of Jews have seen his miracles, and reports about his works have spread throughout the land. Now, at the Festival of Tabernacles (or, Booths) in Jerusalem, many are looking for him.

Opinions about Jesus are greatly divided. "He is a good man," some say. Others respond: "He is not. He misleads the crowd." (John 7:12) Much of this subdued talk occurs during the opening days of the festival. Yet no one has the courage to speak out publicly in Jesus' behalf because there is widespread fear of how the Jewish leaders will react.

Partway through the festival, Jesus shows up at the temple. Many of the people are amazed at his marvelous ability to teach. He never attended the rabbinic schools, so the Jews wonder: "How does this man have such a knowledge of the Scriptures when he has not studied at the schools?"—John 7:15.

"What I teach is not mine," Jesus explains, "but belongs to him who sent me. If anyone desires to do His will, he will know whether the teaching is from God or I speak of my own originality." (John 7:16, 17) Jesus' teaching is in harmony with God's Law, so it should be obvious that he is seeking God's glory, not his own.

Then Jesus says: "Moses gave you the Law, did he not? But not one of you obeys the Law. Why are you seeking to kill me?" Some in the crowd, probably visitors from outside the city, are unaware of such efforts. It seems inconceivable to them that anyone would want to kill a teacher like him. Hence, they conclude that something must be wrong with Jesus for him to make that claim. "You have a demon," they say. "Who is seeking to kill you?"—John 7: 19, 20.

Actually, a year and a half earlier, the Jewish leaders wanted to kill Jesus after he had healed a man on the Sabbath. Jesus now uses a thought-provoking line of reasoning and exposes their unreasonableness. He calls attention to the fact that under the Law, a baby boy is to be circumcised on the eighth day, even if it is the Sabbath. Then he asks: "If a man receives circumcision on a sabbath so that the Law of Moses may not be broken, are you violently angry at me because I made a man completely well on a sabbath? Stop judging by the outward appearance, but judge with righteous judgment."—John 7:23, 24.

Residents of Jerusalem who are aware of the situation comment: "This is the man they [the rulers] are seeking to kill, is it not? And yet see! he is speaking in public, and they say nothing to him. Have the rulers come to know for certain that this is the Christ?" Why, then, do the people not believe that Jesus is the Christ? "We know where this man is from; yet when the Christ comes, no one is to know where he is from," they say.—John 7:25-27.

Right there at the temple, Jesus answers: "You know me and you know where I am from. And I have not come of my own initiative, but the One who sent me is real, and you do not know him. I know him, because I am a representative from him, and that One sent me." (John 7:28, 29) In response to that clear statement, there is an attempt to lay hold of Jesus, either to imprison him or to kill him. However, the attempt fails because it is not yet time for Jesus to die.

Many, though, put faith in Jesus, as they should. He has walked on water, calmed the

winds, miraculously fed thousands with a few loaves and fish, cured the sick, made the lame walk, opened the eyes of the blind, cured lepers, and even raised the dead. Yes, they have good reason to ask: "When the Christ comes, he will not perform more signs than this man has done, will he?"—John 7:31.

When the Pharisees hear the crowd saying these things, they and the chief priests send out officers to arrest Jesus.

◇ When Jesus arrives at the festival, what are people saying about him?

◇ Jesus uses what reasoning to show that he is not violating the Law of God?

◇ Why do many put faith in Jesus?

"NEVER HAS ANY MAN SPOKEN LIKE THIS"

JOHN 7:32-52

Jesus is still in Jerusalem for the Festival of Tabernacles (or, Booths). He is pleased that "many of the crowd put faith in him." That does not please the religious leaders, however. They send officers, who function as religious police, to arrest him. (John 7:31, 32) Yet, Jesus does not try to hide.

Rather, Jesus keeps on teaching publicly in Jerusalem, saying: "I will be with you a little while longer before I go to the One who sent me. You will look for me, but you will not find me, and where I am you cannot come." (John 7:33, 34) The Jews do not understand, so they say among themselves: "Where does this man intend to go, so that we will not find him? He does not intend to go to the Jews dispersed among the Greeks and teach the Greeks, does he? What does he mean when he says, 'You will look for me, but you will not find me, and where I am you cannot come'?" (John 7:35, 36) Jesus, however, is speaking of his death and resurrection to heaven, and his enemies cannot follow him there.

The seventh day of the festival arrives. Each morning of the festival, a priest has poured out water taken from the Pool of Siloam, so that it flowed to the base of the temple's altar. Likely reminding the people of this practice, Jesus cries out: "If anyone is thirsty, let him come to me and drink. Whoever puts faith in me, just as the scripture has said: 'From deep within him streams of living water will flow.'"—John 7: 37, 38.

Jesus is referring to what will happen when his disciples are anointed with holy spirit and called to be in line for heavenly life. This anointing occurs after Jesus' death. Beginning on the day of Pentecost the following year, streams of

life-giving water begin to flow as spirit-anointed disciples share the truth with people.

In response to Jesus' teaching, some say: "This really is the Prophet," evidently referring to the foretold prophet greater than Moses. Others say: "This is the Christ." But some argue: "The Christ is not coming out of Galilee, is he? Does the scripture not say that the Christ is coming from the offspring of David and from Bethlehem, the village where David was?" —John 7:40-42.

So the crowd is divided. Though some want Jesus arrested, no one lays a hand on him. When the officers return to the religious leaders without Jesus, the chief priests and Pharisees ask: "Why did you not bring him in?" The officers reply: "Never has any man spoken like this." The religious leaders angrily resort to ridicule and name-calling: "You have not been misled also, have you? Not one of the rulers or of the Pharisees has put faith in him, has he? But this crowd who do not know the Law are accursed people."—John 7:45-49.

At this, Nicodemus, a Pharisee and a member of the Sanhedrin, dares to speak in Jesus' behalf. Some two and a half years earlier, Nicodemus came to Jesus at night and expressed faith in him. Now Nicodemus says: "Our Law does not judge a man unless it first hears from him and learns what he is doing, does it?" What is their defensive reply? "You are not also out of

Galilee, are you? Search and see that no prophet is to be raised up out of Galilee."—John 7: 51, 52.

The Scriptures do not directly say that a prophet would come out of Galilee. Yet God's Word did point to the Christ as coming from there; it prophesied that "a great light" would be seen in "Galilee of the nations." (Isaiah 9: 1, 2; Matthew 4:13-17) Furthermore, as foretold, Jesus was born in Bethlehem, and he is an offspring of David. Although the Pharisees may be aware of this, they are likely responsible for spreading many of the misconceptions that people have about Jesus.

◇ How may Jesus be calling attention to something that occurs each morning during the festival?
◇ Why do the officers not arrest Jesus, and how do the religious leaders react?
◇ What indicates that the Christ would come out of Galilee?

"THE LIGHT OF THE WORLD"—THE SON OF GOD

JOHN 8:12-36

On the last day of the Festival of Tabernacles, the seventh day, Jesus is teaching in the part of the temple called "the treasury." (John 8: 20; Luke 21:1) This apparently is in the Court of Women, where people deposit their contributions.

At night during the festival, this area of the temple is specially illuminated. Four giant lampstands are there, each with four large basins filled with oil. The light from these lamps is strong enough to illuminate the surroundings to a great distance. What Jesus now says may remind his listeners of this display: "I am the light of the world. Whoever follows me will by no means walk in darkness, but will possess the light of life."—John 8:12.

The Pharisees take exception to Jesus' statement and say: "You bear witness about yourself; your witness is not true." Jesus replies: "Even if I do bear witness about myself, my witness is true, because I know where I came from and where I am going. But you do not know where I came from and where I am going." He adds: "In your own Law it is written: 'The witness of two men is true.' I am one who bears witness about myself, and the Father who sent me bears witness about me."—John 8:13-18.

Not accepting his reasoning, the Pharisees ask: "Where is your Father?" Jesus gives the forthright reply: "You know neither me nor my Father. If you did know me, you would know my Father also." (John 8:19) Even though the Pharisees still want Jesus arrested, no one touches him.

Jesus repeats a statement he has already made: "I am going away, and you will look for me, and yet you will die in your sin. Where I am going, you cannot come." The Jews, completely

misunderstanding Jesus' words, begin to wonder: "He will not kill himself, will he? Because he says, 'Where I am going, you cannot come.'" They do not understand what Jesus means, because they are unaware of his origin. He explains: "You are from the realms below; I am from the realms above. You are from this world; I am not from this world."—John 8:21-23.

Jesus is referring to his prehuman existence in heaven and to his being the promised Messiah, or Christ, whom these religious leaders should be expecting. Nevertheless, they ask with great contempt: "Who are you?"—John 8:25.

In the face of their rejection and opposition, Jesus answers: "Why am I even speaking to you at all?" Still, he directs attention to his Father and explains why the Jews should listen to the Son: "The One who sent me is true, and the very things I heard from him I am speaking in the world."—John 8:25, 26.

Then Jesus expresses confidence in his Father, which these Jews lack: "After you have lifted up the Son of man, then you will know that I am he and that I do nothing of my own initiative; but just as the Father taught me, I speak these things. And the One who sent me is with me; he did not abandon me to myself, because I always do the things pleasing to him."—John 8:28, 29.

Some Jews, though, do put faith in Jesus, and he says to them: "If you remain in my word, you are really my disciples, and you will know the truth, and the truth will set you free."—John 8:31, 32.

To some, this talk of being set free seems strange. They object: "We are Abraham's offspring and never have been slaves to anyone. How is it you say, 'You will become free'?" The Jews know that at times they have been under foreign domination, yet they refuse to be called slaves. Jesus points out, however, that they still are slaves: "Most truly I say to you, every doer of sin is a slave of sin."—John 8:33, 34.

Refusing to admit their slavery to sin puts the Jews in a dangerous position. "The slave does not remain in the household forever," Jesus explains. "The son remains forever." (John 8:35) A slave has no rights to an inheritance, and he may be dismissed at any time. Only the son actually born or adopted into the household remains "forever," that is, as long as he lives.

Thus, the truth about the Son is the truth that sets people free from death-dealing sin forever. "If the Son sets you free, you will be truly free," Jesus declares.—John 8:36.

◇ What occurs at night during the festival, and how does this relate to Jesus' teaching?

◇ Jesus says what about his origin, and what does this reveal about his identity?

◇ In what way are the Jews slaves, but what truth will set them free?

THEIR FATHER—ABRAHAM OR THE DEVIL?

JOHN 8:37-59

Still in Jerusalem for the Festival of Tabernacles (or, Booths), Jesus goes on teaching vital truths. Some Jews present had just said to him: "We are Abraham's offspring and never have been slaves." Jesus responds: "I know that you are Abraham's offspring. But you are seeking to kill me, because my word makes no progress among you. I speak the things I have seen while with my Father, but you do the things you have heard from your father."—John 8:33, 37, 38.

Jesus' point is simple: His Father is different from theirs. Unaware of what Jesus means, the Jews repeat their claim: "Our father is Abraham." (John 8:39; Isaiah 41:8) They are literally his descendants. So they feel that they are of the same faith as God's friend Abraham.

However, Jesus gives a shocking reply: "If you were Abraham's children, you would be doing the works of Abraham." Indeed, a real son imitates his father. "But now you are seeking to kill me," Jesus continues, "a man who has told you the truth that I heard from God. Abraham did not do this." Then Jesus makes the puzzling statement: "You are doing the works of your father."—John 8:39-41.

The Jews still do not grasp to whom Jesus is referring. They claim that they are legitimate sons, saying: "We were not born from immorality; we have one Father, God." Is God really their Father, though? "If God were your Father," Jesus says, "you would love me, for I came from God and I am here. I have not come of my own initiative, but that One sent me." Jesus asks a question and answers it himself: "Why do you not understand what I am saying? Because you cannot listen to my word."—John 8:41-43.

Jesus has tried to show what the consequences of rejecting him are. But now he pointedly says: "You are from your father the Devil, and you wish to do the desires of your father." What is their father like? Jesus identifies him clearly: "That one was a murderer when he began, and he did not stand fast in the truth." Jesus adds: "The one who is from God listens to the sayings of God. This is why you do not listen, because you are not from God."—John 8: 44, 47.

That condemnation angers the Jews, who answer: "Are we not right in saying, 'You are a Samaritan and have a demon'?" By calling Jesus "a Samaritan," they are expressing contempt for him. But Jesus ignores their slur, responding: "I do not have a demon, but I honor my Father, and you dishonor me." That this is a serious matter can be seen by Jesus' startling promise: "If anyone observes my word, he will never see death at all." He does not mean that the apostles and others who follow him will literally never die. Rather, they will never see eternal destruction, "the second death," with no hope of a resurrection.—John 8:48-51; Revelation 21:8.

But the Jews take Jesus' words literally, saying: "Now we do know that you have a demon. Abraham died, also the prophets, but you say, 'If anyone observes my word, he will never taste death at all.' You are not greater than our father Abraham, who died, are you? . . . Who do you claim to be?"—John 8:52, 53.

It is obvious that Jesus is making the point that he is the Messiah. But rather than directly answer their question about his identity, he says: "If I glorify myself, my glory is nothing. It is my Father who glorifies me, the one who you say is your God. Yet you have not known him, but I know him. And if I said I do not know him, I would be like you, a liar."—John 8:54, 55.

Jesus now refers back to the example of their faithful forefather: "Abraham your father rejoiced greatly at the prospect of seeing my day, and he saw it and rejoiced." Yes, believing God's promise, Abraham looked forward to the arrival of the Messiah. "You are not yet 50 years old, and still you have seen Abraham?" the Jews respond in disbelief. Jesus answers: "Most truly I say to you, before Abraham came into existence, I have been." He is referring to his prehuman existence as a mighty spirit in heaven. —John 8:56-58.

The Jews, enraged by Jesus' claim to have lived before Abraham, get ready to stone him. But Jesus leaves unharmed.

◇ How does Jesus show that his Father is different from the father of his enemies?

◇ Why is it unfitting for the Jews to insist that Abraham is their father?

◇ In what way will Jesus' followers "never see death at all"?

JESUS HEALS A MAN BORN BLIND

JOHN 9:1-18

Jesus is still in Jerusalem on the Sabbath. As he and his disciples are walking in the city, they see a beggar who has been blind from birth. The disciples ask Jesus: "Rabbi, who sinned, this man or his parents, so that he was born blind?" —John 9:2.

The disciples know that the man has no invisible soul that existed before he was born, yet they may wonder whether a person might sin while in his mother's womb. Jesus answers: "Neither this man sinned nor his parents, but it was so that the works of God might be made manifest in his case." (John 9:3) So neither this man nor his parents were guilty of a specific error or sin that caused his blindness. Rather, as a result of Adam's sin, all humans are born imperfect and are subject to defects, such as blindness. But the man's blindness provides an opportunity for Jesus to make manifest the works of God, as he has done at other times in healing people of their sicknesses.

Jesus stresses that it is urgent to do these works. "We must do the works of the One who sent me while it is day," he says. "The night is coming when no man can work. As long as I am in the world, I am the world's light." (John 9:4, 5) Yes, soon Jesus' death will plunge him into the darkness of the grave where he can do nothing. In the meantime, he is a source of enlightenment to the world.

But will Jesus heal the man, and if so, how? Jesus spits on the ground and with the saliva makes a paste. He puts some of it on the blind man's eyes and says: "Go wash in the pool of Siloam." (John 9:7) The man obeys. When he does, he can see! Think of his joy at seeing for the first time in his life!

Neighbors and others who knew him to be blind are amazed. "This is the man who used to sit and beg, is it not?" they ask. "This is he," some answer. But others cannot believe it and say: "No, but he looks like him." The man himself responds: "I am he."—John 9:8, 9.

Hence, they ask him: "How, then, were your eyes opened?" He replies: "The man called Jesus made a paste and smeared it on my eyes and said to me, 'Go to Siloam and wash.' So I went and washed and gained sight." They then ask: "Where is that man?" The beggar answers: "I do not know."—John 9:10-12.

The people lead the man to the Pharisees, who also want to know how he gained sight. He tells them: "He put a paste on my eyes, and I washed, and I can see." It would seem natural that the Pharisees would want to rejoice with the healed beggar. Instead, some of them de-

nounce Jesus. "This is not a man from God," they claim, "for he does not observe the Sabbath." Yet others say: "How can a man who is a sinner perform signs of that sort?" (John 9:15, 16) So they are divided.

Faced with these conflicting views, they turn to the man who now can see and ask: "What do you say about him, since it was your eyes that he opened?" He has no doubts about Jesus and responds: "He is a prophet."—John 9:17.

The Jews refuse to believe this. They may think that there is some scheme between Jesus and this man to fool the people. They conclude that one way to settle the matter is to question the beggar's parents about whether he really was blind.

◇ What is the cause of the man's blindness, and what is not?

◇ How do those who know the blind man react to his being healed?

◇ How are the Pharisees divided over the man's being healed?

PHARISEES CONFRONT THE MAN WHO WAS BLIND

JOHN 9:19-41

The Pharisees cannot accept that Jesus gave sight to the man who was born blind, so they call in his parents. The parents know that they face the possibility of being "expelled from the synagogue." (John 9:22) Such cutting off of fellowship from other Jews would have severe social and economic consequences for the family.

The Pharisees ask two questions: "Is this your son who you say was born blind? How, then, does he now see?" The parents reply: "We know that this is our son and that he was born blind. But how it is that he now sees, we do not know; or who opened his eyes, we do not know." Even if their son had told them what had happened, the parents are cautious as to how they respond and say: "Ask him. He is of age. He must speak for himself."—John 9:19-21.

Hence, the Pharisees call the man back and intimidate him by claiming that they have evidence against Jesus. "Give glory to God," they demand. "We know that this man is a sinner." Deflecting their charge, the man who was blind says: "Whether he is a sinner, I do not know." Yet he states: "One thing I do know, that I was blind, but now I can see."—John 9:24, 25.

Unwilling to leave the matter at that, the Pharisees continue: "What did he do to you? How did he open your eyes?" The man shows some courage in replying: "I told you already, and yet you did not listen. Why do you want to hear it again? You do not want to become his disciples also, do you?" Enraged, the Pharisees charge: "You are a disciple of that man, but we are disciples of Moses. We know that God has spoken to Moses, but as for this man, we do not know where he is from."—John 9:26-29.

Expressing wonderment, the beggar comments: "This is certainly amazing, that you do not know where he is from, and yet he opened my eyes." The man then makes a logical argument as to whom God hears and approves: "We know that God does not listen to sinners, but if anyone is God-fearing and does his will, he listens to this one. From of old it has never been heard that anyone opened the eyes of one born blind." This leads to the conclusion: "If this man were not from God, he could do nothing at all." —John 9:30-33.

Unable to refute the beggar's reasoning, the Pharisees revile him, saying: "You were altogether born in sin, and yet are you teaching us?" They throw him out.—John 9:34.

When Jesus hears what happened, he finds the man and asks: "Are you putting faith in the Son of man?" The healed man responds: "And who is he, sir, so that I may put faith in him?" Leaving no doubt, Jesus says: "You have seen him, and in fact, he is the one speaking with you."—John 9:35-37.

The man replies: "I do put faith in him, Lord." Showing faith and respect, the man bows down before Jesus, who makes a profound statement: "For this judgment I came into this world, that those not seeing might see and those seeing might become blind."—John 9:38, 39.

The Pharisees, who happen to be there, know that they are not sightless. But what of their presumed role as spiritual guides? They ask defensively: "We are not blind also, are we?" Jesus says: "If you were blind, you would have no sin. But now you say, 'We see.' Your sin remains." (John 9:40, 41) Had they not been teachers in Israel, rejecting Jesus as the Messiah might be understandable. But with their knowledge of the Law, their rejection of him is a serious sin.

◇ Why are the parents of the once blind beggar afraid when they are called before the Pharisees, and how do they answer?

◇ The Pharisees become enraged at what logical argument?

◇ Why do the Pharisees have no excuse for opposing Jesus?

JESUS SENDS 70 DISCIPLES TO PREACH

LUKE 10:1-24

It is now late in the year 32 C.E., about three years since Jesus' baptism. He and his disciples recently were at the Festival of Tabernacles in Jerusalem. They likely are still nearby. (Luke 10: 38; John 11:1) In fact, Jesus spends most of the remaining six months of his ministry in Judea or across the Jordan River in the district of Perea. Preaching is needed in these areas too.

Earlier, after the Passover of 30 C.E., Jesus spent some months preaching in Judea and traveling through Samaria. Then about the time of the Passover of 31 C.E., Jews in Jerusalem tried to kill him. For the next year and a half, Jesus taught mainly up north, in Galilee. During that time, many became his followers. In Galilee, Jesus trained his apostles and then sent them out with the instruction: "Preach, saying: 'The Kingdom of the heavens has drawn near.'" (Matthew 10:5-7) Now he organizes a witnessing campaign in Judea.

To start this campaign, Jesus chooses 70 disciples and sends them out by twos. Thus, there are 35 teams of Kingdom preachers in the territory, where "the harvest is great, but the workers are few." (Luke 10:2) They are to go in advance into places where Jesus might follow. The 70 are to cure the sick and spread the same message that Jesus has been proclaiming.

These disciples are not to focus on teaching in synagogues. Jesus tells them to go to people's homes. "Wherever you enter into a house," he instructs, "say first: 'May this house have peace.' And if a friend of peace is there, your peace will rest upon him." What is to be their message? Jesus says: "Tell them: 'The Kingdom of God has come near to you.'"—Luke 10:5-9.

The instructions Jesus gives the 70 are similar to those he gave when sending out the 12 apostles about a year earlier. He warns them that not all will receive them well. Their efforts, though, will prepare receptive ones so that when Jesus arrives shortly afterward, many will be eager to meet the Master and learn from him.

Before long, the 35 pairs of Kingdom preachers return to Jesus. They tell him joyfully: "Lord, even the demons are made subject to us by the use of your name." This fine report surely thrills Jesus, for he responds: "I see Satan already fallen like lightning from heaven. Look! I have given you the authority to trample underfoot serpents and scorpions."—Luke 10:17-19.

Jesus thus assures his followers that they will be able to prevail over injurious things, symbolically trampling on serpents and scorpions.

Moreover, they can be certain that in the future Satan will fall from heaven. Jesus also helps the 70 to see what is really important in the long run. He says: "Do not rejoice because the spirits are made subject to you, but rejoice because your names have been written in the heavens." —Luke 10:20.

Jesus is overjoyed and publicly praises his Father for using these humble servants of his in such a powerful way. Turning to his disciples, he tells them: "Happy are the eyes that see the things you are seeing. For I say to you, many prophets and kings desired to see the things you are observing but did not see them, and to hear the things you are hearing but did not hear them."—Luke 10:23, 24.

◇ Where does Jesus preach during his final six months, and why does he concentrate his efforts there?
◇ How were the 70 disciples to find people?
◇ Though the 70 disciples accomplish much, what does Jesus say is of greater importance?

A SAMARITAN PROVES TO BE A REAL NEIGHBOR

LUKE 10:25-37

While Jesus is still near Jerusalem, various Jews approach him. Some want to learn from him and others want to test him. One of them, an expert on the Law, presents the question: "Teacher, what do I need to do to inherit everlasting life?"—Luke 10:25.

Jesus detects that the man is not simply asking for information. He may be trying to get Jesus to reply in a way that will offend the Jews. Jesus realizes that this man already has a definite viewpoint. So he wisely responds in a way that gets the man to reveal what *he* is thinking.

Jesus asks: "What is written in the Law? How do you read?" This man has studied God's Law, so he bases his response on it. He quotes from Deuteronomy 6:5 and Leviticus 19:18, saying: "'You must love Jehovah your God with your whole heart and with your whole soul and with your whole strength and with your whole mind' and 'your neighbor as yourself.'" (Luke 10:26, 27) Is that the answer?

Jesus tells the man: "You answered correctly; keep doing this and you will get life." But does that end the discussion? The man does not want just a factual answer; he is seeking "to prove himself righteous," to have confirmation that his views are correct and that he is thus justified in how he treats others. So he asks: "Who really is my neighbor?" (Luke 10:28, 29) That seemingly simple question has deep implications. How so?

The Jews believe that the term "neighbor" applies only to those who keep the Jewish traditions, and it might seem that Leviticus 19:18 supports that. In fact, a Jew may claim that it is even "unlawful" to have fellowship with a non-Jew. (Acts 10:28) Thus this man and possibly some of Jesus' own disciples view themselves as righteous if they treat fellow Jews kindly. But they may treat a non-Jew unkindly; he is not really a "neighbor."

How can Jesus correct this view without offending this man and other Jews? He does so by telling a story: "A man was going down from Jerusalem to Jericho and fell victim to robbers, who stripped him, beat him, and went off, leaving him half-dead." Jesus continues: "By coincidence a priest was going down on that road, but when he saw him, he passed by on the opposite side. Likewise, a Levite, when he came to the place and saw him, passed by on the opposite side. But a certain Samaritan traveling the road came upon him, and at seeing him, he was moved with pity."—Luke 10:30-33.

The man to whom Jesus tells this story certainly knows that many priests and Levite temple assistants live in Jericho. To return from the temple, they must travel down a road some 14 miles. That route can be dangerous, with robbers lurking along it. If a priest and a Levite find a fellow Jew in distress, should they not help him? In his story, Jesus relates that they did not. The one who did was a Samaritan, a man from a people whom the Jews despise.—John 8:48.

How did the Samaritan help the injured Jew? Jesus goes on: "He approached him and bandaged his wounds, pouring oil and wine on them. Then he mounted him on his own animal and brought him to an inn and took care of him. The next day he took out two denarii, gave them to the innkeeper, and said: 'Take care of him, and whatever you spend besides this, I will repay you when I return.'"—Luke 10:34, 35.

After telling the story, the Master Teacher, Jesus, asks the man this thought-provoking question: "Who of these three seems to you to have made himself neighbor to the man who fell victim to the robbers?" Perhaps the man feels uncomfortable in answering "the Samaritan," so he replies: "The one who acted mercifully toward him." Jesus then makes the lesson of his story unmistakably clear, urging: "Go and do the same yourself."—Luke 10:36, 37.

What an effective method of teaching! Had Jesus simply told the man that non-Jews also are his neighbors, would the man and the other Jews listening have accepted that? Likely not. However, by relating a rather simple story, using details that the listeners can identify with, the answer to the question, "Who really is my neighbor?" becomes obvious. The person who proves to be the *real neighbor* is the one who exercises the love and kindness that the Scriptures command us to show.

◇ Why might a certain man question Jesus about how to gain everlasting life?
◇ Who do the Jews believe are their neighbors, and why?
◇ How does Jesus make clear the correct view of who is our neighbor?

LESSONS ABOUT HOSPITALITY AND PRAYER

LUKE 10:38–11:13

On the eastern slope of the Mount of Olives, about two miles from Jerusalem, lies the village of Bethany. (John 11:18) Jesus goes there and enters the house of two sisters, Martha and Mary. They and their brother, Lazarus, are Jesus' friends, and they warmly welcome him.

It is an honor to have the Messiah as a visitor. Martha is eager to provide well for Jesus, so she sets to work preparing an elaborate meal. While Martha works, her sister, Mary, sits at Jesus' feet and listens to him. In time, Martha says to Jesus: "Lord, does it not matter to you that my sister has left me alone to attend to things? Tell her to come and help me."—Luke 10:40.

Rather than criticizing Mary, Jesus counsels Martha for being overly concerned with material provisions: "Martha, Martha, you are anxious and disturbed about many things. A few things, though, are needed, or just one. For her part, Mary chose the good portion, and it will not be taken away from her." (Luke 10:41, 42) Yes, Jesus points out that it is not necessary to spend a lot of time preparing many dishes. Just a simple meal will suffice.

Martha's intentions are good. She wants to be hospitable. But her anxious attention to the meal means that she is missing out on valuable instruction from God's own Son! Jesus emphasizes that Mary made a wise choice, one that will be of lasting benefit to her as well as a lesson for all of us to remember.

On another occasion, Jesus provides a different but equally important lesson. A disciple asks him: "Lord, teach us how to pray, just as John also taught his disciples." (Luke 11:1) Jesus had already done so about a year and a half earlier in his Sermon on the Mount. (Matthew 6:9-13) However, this disciple may not have been present then, so Jesus repeats the key points. Then he gives an illustration to emphasize the need to be persistent in prayer.

"Suppose one of you has a friend and you go to him at midnight and say to him, 'Friend, lend me three loaves, because one of my friends has just come to me on a journey and I have nothing to offer him.' But that one replies from inside: 'Stop bothering me. The door is already locked, and my young children are with me in bed. I cannot get up and give you anything.' I tell you, even if he will not get up and give him anything because of being his friend, certainly because of his bold persistence he will get up and give him whatever he needs."—Luke 11:5-8.

Jesus is not implying that Jehovah is unwilling to respond to petitions, as was the friend. Rather, he is showing that if an unwilling friend will respond to persistent requests, certainly our loving heavenly Father will respond to the sincere petitions of his faithful servants! Jesus continues: "I say to you, keep on asking, and it will be given you; keep on seeking, and you will find; keep on knocking, and it will be opened to you. For everyone asking receives, and everyone seeking finds, and to everyone knocking, it will be opened."—Luke 11:9, 10.

Jesus then underscores his point by making a comparison to human fathers: "Which father among you, if his son asks for a fish, will hand him a serpent instead of a fish? Or if he also asks for an egg, will hand him a scorpion? Therefore, if you, although being wicked, know how to give good gifts to your children, how much more so will the Father in heaven give holy spirit to those asking him!" (Luke 11:11-13) What a fine assurance that our Father is willing to hear us and respond to our needs!

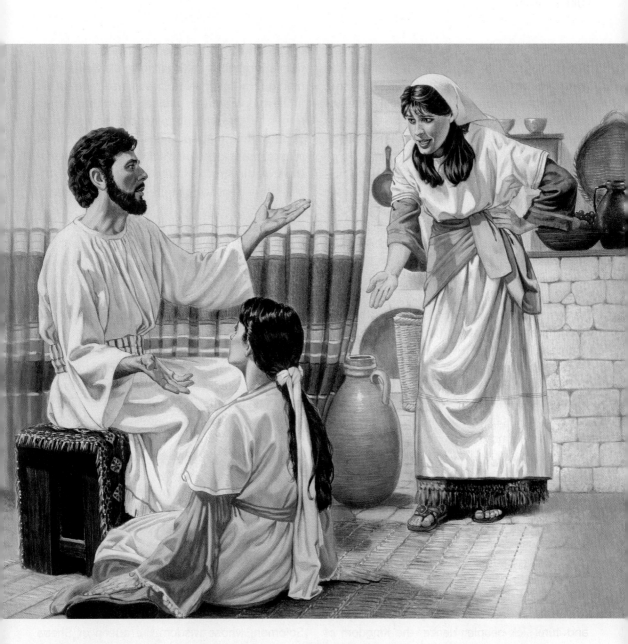

◇ How do Martha and Mary differ in their focus, and what lesson can we learn from this?

◇ Why does Jesus repeat his instructions on prayer?

◇ How does Jesus illustrate the need to persist in prayer?

JESUS REVEALS THE SOURCE OF HAPPINESS

LUKE 11:14-36

Jesus has just repeated his instructions about prayer, but that is not the only subject that comes up more than once during his ministry. When he was performing miracles in Galilee, Jesus faced the false charge that he did so by means of power from the ruler of the demons. Now in Judea this charge arises again.

When Jesus casts out of a man a demon that prevents him from speaking, the crowds are amazed. Not his critics, though. They bring up the same false accusation: "He expels the demons by means of Beelzebub, the ruler of the demons." (Luke 11:15) Others, seeking more evidence as to Jesus' identity, ask him for a sign from heaven.

Realizing that they are trying to test him, Jesus answers them as he did similar critics encountered in Galilee. He says that every kingdom divided against itself will fall, reasoning: "If Satan is also divided against himself, how will his kingdom stand?" Then Jesus tells them directly: "If it is by means of God's finger that I expel the demons, the Kingdom of God has really overtaken you."—Luke 11:18-20.

Jesus' mention of "God's finger" should call to his listeners' minds what happened earlier in Israel's history. Those in Pharaoh's court who saw Moses perform a miracle exclaimed: "It is the finger of God!" It was also "God's finger" that wrote the Ten Commandments on two stone tablets. (Exodus 8:19; 31:18) Similarly, "God's finger"—his holy spirit, or active force— is what is now enabling Jesus to expel demons and cure sick people. Hence, the Kingdom of God has indeed overtaken these opposers, because the designated King of the Kingdom, Jesus, is right there performing these works.

Jesus' ability to expel demons is evidence of his power over Satan, just as when a stronger man approaches and overpowers a well-armed man guarding a palace. Jesus also repeats his illustration about an unclean spirit that leaves a man. If the man does not fill the void with good things, that spirit will return with seven others, making the man's final condition worse than at the first. (Matthew 12:22, 25-29, 43-45) So it is proving to be with the nation of Israel.

A woman listening to Jesus is moved to exclaim: "Happy is the womb that carried you and the breasts that nursed you!" Jewish women hoped to be the mother of a prophet, particularly of the Messiah. So this woman might think that Mary can be especially happy as the mother of such a teacher. Yet Jesus corrects the woman as to the true source of happiness: "No, rather, happy are those hearing the word of God and keeping it!" (Luke 11:27, 28) Jesus has never suggested that Mary should be given special honor. Rather, true happiness for any man or woman is found in being a faithful servant of God, not in any physical ties or accomplishments.

As Jesus did in Galilee, he rebukes the people for demanding a sign from heaven. He says that no sign will be given them except "the sign of Jonah." Jonah served as a sign both by his three days in the fish and by his bold preaching, which moved the Ninevites to repent. Jesus says: "But look! something more than Jonah is here." (Luke 11:29-32) Jesus also is more than Solomon, whose wisdom the queen of Sheba came to hear.

"After lighting a lamp," Jesus adds, "a person puts it, not in a hidden place nor under a basket, but on the lampstand." (Luke 11:33) He

may mean that teaching and performing miracles before these people is like hiding the light of a lamp. Because their eyes are not focused, they miss the purpose of his works.

Jesus has just expelled a demon and has caused a man who was speechless to speak. That should motivate people to glorify God and tell others what Jehovah is accomplishing. So Jesus has words of warning for his critics: "Be alert, therefore, that the light that is in you is not darkness. Therefore, if your whole body is bright with no part of it dark, it will all be as bright as when a lamp gives you light by its rays."—Luke 11:35, 36.

◇ How do some in Judea respond to Jesus' healing a man?
◇ What is "God's finger," and how has God's Kingdom overtaken Jesus' listeners?
◇ How can people find true happiness?

DINING WITH A PHARISEE

LUKE 11:37-54

While in Judea, Jesus accepts a meal invitation from a Pharisee. It is likely during the day, rather than an evening meal. (Luke 11:37, 38; compare Luke 14:12.) Before eating, the Pharisees carry out ritual washing of their hands up to the elbow. But Jesus does not. (Matthew 15:1, 2) It would not violate God's Law to wash to that extent, yet it is not something God requires.

The Pharisee is surprised that Jesus does not follow that tradition. Jesus detects this and says: "Now you Pharisees, you cleanse the outside of the cup and dish, but inside you are full of greediness and wickedness. Unreasonable ones! The one who made the outside made also the inside, did he not?"—Luke 11:39, 40.

Having clean hands before eating is not the issue, but religious hypocrisy is. The Pharisees and others who ritualistically wash their hands fail to cleanse their hearts from wickedness. So Jesus counsels them: "Give as gifts of mercy the things that are from within, and look! everything about you will be clean." (Luke 11:41) How true! Giving should spring from a loving heart, not from a desire to impress others by a pretense of righteousness.

It is not that these men do not give. Jesus points out: "You give the tenth of the mint and of the rue and of every other garden herb, but you disregard the justice and the love of God! These things you were under obligation to do, but not to disregard those other things." (Luke 11:42) God's Law called for the paying of tithes (a tenth part) of crops. (Deuteronomy 14:22) That included the mint and the rue, herbs or plants used to flavor food. The Pharisees scrupulously paid a tenth of these herbs, but what of the more important requirements of the Law,

such as to exercise justice and to be modest before God?—Micah 6:8.

Jesus goes on to say: "Woe to you Pharisees, because you love the front seats in the synagogues and the greetings in the marketplaces! Woe to you, because you are as those graves that are not clearly visible, that men walk on and do not know it!" (Luke 11:43, 44) Yes, people could stumble on such graves and become ceremonially unclean. Jesus uses that fact to underscore that the uncleanness of the Pharisees is not apparent.—Matthew 23:27.

One man who is well-versed in God's Law complains: "Teacher, in saying these things, you insult us also." Yet such men need to realize that they are failing to help the people. Jesus says: "Woe also to you who are versed in the Law, because you load men down with loads hard to carry, but you yourselves do not touch the loads with one of your fingers! Woe to you, because you build the tombs of the prophets, but your forefathers killed them!"—Luke 11:45-47.

The loads that Jesus refers to are the oral traditions and the Pharisees' interpretation of the Law. These men are not making life easier for the people. Rather, they insist that all must keep what become heavy burdens. Their ancestors killed God's prophets, from Abel onward. Now they, who make it seem as if they are honoring the prophets by building tombs for them, are imitating the attitude and actions of their forefathers. They are even seeking to kill God's foremost Prophet. Jesus says that God will hold an accounting with this generation. And that became a reality about 38 years later, in 70 C.E.

Jesus continues: "Woe to you who are versed in the Law, because you took away the key of knowledge. You yourselves did not go in, and you hinder those going in!" (Luke 11:52) These men, who should be unlocking the meaning of God's Word, are instead taking away the opportunity for people to know and understand it.

How do the Pharisees and scribes react? As Jesus departs, they begin to oppose him angrily and to assail him with questions. They are not asking out of a desire to learn. Instead, they want to trick Jesus into saying something for which they can have him arrested.

◇ Why does Jesus condemn the Pharisees and scribes?

◇ The people are pressured to carry what loads?

◇ What lies ahead for those who oppose Jesus and seek to kill him?

JESUS GIVES COUNSEL ABOUT RICHES

LUKE 12:1-34

As Jesus dines at the Pharisee's house, thousands gather outside awaiting him. He has had similar experiences with the crowds in Galilee. (Mark 1:33; 2:2; 3:9) Here in Judea, many want to see and hear him, showing an attitude quite different from that of the Pharisees at the meal.

What Jesus says first has special meaning for his disciples: "Watch out for the leaven of the Pharisees, which is hypocrisy." Jesus has given this warning before, but what he saw at the meal shows how urgent this counsel is. (Luke 12:1; Mark 8:15) The Pharisees may try to conceal their wickedness with a show of piety, but they are a danger that needs to be exposed. Jesus explains: "There is nothing carefully concealed that will not be revealed, and nothing secret that will not become known." —Luke 12:2.

Perhaps many of the people crowding around Jesus are Judeans who had not heard him teach in Galilee. Thus, he repeats key thoughts that he expressed earlier. He urges all who are listening: "Do not fear those who kill the body and after this are not able to do anything more." (Luke 12:4) As he has done before, he stresses the need for his followers to trust that God will care for them. They also need to acknowledge the Son of man and realize that God can help them.—Matthew 10:19, 20, 26-33; 12: 31, 32.

Then a man in the crowd brings up his immediate concern: "Teacher, tell my brother to divide the inheritance with me." (Luke 12:13) The Law says that the firstborn son receives two parts of the inheritance, so there should be no dispute. (Deuteronomy 21:17) It seems, though, that this man wants more than his legal share.

Jesus wisely refuses to take sides. "Man, who appointed me judge or arbitrator between you two?" he asks.—Luke 12:14.

Jesus then gives this admonition to all: "Keep your eyes open and guard against every sort of greed, because even when a person has an abundance, his life does not result from the things he possesses." (Luke 12:15) No matter how much wealth a man may have, will he not at some point die and leave everything behind? Jesus emphasizes that point with a memorable illustration that also shows the value of having a good name with God:

"The land of a rich man produced well. So he began reasoning within himself, 'What should I do now that I have nowhere to gather my crops?' Then he said, 'I will do this: I will tear down my storehouses and build bigger ones, and there I will gather all my grain and all my goods, and I will say to myself: "You have many good things stored up for many years; take it easy, eat, drink, enjoy yourself."' But God said to him, 'Unreasonable one, this night they are demanding your life from you. Who, then, is to have the things you stored up?' So it goes with the man who stores up treasure for himself but is not rich toward God."—Luke 12:16-21.

Both Jesus' disciples and the others hearing him could become ensnared by seeking or piling up wealth. Or the cares of life could distract them from serving Jehovah. So Jesus repeats the fine counsel he gave about a year and a half earlier in the Sermon on the Mount:

"Stop being anxious about your lives as to what you will eat or about your bodies as to what you will wear. . . . Consider the ravens: They neither sow seed nor reap; they have neither barn nor storehouse; yet God feeds them.

Are you not worth much more than birds? . . . Consider how the lilies grow: They neither toil nor spin; but I tell you that not even Solomon in all his glory was arrayed as one of these. . . . So stop seeking what you will eat and what you will drink, and stop being in anxious suspense . . . Your Father knows you need these things. . . . Keep seeking his Kingdom, and these things will be added to you."—Luke 12:22-31; Matthew 6: 25-33.

Who will be seeking God's Kingdom? Jesus reveals that a relatively small number, a "little flock," of faithful humans will be doing so. Later it will be revealed that their number is just 144,000. What is in store for them? They have Jesus' assurance: "Your Father has approved of giving you the Kingdom." These will not concentrate on gaining treasures on earth, which thieves could steal. Rather, their heart will be on "never-failing treasure in the heavens," where they will reign with Christ.—Luke 12:32-34.

◇ How does Jesus respond to a question about inheritance?
◇ Why is the illustration that Jesus gives worth our serious attention?
◇ What does Jesus reveal about those who will be in the Kingdom with him?

KEEP READY, FAITHFUL STEWARD!

LUKE 12:35-59

Jesus has explained that only a "little flock" will receive a place in the heavenly Kingdom. (Luke 12:32) But receiving that marvelous reward is not something to be treated lightly. In fact, he goes on to stress how important it will be for a person to have the right attitude if he is to be part of the Kingdom.

Accordingly, Jesus admonishes his disciples to keep ready for his return. He says: "Be dressed and ready and have your lamps burning, and you should be like men waiting for their master to return from the marriage, so when he comes and knocks, they may at once open to him. Happy are those slaves whom the master on coming finds watching!"—Luke 12:35-37.

The disciples can easily grasp the attitude that Jesus is illustrating. The servants he mentions are ready, awaiting their master's return. Jesus explains: "If [the master] comes in the second watch [from about nine in the evening to midnight], even if in the third [from midnight to about three in the morning], and finds them ready, happy are they!"—Luke 12:38.

This is much more than counsel about being diligent house servants, or workers. That is clear from the way Jesus, the Son of man, brings himself into the illustration. He tells his disciples: "You also, keep ready, because at an hour that you do not think likely, the Son of man is coming." (Luke 12:40) So at some future point, Jesus will come. He wants his followers —particularly those of the "little flock"—to be ready.

Peter wants to understand Jesus' meaning clearly, so he asks: "Lord, are you telling this illustration just to us or also to everyone?" Rather than answer Peter directly, Jesus sets out a related illustration: "Who really is the faithful steward, the discreet one, whom his master will appoint over his body of attendants to keep giving them their measure of food supplies at the proper time? Happy is that slave if his master on coming finds him doing so! I tell you truthfully, he will appoint him over all his belongings."—Luke 12:41-44.

In the earlier illustration, "the master" obviously refers to Jesus, the Son of man. Logically, "the faithful steward" involves men who are part of the "little flock" and who will be given the Kingdom. (Luke 12:32) Here Jesus is saying that certain members of this group will be giving "his body of attendants" their sustenance, "their measure of food supplies at the proper time." So Peter and the other disciples whom Jesus is teaching and feeding spiritually can conclude that there will be a future period during which the Son of man will come. And in that period, there will be a functioning arrangement for the spiritual feeding of Jesus' followers, the Master's "body of attendants."

Jesus emphasizes in another way why his disciples need to be alert and to give attention to their attitude. That is because it is possible to grow lax and even go to the point of opposing one's fellows: "But if ever that slave should say in his heart, 'My master delays coming,' and starts to beat the male and female servants and to eat and drink and get drunk, the master of that slave will come on a day that he is not expecting him and at an hour that he does not know, and he will punish him with the greatest severity and assign him a part with the unfaithful ones."—Luke 12:45, 46.

Jesus says that he has come "to start a fire on the earth." And he has, raising issues that cause great heat of controversy and result in the consuming of false teachings and traditions. This even separates individuals who might be expected to be united, dividing "father against son and son against father, mother against daughter and daughter against mother, mother-in-law against daughter-in-law and daughter-in-law against mother-in-law."—Luke 12:49, 53.

These comments have been especially for his disciples. Then Jesus turns to the crowds. Most of the people have stubbornly refused to accept the evidence that he is the Messiah, so he tells them: "When you see a cloud rising in the west, at once you say, 'A storm is coming,' and it happens. And when you see that a south wind is blowing, you say, 'There will be a heat wave,' and it occurs. Hypocrites, you know how to examine the appearance of earth and sky, but why do you not know how to examine this particular time?" (Luke 12:54-56) They clearly are not ready.

◇ Who is "the master," and who is "the faithful steward"?

◇ Why can the disciples conclude that there will be a faithful steward in the future, and what is this steward's role?

◇ Why is Jesus' counsel to "keep ready" so important?

WHY DESTRUCTION IS AHEAD

LUKE 13:1-21

Jesus has tried in many ways to move the people to think about their standing with God. Another occasion arises after his discussion with people outside the house of a Pharisee.

Some of them mention a tragic event. They speak about "the Galileans whose blood [the Roman Governor Pontius] Pilate had mixed with their sacrifices." (Luke 13:1) What do they mean?

Perhaps these Galileans were the ones killed when thousands of Jews protested Pilate's use of money from the temple treasury to construct an aqueduct to bring water into Jerusalem. Pilate may have acquired the money with the cooperation of the temple authorities. Those relating this tragedy may feel that the Galileans suffered the calamity because they were guilty of wicked deeds. Jesus disagrees.

He asks: "Do you think that those Galileans were worse sinners than all other Galileans because they have suffered these things?" His answer is no. But he uses the incident to warn the Jews: "Unless you repent, you will all likewise be destroyed." (Luke 13:2, 3) Jesus then refers to another tragedy that may have occurred recently and may have been related to the construction of that aqueduct, asking:

"Those 18 on whom the tower in Siloam fell, killing them—do you think that they had greater guilt than all other men who live in Jerusalem?" (Luke 13:4) The crowd may feel that those individuals died because of some personal badness. Again Jesus disagrees. He knows that "time and unexpected events" happen and are likely responsible for this tragedy too. (Ecclesiastes 9:11) The people, though, should take a lesson from the event. "Unless you repent, you will all be destroyed, as they were," Jesus says.

(Luke 13:5) But why is he stressing this lesson now?

It has to do with where he is in the course of his ministry, and he illustrates the matter this way: "A man had a fig tree planted in his vineyard, and he came looking for fruit on it but found none. Then he said to the vinedresser, 'Here it is three years that I have come looking for fruit on this fig tree, but have found none. Cut it down! Why should it keep the ground useless?' In reply he said to him, 'Master, leave it alone for one more year until I dig around it and put on manure. If it produces fruit in the future,

well and good; but if not, then cut it down.'" —Luke 13:6-9.

For more than three years, Jesus has been trying to cultivate faith among the Jews. Yet, relatively few have become disciples and can be considered fruitage of his labors. Now, in the fourth year of his ministry, he is intensifying his efforts. It is as if he were digging and putting fertilizer around the Jewish fig tree by preaching and teaching in Judea and Perea. With what results? Only a small number of Jews respond. As a whole, the nation refuses to repent and is now in line for destruction.

That lack of response on the part of most once again comes to the fore shortly after-

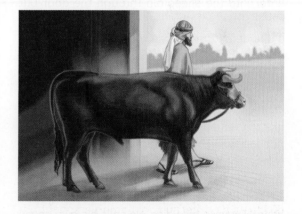

ward on a Sabbath. Jesus is teaching in a synagogue. He sees a woman who, because a demon is afflicting her, has been bent double for 18 years. Showing compassion, Jesus tells her: "Woman, you are released from your weakness." (Luke 13:12) Jesus lays his hands on her, and instantly she straightens up and starts to glorify God.

That angers the presiding officer of the synagogue, who says: "There are six days on which work ought to be done; so come and be cured on those days, and not on the Sabbath day."

(Luke 13:14) That officer is not denying that Jesus has the power to heal; rather, he is condemning the people for coming to be healed on the Sabbath! Jesus responds with clear logic: "Hypocrites, does not each one of you on the Sabbath untie his bull or his donkey from the stall and lead it away to give it something to drink? Should not this woman, who is a daughter of Abraham and whom Satan held bound for 18 years, be released from this bondage on the Sabbath day?"—Luke 13:15, 16.

The opposers feel shame, but the crowds rejoice over the glorious things they are seeing Jesus do. Then Jesus repeats here in Judea two prophetic illustrations regarding the Kingdom, which he had related earlier from a boat on the Sea of Galilee.—Matthew 13:31-33; Luke 13:18-21.

◇ What two tragedies does Jesus use to provide a warning, and what is the warning?
◇ How does the illustration of the unfruitful fig tree highlight the situation of the Jewish nation?
◇ Over what is the presiding officer of the synagogue critical, and how does Jesus expose the man's hypocrisy?

THE FINE SHEPHERD AND THE SHEEPFOLDS

JOHN 10:1-21

As Jesus continues teaching in Judea, he now draws on something that his listeners can easily picture—sheep and sheepfolds. But he is speaking illustratively. The Jews may recall David's words: "Jehovah is my Shepherd. I will lack nothing. In grassy pastures he makes me lie down." (Psalm 23:1, 2) Another psalmist invited the nation: "Let us kneel before Jehovah our Maker. For he is our God, and we are the people of his pasture." (Psalm 95:6, 7) Yes, the Israelites under the Law were long likened to a flock of sheep.

These "sheep" have been in a "sheepfold" in that they were born under the Mosaic Law covenant. The Law served as a fence, separating them from the corrupting practices of people not under this arrangement. Some Israelites, however, mistreated God's flock. Jesus states: "Most truly I say to you, the one who does not enter into the sheepfold through the door but climbs in by another way, that one is a thief and a plunderer. But the one who enters through the door is the shepherd of the sheep."—John 10: 1, 2.

The people may think of men who have claimed to be the Messiah, or Christ. These are like thieves and plunderers. The people should not follow such impostors. Rather, they should follow "the shepherd of the sheep," about whom Jesus says:

"The doorkeeper opens to this one, and the sheep listen to his voice. He calls his own sheep by name and leads them out. When he has brought all his own out, he goes ahead of them, and the sheep follow him, because they know his voice. They will by no means follow a stranger but will flee from him, because they do not know the voice of strangers."—John 10:3-5.

Earlier, John the Baptist, like a doorkeeper, identified Jesus as the one whom those symbolic sheep under the Law should follow. And some sheep, in Galilee and right here in Judea, have recognized Jesus' voice. To where would he 'lead them out'? And what would result from following him? Some hearing this illustration may wonder, because 'they do not understand what he is saying to them.'—John 10:6.

Jesus explains: "Most truly I say to you, I am the door for the sheep. All those who have come in place of me are thieves and plunderers; but the sheep have not listened to them. I am the door; whoever enters through me will be saved, and that one will go in and out and find pasturage."—John 10:7-9.

Clearly, Jesus is introducing something new. His listeners know that he is not the door to the Law covenant, which has existed for centuries. So he must be saying that the sheep he 'leads out' are to enter another sheepfold. With what result?

Further explaining his role, Jesus says: "I have come that they may have life and have it in abundance. I am the fine shepherd; the fine shepherd surrenders his life in behalf of the sheep." (John 10:10, 11) Jesus had earlier comforted his disciples by saying: "Have no fear, little flock, for your Father has approved of giving you the Kingdom." (Luke 12:32) Indeed, those who make up the "little flock" are ones Jesus will lead into a new sheepfold, so that they may "have life and have it in abundance." What a blessing to be part of that flock!

Jesus does not end the matter there, though. He observes: "I have other sheep, which are not of this fold; those too I must bring in, and they will listen to my voice, and they will become one

flock, one shepherd." (John 10:16) These "other sheep" are "not of this fold." Hence, they must be of yet another fold, different from the "little flock" who will inherit the Kingdom. These two folds, or pens of sheep, have different destinies. Still, the sheep in both folds will benefit from Jesus' role. He says: "This is why the Father loves me, because I surrender my life." —John 10:17.

Many of the crowd respond: "He has a demon and is out of his mind." Yet others show that they are listening with interest and are inclined to follow the Fine Shepherd. They say: "These are not the sayings of a demonized man. A demon cannot open blind people's eyes, can it?" (John 10:20, 21) They evidently are referring to Jesus' earlier curing of the man born blind.

◇ What could the Jews understand as Jesus mentions sheep and sheepfolds?
◇ Who does Jesus say is the Fine Shepherd, and to what will he lead the sheep?
◇ Into what two folds are the sheep who follow Jesus to be led?

ONE WITH THE FATHER, BUT NOT GOD

JOHN 10:22-42

Jesus has come to Jerusalem for the Festival of Dedication (or, Hanukkah). This festival commemorates the rededication of the temple. Over a century earlier, Syrian King Antiochus IV Epiphanes built an altar over the great altar at God's temple. Later, sons of a Jewish priest recaptured Jerusalem and rededicated the temple to Jehovah. Since then, an annual celebration is held on Chislev 25, the month corresponding to the late part of November and the early part of December.

It is wintertime, the season of cold weather. Jesus is walking in the temple in the colonnade of Solomon. Here Jews encircle him and demand: "How long are you going to keep us in suspense? If you are the Christ, tell us plainly." (John 10:22-24) How will Jesus respond? He replies: "I told you, and yet you do not believe." Jesus has not told them *directly* that he is the Christ, as he told the Samaritan woman at the well. (John 4:25, 26) He has, though, revealed his identity in saying: "Before Abraham came into existence, I have been."—John 8:58.

Jesus wants people to conclude for themselves that he is the Christ by comparing his works with what was foretold the Christ would do. This is why he at other times told his disciples not to tell anyone that he was the Messiah. But now he tells these hostile Jews outright: "The works that I am doing in my Father's name, these bear witness about me. But you do not believe."—John 10:25, 26.

Why do they not believe that Jesus is the Christ? He says: "You do not believe, because you are not my sheep. My sheep listen to my voice, and I know them, and they follow me. I give them everlasting life, and they will by no means ever be destroyed, and no one will snatch them out of my hand. What my Father has given me is something greater than all other things." Jesus then tells them how close his relationship with his Father is, saying: "I and the Father are one." (John 10:26-30) Jesus is here on earth and his Father is in heaven, so he cannot mean that he and his Father are literally one. Rather, they are one in purpose, being united.

Jesus' words so anger the Jews that they again pick up stones to kill him. This does not frighten Jesus. "I displayed to you many fine works from the Father," he says. "For which of those works are you stoning me?" They respond: "We are stoning you, not for a fine work, but for blasphemy; for you . . . make yourself a god." (John 10:31-33) Jesus never claimed to be a god, so why this accusation?

Well, Jesus is saying that he has powers that the Jews believe belong to God alone. For example, regarding the "sheep" he said: "I give them everlasting life," which is something humans cannot do. (John 10:28) The Jews are overlooking the fact that Jesus has openly admitted that he received authority from his Father.

In refuting their false charge, Jesus asks: "Is it not written in your Law [at Psalm 82:6], 'I said: "You are gods"'? If he called 'gods' those against whom the word of God came . . . do you say to me whom the Father sanctified and sent into the world, 'You blaspheme,' because I said, 'I am God's Son'?"—John 10:34-36.

Yes, the Scriptures call even unjust human judges "gods." So how can these Jews fault Jesus for saying "I am God's Son"? He points to something that should convince them: "If I am not doing the works of my Father, do not believe me. But if I am doing them, even though you do

not believe me, believe the works, so that you may come to know and may continue knowing that the Father is in union with me and I am in union with the Father."—John 10:37, 38.

In response, the Jews try to seize Jesus, but he again escapes. He leaves Jerusalem and goes across the Jordan River to the area where John began baptizing nearly four years earlier. This apparently is not far from the southern end of the Sea of Galilee.

Crowds come to Jesus and say: "John did not perform a single sign, but all the things John said about this man were true." (John 10:41) Thus, many Jews put faith in Jesus.

◊ Why does Jesus call the people's attention to his works?

◊ How are Jesus and his Father one?

◊ How does Jesus' quotation from the Psalms disprove the Jews' charge that he is making himself a god or equal to God?

JESUS' LATER MINISTRY EAST OF THE JORDAN

"MANY PUT
FAITH IN HIM."
—JOHN 10:42

JESUS' MINISTRY IN PEREA

LUKE 13:22–14:6

Jesus has been teaching and curing people in Judea and Jerusalem. Then he crosses the Jordan River to teach from city to city in the district of Perea. Soon, though, he will be back in Jerusalem.

While Jesus is in Perea, a man asks: "Lord, are those being saved few?" The man may know of debates among the religious leaders over whether many will be saved or only a few. Jesus shifts the issue from how many will be saved to what must be done in order to be saved. "Exert yourselves vigorously to get in through the narrow door," he says. Yes, effort, a struggle, is required. Why so? Jesus explains: "Many, I tell you, will seek to get in but will not be able." —Luke 13:23, 24.

To illustrate the need for vigorous effort, Jesus says: "When the householder gets up and locks the door, you will stand outside knocking at the door, saying, 'Lord, open to us.' . . . But he will say to you, 'I do not know where you are from. Get away from me, all you workers of unrighteousness!'"—Luke 13: 25-27.

This illustrates the plight of a person who comes late—apparently when it is convenient for him—and finds that the door is shut and locked. He should have come earlier, even if that was inconvenient. It is like that with many who could have benefited from Jesus' being there teaching them. They failed to seize the opportunity to make true worship their chief purpose in life. Those to whom Jesus has been sent have not, for the most part, accepted God's provision for salvation. Jesus says that they will 'weep and gnash their teeth' when they are thrown outside. Yet people "from east and west and from north and south," yes, from all nations,

"will recline at the table in the Kingdom of God." —Luke 13:28, 29.

Jesus explains: "There are those last [such as non-Jews and downtrodden Jews] who will be first, and there are those first [religiously favored Jews who take pride in being descendants of Abraham] who will be last." (Luke 13: 30) Their being "last" means that such ungrateful ones will not be in the Kingdom of God at all.

Some Pharisees now come to Jesus and advise him: "Get out and go away from here, because Herod [Antipas] wants to kill you." Perhaps King Herod himself started this rumor to cause Jesus to flee the territory. Herod may be afraid that somehow he will become involved in the death of another prophet, even as he was in the killing of John the Baptist. But Jesus tells the Pharisees: "Go and tell that fox, 'Look! I am casting out demons and healing people today and tomorrow, and on the third day I will be finished.'" (Luke 13:31, 32) In calling Herod a "fox," Jesus may be alluding to how crafty foxes can be. However, Jesus will not be manipulated or rushed by Herod or anyone else. He is going to carry out the assignment his Father gave him, doing so according to God's schedule, not man's.

Jesus moves on in his journey toward Jerusalem because, as he says, "it cannot be that a prophet should be put to death outside of Jerusalem." (Luke 13:33) No Bible prophecy said that the Messiah must die in that city, so why does Jesus speak of being killed there? Because Jerusalem is the capital, where the 71-member Sanhedrin high court is located and where those accused of being false prophets would be tried. Furthermore, that is where animal sacrifices are offered. Thus, Jesus realizes that it would be inadmissible for him to be killed elsewhere.

"Jerusalem, Jerusalem, the killer of the prophets and stoner of those sent to her," Jesus laments, "how often I wanted to gather your children together the way a hen gathers her brood of chicks under her wings! But you did not want it. Look! Your house is abandoned to you." (Luke 13:34, 35) The nation is rejecting the Son of God and must face the consequences!

Before Jesus gets to Jerusalem, a leader of the Pharisees invites him to his house for a meal on the Sabbath. Those invited watch closely to see what Jesus might do about a man present who is suffering from dropsy (a severe accumulation of fluid, often in the legs and feet). Jesus asks the Pharisees and the experts in the Law: "Is it lawful to cure on the Sabbath or not?" —Luke 14:3.

Nobody answers. Jesus heals the man and then asks them: "Who of you, if his son or bull falls into a well, will not immediately pull him out on the Sabbath day?" (Luke 14:5) Again, they have no response to his sound reasoning.

◇ What does Jesus show is needed for salvation, and why are many locked out?
◇ Who are the "last" that become "first," and the "first" that become "last"?
◇ About what may King Herod be concerned?
◇ Why does Jesus indicate that he will be killed in Jerusalem?

INVITATIONS TO A MEAL—WHOM DOES GOD INVITE?

LUKE 14:7-24

After he has healed the man suffering from dropsy, Jesus is still at the house of the Pharisee. Jesus observes other guests choosing prominent places at the meal, and he uses this as an opportunity to teach a lesson about humility.

"When you are invited by someone to a marriage feast," Jesus says, "do not recline in the most prominent place. Perhaps someone more distinguished than you may also have been invited. Then the one who invited you both will come and say to you, 'Let this man have your place.' Then you will proceed with shame to take the lowest place."—Luke 14:8, 9.

Jesus next says: "When you are invited, go and recline in the lowest place, so that when the man who invited you comes, he will say to you, 'Friend, go on up higher.' Then you will have honor in front of all your fellow guests." This is much more than simply displaying good manners. Jesus explains: "For everyone who exalts himself will be humbled, and whoever humbles himself will be exalted." (Luke 14:10, 11) Yes, he is encouraging his listeners to cultivate humility.

Then Jesus states another lesson for the Pharisee who invited him—how to provide a dinner that has real merit with God. "When you spread a dinner or an evening meal, do not call your friends or your brothers or your relatives or your rich neighbors. Otherwise, they might also invite you in return, and it would become a repayment to you. But when you spread a feast, invite the poor, the crippled, the lame, the blind; and you will be happy, because they have nothing with which to repay you."—Luke 14:12-14.

It is natural to invite friends, relatives, or neighbors to a meal, and Jesus is not saying

that this is wrong. He stresses, however, that providing a meal for the needy, such as the poor, crippled, or blind, can bring a rich blessing. Jesus explains to his host: "You will be repaid in the resurrection of the righteous ones." A fellow guest concurs, saying: "Happy is the one who dines in the Kingdom of God." (Luke 14:15) He sees what a privilege this would be. However, not all have such appreciation, as Jesus goes on to illustrate:

"A man was spreading a grand evening meal, and he invited many. He sent his slave out . . . to say to the invited ones, 'Come, because everything is now ready.' But they all alike began to make excuses. The first said to him, 'I bought a field and need to go out and see it; I ask you, have me excused.' And another said, 'I bought five yoke of cattle and am going to examine them; I ask you, have me excused.' Still another said, 'I just got married, and for this reason I cannot come.'"—Luke 14:16-20.

Those are weak excuses! A man normally examines a field or livestock before the purchase, so it is not urgent to look at them afterward. The third man is not preparing to marry. He is already married, so that should not prevent him from accepting an important invitation. On hearing these excuses, the master angrily tells his slave:

"Go out quickly to the main streets and the alleys of the city, and bring in here the poor and crippled and blind and lame." After the slave does so, there is still room. The master then tells his slave: "Go out to the roads and the lanes and compel them to come in, so that my house may be filled. For I say to you, none of those men who were invited will taste my evening meal."—Luke 14:21-24.

What Jesus has just related well illustrates how Jehovah God had Jesus Christ extend an invitation to individuals to be in line for the Kingdom of the heavens. The Jews, especially the religious leaders, were the first to be invited. In the main, they rejected the invitation throughout Jesus' ministry. But the invitation would not stop with them. Jesus clearly is suggesting that in the future a second invitation would be extended to lowly ones of the Jewish nation and to proselytes. Thereafter, there would be a third and final invitation to people whom the Jews viewed as unsuitable before God.—Acts 10:28-48.

Yes, what Jesus is saying truly confirms the words of one of his fellow guests, who said: "Happy is the one who dines in the Kingdom of God."

◇ How does Jesus convey a lesson about humility?

◇ How can a host provide a meal that has real merit with God, and why will it bring the host happiness?

◇ What point is Jesus making in his illustration of the evening meal?

DISCIPLESHIP—HOW SERIOUS?

LUKE 14:25-35

Jesus has taught valuable lessons while having a meal at the house of a leader of the Pharisees. As Jesus continues his trip toward Jerusalem, large crowds travel with him. Why? Are they really interested in being his true followers, no matter what that may require of them?

As they travel along the way, Jesus says something to them that may shock some: "If anyone comes to me and does not hate his father and mother and wife and children and brothers and sisters, yes, and even his own life, he cannot be my disciple." (Luke 14:26) But what does he mean in saying this?

Jesus is not saying that all who become his followers must literally hate their relatives. Rather, he means that they must hate them in the sense of loving them less than they love Jesus, not being like the man in his illustration of the evening meal who turned down an important invitation because he just got married. (Luke 14:20) The Jews' ancestor Jacob is said to have "hated" Leah and loved Rachel, meaning that he loved Leah less than her sister Rachel.—Genesis 29:31; footnote.

Note that Jesus says that a disciple should hate "even his own life," or soul. This means that a true disciple must love Jesus more than he loves his own life, even being willing to lose his life if necessary. Clearly, becoming a disciple of Christ is a serious responsibility. It is not to be undertaken casually, without careful thought.

Discipleship may involve hardship and persecution, for Jesus says: "Whoever does not carry his torture stake and come after me cannot be my disciple." (Luke 14:27) Yes, a true disciple of Jesus must be willing to undergo a burden of reproach such as Jesus faced. Jesus

has even said that he will die at the hands of his enemies.

So the crowds traveling with Jesus need to analyze very carefully what it means to be a disciple of Christ. Jesus emphasizes this with an illustration. "For example," he says, "who of you wanting to build a tower does not first sit down and calculate the expense to see if he has enough to complete it? Otherwise, he might lay its foundation but not be able to finish it." (Luke

14:28, 29) Thus, before becoming Jesus' disciples, those traveling with him toward Jerusalem should have firmly decided to carry out the responsibility fully. He underscores that thought with another illustration:

"What king marching out against another king in war does not first sit down and take counsel whether he is able with 10,000 troops to stand up to the one who comes against him with 20,000? If, in fact, he cannot do so, then while that one is yet far away, he sends out a body of ambassadors and sues for peace." To emphasize his point, Jesus says: "In the same way, you may be sure that not one of you who does not say good-bye to all his belongings can be my disciple."—Luke 14:31-33.

Of course, Jesus is not saying that only for the crowds following him on the road. All who learn of Christ must be willing to do what he is saying here. This means that they need to be ready to sacrifice everything they have—their belongings, even their life—if they are to be his disciples. That is something to think and pray about.

Now Jesus brings up a matter that he touched on in his Sermon on the Mount when he said that his disciples are "the salt of the earth." (Matthew 5:13) He likely meant that even as literal salt is a preservative, his disciples have a preserving effect on people, protecting them from spiritual and moral decay. Now, as his ministry draws to a close, he says: "Salt, to be sure, is fine. But if the salt loses its strength, with what will it be seasoned?" (Luke 14:34) His listeners know that some salt available then was impure, mixed with earthy matter and thus of little use.

So Jesus is showing that even those who have long been his disciples must not let their determination grow weak. If that were to hap-

pen, they would become useless, like salt that has lost its strength. The world might then ridicule them. More than that, they would be unfit before God, even bringing reproach upon his name. Jesus stresses the importance of avoiding that outcome, saying: "Let the one who has ears to listen, listen."—Luke 14:35.

◇ What does Jesus mean in saying that a disciple must "hate" his relatives and even "his own life"?
◇ What is Jesus teaching by means of his illustrations about building a tower and about a king with an army?
◇ What is the point of Jesus' comments about salt?

REJOICING OVER THE SINNER WHO REPENTS

LUKE 15:1-10

At various times during his ministry, Jesus has emphasized the importance of humility. (Luke 14:8-11) He is eager to find men and women who desire to serve God humbly. Up till now, some of them may still be notorious sinners.

The Pharisees and scribes notice that such individuals—people whom they consider unworthy—are drawn to Jesus and his message. They complain: "This man welcomes sinners and eats with them." (Luke 15:2) The Pharisees and scribes feel superior and treat the common people like dirt under their feet. Reflecting the contempt they have for such ones, the leaders use the Hebrew expression *'am ha·'a'rets,* "people of the land [earth]" to refer to them.

In contrast, Jesus treats all with dignity, kindness, and compassion. Many of the lowly ones, including some who are known to be practicing sin, are thus eager to listen to Jesus. How, though, does Jesus feel about and respond to the criticism that he is receiving for helping such lowly ones?

The answer becomes clear as he presents a touching illustration, similar to one he earlier gave in Capernaum. (Matthew 18:12-14) Jesus presents things as if the Pharisees are righteous and safe in the fold of God. In contrast, the lowly people are presented as ones who have gone astray and who are in a lost state. Jesus says:

"What man among you with 100 sheep, on losing one of them, will not leave the 99 behind in the wilderness and go after the lost one until he finds it? And when he has found it, he puts it on his shoulders and rejoices. And when he gets home, he calls his friends and his neighbors together, saying to them, 'Rejoice with me, for I have found my sheep that was lost.'"—Luke 15:4-6.

What application does Jesus make? He explains: "I tell you that in the same way, there will be more joy in heaven over one sinner who repents than over 99 righteous ones who have no need of repentance."—Luke 15:7.

Jesus' mention of repentance must strike the Pharisees. They consider themselves to be righteous and feel they have no need of repentance. When some of them criticized Jesus a couple of years earlier because he was eating with tax collectors and sinners, he replied: "I came to call, not righteous people, but sinners." (Mark 2:15-17) The self-righteous Pharisees fail to see

their need to repent, and thus they bring no joy in heaven. It is just the opposite when sinners truly repent.

Reinforcing his point that the restoration of lost sinners is a cause for great rejoicing in heaven, Jesus presents another illustration, one set in a family home: "What woman who has ten drachma coins, if she loses one of the drachmas, does not light a lamp and sweep her house and search carefully until she finds it? And when she has found it, she calls her friends and neighbors together, saying, 'Rejoice with me, for I have found the drachma coin that I had lost.'"—Luke 15:8, 9.

The application Jesus makes is similar to the one he made after giving the illustration of the lost sheep. He now says: "In the same way, I tell you, joy arises among the angels of God over one sinner who repents."—Luke 15:10.

Imagine, God's angels show deep interest in the restoration of lost sinners! That is particularly significant because the sinners who repent and gain a place in God's heavenly Kingdom will have a position higher than that of the angels themselves! (1 Corinthians 6:2, 3) Yet the angels do not feel jealous. How, then, should we feel when a sinner turns to God in full repentance?

◇ Why does Jesus associate with known sinners?
◇ How do the Pharisees view the common people and Jesus' having dealings with such ones?
◇ What lesson does Jesus teach with two illustrations?

THE SON WHO WAS LOST RETURNS

LUKE 15:11-32

Jesus has given the illustrations of the lost sheep and the lost drachma coin while likely still in Perea east of the Jordan River. The message that both teach is that we should rejoice when a sinner repents and returns to God. The Pharisees and the scribes have been critical of Jesus because he welcomes people of that sort. But do such critics learn something from Jesus' two illustrations? Do they grasp how our Father in heaven feels toward repentant sinners? Jesus now gives a touching illustration that emphasizes this same important lesson.

The illustration involves a father who has two sons, the younger son being the principal character of this illustration. Both the Pharisees and the scribes, as well as others hearing what Jesus relates, should be able to learn from what is said about this younger son. However, not to be overlooked is what Jesus relates about the father and the older son, for the attitudes they display are instructive too. So think about all three of these men as Jesus tells the illustration:

"A man had two sons," Jesus begins. "The younger one said to his father, 'Father, give me the share of the property that should come to me.' So he divided his belongings between them." (Luke 15:11, 12) Note that this younger son is not seeking his inheritance because his father has died. The father is still alive. Yet the son wants his portion *now* so that he can be independent and do with it as he chooses. And what is that?

"A few days later," Jesus explains, "the younger son gathered all his things together and traveled to a distant country and there squandered his property by living a debauched life." (Luke 15:13) Rather than remaining in the security of his home, with a father who cared for his children and provided for them, this son goes off to another land. There he squanders all his inheritance in wanton indulgence, pursuing sensual pleasures. Then he comes into hard times, as Jesus goes on to relate:

"When he had spent everything, a severe famine occurred throughout that country, and he fell into need. He even went and attached himself to one of the citizens of that country, who sent him into his fields to herd swine. And he longed to be filled with the carob pods that the swine were eating, but no one would give him anything."—Luke 15:14-16.

God's Law categorized pigs as unclean, yet this son has to work as a herder of swine. He is racked with hunger, which reduces him to wanting to eat what normally is food only for animals, the pigs he is herding. In the son's calamity and despair, "he came to his senses." What does he do? He says to himself: "How many of my father's hired men have more than enough bread, while I am dying here from hunger! I will get up and travel to my father and say to him: 'Father, I have sinned against heaven and against you. I am no longer worthy of being called your son. Make me as one of your hired men.'" Then he gets up and goes to his father.—Luke 15:17-20.

How will his father react? Will he turn on his son angrily and scold him about the folly of leaving home in the first place? Will the father display an indifferent, unwelcoming attitude? If it were you, how would you react? What if it were your son or daughter?

◇ To whom does Jesus tell this illustration, and why?

◇ Who may be considered the principal character, and what happens to him?

THE LOST SON IS FOUND

Jesus describes how the father feels and acts: "While [the son] was still a long way off, his father caught sight of him and was moved with pity, and he ran and embraced him and tenderly kissed him." (Luke 15:20) Even if the father has heard of his son's debauched living, he welcomes his son back. Will the Jewish leaders, who claim to know and worship Jehovah, see from this how our heavenly Father feels toward repentant sinners? Will they also recognize that Jesus has been showing the same welcoming spirit?

The discerning father can likely conclude from his son's sad, downcast countenance that he is repentant. Still, the father's loving initiative to greet him makes it easier for his son to confess his sins. Jesus relates: "Then the son said to him, 'Father, I have sinned against heaven and against you. I am no longer worthy of being called your son.'"—Luke 15:21.

The father orders his slaves: "Quick! bring out a robe, the best one, and clothe him with it, and put a ring on his hand and sandals on his feet. Also bring the fattened calf, slaughter it, and let us eat and celebrate, for this son of mine was dead but has come to life again; he was lost and has been found." Then they start "to enjoy themselves."—Luke 15:22-24.

Meanwhile, the father's older son is in the field. Jesus says about him: "As he returned and got near the house, he heard music and dancing. So he called one of the servants to him and asked what was happening. He said to him, 'Your brother has come, and your father slaughtered the fattened calf because he got him back in good health.' But he became angry and refused to go in. Then his father came out and began to plead with him. In reply he said to his father, 'Look! These many years I have slaved for you and never once did I disobey your orders, and yet you never once gave me a

young goat to enjoy with my friends. But as soon as this son of yours arrived who squandered your belongings with prostitutes, you slaughtered the fattened calf for him.'"—Luke 15:25-30.

Who, like the older son, have been critical of the mercy and attention that Jesus has accorded the common people and sinners? The scribes and the Pharisees. Their criticism of Jesus' welcoming sinners has prompted this illustration. Of course, anyone critical of God's showing mercy should take the lesson to heart.

Jesus concludes his illustration by relating the father's appeal to his older son: "My son, you have always been with me, and all the things that are mine are yours. But we just had to celebrate and rejoice, for your brother was dead but has come to life; he was lost and has been found."—Luke 15:31, 32.

Jesus does not reveal what the older son eventually does. However, after Jesus' death and resurrection, "a large crowd of priests began to be obedient to the faith." (Acts 6:7) That might have included some of the very ones who hear Jesus relate this powerful illustration about the son who was lost. Yes, it was possible even for them to come to their senses, repent, and return to God.

From that day forward, Jesus' disciples can and should take to heart key lessons that he set out in this fine illustration. An initial lesson is how truly wise it is to remain in the security of God's people, under the care of our Father who loves us and provides for us, instead of wandering off after tempting pleasures in "a distant country."

Another lesson is that if any of us should deviate from God's way, we must humbly return to our Father so as to enjoy his favor again.

Still another lesson can be seen by the contrast between the father's receptive, forgiving spirit and the older brother's resentful, unwelcoming attitude. Clearly, God's servants want to be forgiving and welcoming if one who had strayed truly repents and returns to 'the Father's house.' Let us rejoice that our brother who 'was dead has come to life' and that he who 'was lost has been found.'

◇ When the younger son returns, how does his father respond?
◇ How does the compassionate father reflect the ways of Jehovah and Jesus?
◇ In what sense does the older son's reaction mirror the way the scribes and the Pharisees behave?
◇ What lessons do you find in Jesus' illustration?

PLAN AHEAD—USE PRACTICAL WISDOM

LUKE 16:1-13

The illustration of the lost son, which Jesus just related, should have impressed on listening tax collectors, scribes, and Pharisees that God is willing to forgive repentant sinners. (Luke 15: 1-7, 11) Now Jesus addresses his disciples. He uses another illustration, this time about a rich man who learns that his house manager, or steward, has not acted properly.

Jesus relates that the steward has been accused of mishandling his master's goods. So the master says that the steward will be dismissed. "What am I to do," the steward wonders, "seeing that my master is taking the stewardship away from me? I am not strong enough to dig, and I am ashamed to beg." To deal with what lies ahead, he concludes: "I know what I will do, so that when I am removed from the stewardship, people will welcome me into their homes." He immediately calls those who are in debt, asking them: "How much do you owe my master?"—Luke 16:3-5.

The first one answers: "A hundred measures of olive oil." That is some 580 gallons of oil. The debtor might have had an extensive olive grove or been a merchant who sold oil. The steward tells him: "Take back your written agreement and sit down and quickly write 50 [290 gallons]."—Luke 16:6.

The steward asks another one: "Now you, how much do you owe?" The reply is: "A hundred large measures of wheat." That is some 20,000 dry quarts. The steward tells this debtor: "Take back your written agreement and write 80." He thus reduces the debt by 20 percent. —Luke 16:7.

The steward is still in charge of his master's financial affairs, so in a sense he does have jurisdiction over reducing what others owe the master. By reducing the amounts owed, the steward is making friends of those who may do him favors after he loses his job.

At some point the master learns what has happened. Though what was done means a loss to him, he is impressed with the steward and commends him because "though unrighteous," he "acted with practical wisdom." Jesus adds: "The sons of this system of things are wiser in a practical way toward their own generation than the sons of the light are."—Luke 16:8.

Jesus is not condoning the steward's methods, nor is he encouraging crafty business dealings. What, then, is his point? He urges the disciples: "Make friends for yourselves by means of the unrighteous riches, so that when such fail, they may receive you into the everlasting dwelling places." (Luke 16:9) Yes, there is a lesson here about being farsighted and using practical wisdom. God's servants, "the sons of the light," need to use their material assets in a wise way, with the everlasting future in mind.

Only Jehovah God and his Son can receive someone into the heavenly Kingdom or the Paradise on earth under that Kingdom. We should diligently cultivate friendship with them by using what material riches we have in supporting Kingdom interests. Our everlasting future will thus be assured when gold, silver, and other material riches fail or perish.

Jesus also says that those who are faithful in caring for and using whatever riches or material things they have will be faithful in caring for matters of greater importance. "Therefore," Jesus points out, "if you have not proved yourselves faithful in connection with the unrighteous riches, who will entrust you with what is true [such as Kingdom interests]?" —Luke 16:11.

Jesus is showing his disciples that much will be asked of them if they are to be received "into the everlasting dwelling places." One cannot be a true servant of God and at the same time be a slave to unrighteous, material riches. Jesus concludes: "No servant can be a slave to two masters, for either he will hate the one and love the other, or he will stick to the one and despise the other. You cannot be slaves to God and to Riches."—Luke 16:9, 13.

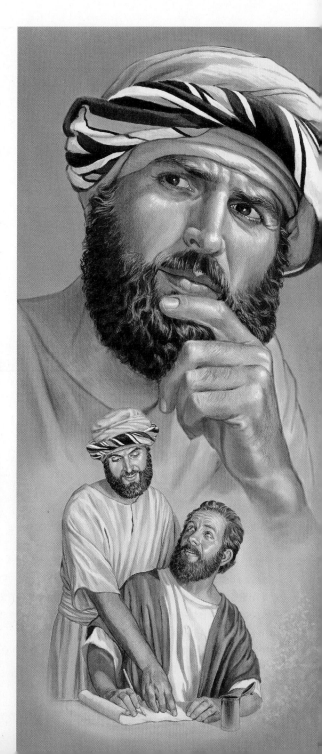

◇ In Jesus' illustration, how does the steward make friends of those who can help him later?

◇ What are "unrighteous riches," and how can a Christian "make friends" by means of them?

◇ Who can receive us "into the everlasting dwelling places" if we are faithful in using whatever "unrighteous riches" we have?

A CHANGE FOR THE RICH MAN AND FOR LAZARUS

LUKE 16:14-31

Jesus has been giving his disciples fine counsel about the use of material riches. But his disciples are not the only ones listening. Pharisees are also present, and they ought to take to heart Jesus' counsel. Why? Because they are "money lovers." On hearing what Jesus is saying, they 'begin to sneer at him.'—Luke 15:2; 16: 13, 14.

That does not intimidate Jesus, though. He says to them: "You are those who declare yourselves righteous before men, but God knows your hearts. For what is considered exalted by men is a disgusting thing in God's sight."—Luke 16:15.

The Pharisees have long been "exalted by men," but this is a time of change, a time for the tables to turn. The highly exalted ones who are rich in worldly goods, political power, and religious influence are to be brought down. The common people who recognize their spiritual need are to be raised up. Jesus makes it clear that a major change is taking place, saying:

"The Law and the Prophets were until John. From then on, the Kingdom of God is being declared as good news, and every sort of person is pressing forward toward it. Indeed, it is easier for heaven and earth to pass away than for one stroke of a letter of the Law to go unfulfilled." (Luke 3:18; 16:16, 17) How do Jesus' words indicate that a change is occurring?

The Jewish religious leaders proudly profess adherence to the Law of Moses. Recall that when Jesus restored sight to a man in Jerusalem, the Pharisees pridefully said: "We are disciples of Moses. We know that God has spoken to Moses." (John 9:13, 28, 29) One purpose of the Law given through Moses was to lead humble ones to the Messiah, that is, to Jesus.

John the Baptist identified Jesus as the Lamb of God. (John 1:29-34) Starting with John's ministry, humble Jews, especially among the poor, have been hearing about "the Kingdom of God." Yes, there is "good news" for all wanting to be subjects of God's Kingdom and benefit from it.

The Mosaic Law is not going unfulfilled; rather, it has led to the Messiah. Moreover, the obligation to keep it is ending. For example, the Law allowed for divorce on various grounds, but now Jesus explains that "everyone who divorces his wife and marries another commits adultery, and whoever marries a woman divorced from her husband commits adultery." (Luke 16:18) How such pronouncements enrage the legalistically minded Pharisees!

Jesus now relates an illustration that underscores the magnitude of the change that is taking place. It features two men—each of whose status, or situation, changes dramatically. In considering the illustration, bear in mind that among those hearing it are money-loving Pharisees who are being exalted by men.

"There was a rich man," Jesus says, "who used to dress in purple and linen, enjoying himself day after day with magnificence. But a beggar named Lazarus used to be put at his gate, covered with ulcers and desiring to be filled with the things dropping from the table of the rich man. Yes, even the dogs would come and lick his ulcers."—Luke 16:19-21.

The Pharisees are money lovers, so is there any doubt whom Jesus is illustrating by this "rich man"? These Jewish religious leaders also like to deck themselves out in costly, fancy clothing. And beyond whatever actual wealth they might have, they seem rich in the privileges they enjoy and opportunities they have. Yes, illustrating them by a man clothed in royal purple reflects their favored position, and the white linen reflects their self-righteousness.—Daniel 5:7.

How do these rich, proud leaders view the poor, the common people? They contemptuously consider them 'am ha·'a'rets, or people of the land (earth), who neither know the Law nor deserve to be taught it. (John 7:49) That reflects the situation of the "beggar named Lazarus," who hungers for even the meager "things

◇ What contrast exists between the situation of the Jewish religious leaders and that of the common people?

◇ As Jesus indicates, what change takes place beginning with John's ministry?

◇ Who are like the rich man in Jesus' illustration, and who are like Lazarus?

dropping from the table of the rich man." Like Lazarus covered with ulcers, the common people are looked down on, as if they are spiritually diseased.

That sad situation has existed for some time, but Jesus knows that the time has come for a great change in the condition of both those who are like the rich man and those who are like Lazarus.

THE CHANGE FOR THE RICH MAN AND FOR LAZARUS

Jesus goes on to describe this dramatic change in circumstances. "Now in the course of time," he says, "the beggar died and was carried off by the angels to Abraham's side. Also, the rich man died and was buried. And in the Grave he lifted up his eyes, being in torment, and he saw Abraham from afar and Lazarus by his side."—Luke 16:22, 23.

Those listening to Jesus know that Abraham is long dead and in the Grave. The Scriptures make it clear that no one in the Grave, or Sheol, can see or speak, including Abraham. (Ecclesiastes 9:5, 10) What, then, do these religious leaders think that Jesus means with this illustration? What might he be indicating about the common people and the money-loving religious leaders?

Jesus has just pointed to a change by saying that 'the Law and the Prophets were until John the Baptist, but from then on the Kingdom of God is being declared as good news.' Hence, it is with the preaching of John and Jesus Christ that both Lazarus and the rich man die to their former circumstances, or condition, and they experience new positions relative to God.

Specifically, those of the humble or poor class have long been spiritually deprived. But

they are being helped by and are responding to the message about the Kingdom presented first by John the Baptist and then by Jesus. Formerly, they had to get by with what amounted to little 'things dropped from the spiritual table' of the religious leaders. Now they are being fed with essential Scriptural truths, particularly the wonderful things Jesus is explaining. It is as if they finally are in the favored position in the eyes of Jehovah God.

In contrast, those in the rich and influential class of religious leaders refuse to accept the Kingdom message that John proclaimed and that Jesus has been preaching throughout the land. (Matthew 3:1, 2; 4:17) In fact, they are angered, or tormented, by that message, which points to a coming fiery judgment from God. (Matthew 3:7-12) It would be a relief to the money-loving religious leaders if Jesus and his disciples would let up on declaring God's message. Those leaders are like the rich man in the illustration, who says: "Father Abraham, have mercy on me, and send Lazarus to dip the tip of his finger in water and cool my tongue, for I am in anguish in this blazing fire."—Luke 16:24.

But that is not to happen. Most of the religious leaders will not change. They had refused to "listen to Moses and the Prophets," which writings should have led them to accept Jesus as God's Messiah and King. (Luke 16:29, 31; Galatians 3:24) Nor do they humble themselves and let themselves be persuaded by those poor ones who accept Jesus and now have divine favor. Jesus' disciples, for their part, cannot compromise or water down the truth just to satisfy the religious leaders or give them relief. In his illustration, Jesus describes this reality in the words uttered by "Father Abraham" to the rich man:

"Child, remember that you had your fill of good things in your lifetime, but Lazarus for his part received bad things. Now, however, he is being comforted here, but you are in anguish. And besides all these things, a great chasm has been fixed between us and you, so that those who want to go over from here to you cannot, neither may people cross over from there to us." —Luke 16:25, 26.

How just and fitting it is that such a dramatic change takes place! It amounts to a reversal of position between the proud religious leaders and the humble ones who accept Jesus' yoke and are finally being refreshed and fed spiritually. (Matthew 11:28-30) This change will be even more evident in a few months when the Law covenant is replaced by the new covenant. (Jeremiah 31:31-33; Colossians 2:14; Hebrews 8:7-13) When God pours out holy spirit on the day of Pentecost 33 C.E., it will be unmistakably clear that, rather than the Pharisees and their religious allies, Jesus' disciples have God's favor.

◇ How does Jesus indicate a change in circumstances?

◇ The message preached by John and Jesus finds what response among the religious leaders, and how does Jesus illustrate this?

◇ The religious leaders would like what to happen, but why will it not occur?

◇ When will the chasm between the religious leaders and Jesus' disciples become even greater?

TEACHING IN PEREA ON THE WAY TO JUDEA

LUKE 17:1-10   JOHN 11:1-16

For a while, Jesus has been in the area "across the Jordan" called Perea. (John 10:40) He now travels south toward Jerusalem.

Jesus is not alone. His disciples are traveling with him, as well as "large crowds," including tax collectors and sinners. (Luke 14:25; 15:1) Pharisees and scribes, who are critical of what Jesus is saying and doing, are also there. They have much to think about after hearing Jesus relate the illustrations about the lost sheep, the lost son, and the rich man and Lazarus.—Luke 15:2; 16:14.

Perhaps with the criticism and sneering of his opposers fresh in mind, Jesus turns his attention to his disciples. He touches on some points that he earlier taught in Galilee.

For example, Jesus says: "It is unavoidable that causes for stumbling should come. Nevertheless, woe to the one through whom they come! . . . Pay attention to yourselves. If your brother commits a sin, rebuke him, and if he repents, forgive him. Even if he sins seven times a day against you and he comes back to you seven times, saying, 'I repent,' you must forgive him." (Luke 17:1-4) That last comment may remind Peter of the question he had asked about forgiving up to seven times.—Matthew 18:21.

Will the disciples be able to act in harmony with Jesus' words? When they say to Jesus, "Give us more faith," he assures them: "If you had faith the size of a mustard grain, you would say to this black mulberry tree, 'Be uprooted and planted in the sea!' and it would obey you." (Luke 17:5, 6) Yes, even a degree of faith can accomplish great things.

Jesus goes on to teach the importance of having a humble, balanced view of oneself, saying to the apostles: "Which one of you who has a slave plowing or shepherding would say to him when he comes in from the field, 'Come here at once and dine at the table'? Rather, will he not say to him, 'Get something ready for me to have my evening meal, and put on an apron and serve me until I finish eating and drinking, and afterward you can eat and drink'? He will not feel gratitude to the slave because he did what was assigned, will he? Likewise, when you have done all the things assigned to you, say: 'We are good-for-nothing slaves. What we have done is what we ought to have done.'"—Luke 17: 7-10.

Each servant of God should understand the importance of putting God's interests first. Furthermore, each should remember the privilege that he has to worship God as a member of his household.

Apparently soon after this, a messenger sent by Mary and Martha arrives. They are the sisters of Lazarus, and they live in Bethany of Judea. The messenger relates: "Lord, see! the one you have affection for is sick."—John 11:1-3.

Though learning that his friend Lazarus is very ill, Jesus is not paralyzed by grief. Instead, he says: "This sickness is not meant to end in death, but is for the glory of God, so that the Son of God may be glorified through it." He remains where he is for two days then tells his disciples: "Let us go into Judea again." They protest: "Rabbi, just lately the Judeans were seeking to stone you, and are you going there again?"—John 11:4, 7, 8.

Jesus responds: "There are 12 hours of daylight, are there not? If anyone walks in daylight, he does not stumble into anything, because he sees the light of this world. But if anyone walks in the night, he stumbles, because the light is not in him." (John 11:9, 10) He apparently means that the time God has allotted for Jesus' ministry is not yet completed. Until it is, Jesus needs to use to the full the short time left for him.

Jesus adds: "Lazarus our friend has fallen asleep, but I am traveling there to awaken him." Evidently thinking that Lazarus is simply rest-ing and that he will recover, the disciples say: "Lord, if he is sleeping, he will get well." Jesus tells them outspokenly: "Lazarus has died . . . But let us go to him."—John 11:11-15.

Aware that Jesus could be killed in Judea, yet desiring to support him, Thomas urges his fellow disciples: "Let us also go, so that we may die with him."—John 11:16.

◇ Where has Jesus been preaching?

◇ What teachings does Jesus repeat, and what situation does he use to illustrate his point about humility?

◇ Jesus receives what news, and why does Thomas mention dying with Jesus?

"THE RESURRECTION AND THE LIFE"

JOHN 11:17-37

Coming from Perea, Jesus arrives at the outskirts of Bethany, a village about two miles east of Jerusalem. Mary and Martha, the sisters of Lazarus, are mourning his recent death. Many have come to console them.

Then someone tells Martha that Jesus is approaching, and she hurries to meet him. Martha tells Jesus what she and her sister have likely been thinking for four days: "Lord, if you had been here, my brother would not have died."

However, it is not that she has no hope. "I know that whatever you ask God for, God will give you," Martha says. (John 11:21, 22) She feels that Jesus might yet help her brother.

Jesus responds: "Your brother will rise." Martha concludes that he is referring to a future resurrection on earth, the hope that Abraham and others had. And she expresses her belief that this will surely occur: "I know he will rise in the resurrection on the last day."—John 11:23, 24.

Yet, could it be that Jesus can provide immediate relief in this case? He reminds Martha that he has God-given power over death, saying: "The one who exercises faith in me, even though he dies, will come to life; and everyone who is living and exercises faith in me will never die at all."—John 11:25, 26.

Jesus is not suggesting that his disciples then alive will never die. Even he must die, as he has told his apostles. (Matthew 16:21; 17:22, 23) Jesus is stressing that exercising faith in him can lead to everlasting life. For many, such life will be gained through a resurrection. However, faithful ones alive at the end of this system may never have to die at all. In either case, everyone who exercises faith in him can be sure of never facing permanent death.

But can Jesus, who just said, "I am the resurrection and the life," help Lazarus, now dead for days? Jesus asks Martha: "Do you believe this?" She answers: "Yes, Lord, I have believed that you are the Christ, the Son of God, the one coming into the world." With faith that Jesus can do something that very day, Martha hurries home and tells her sister privately: "The Teacher is here and is calling you." (John 11:25-28) At that, Mary leaves the house, soon to be followed by others, who assume that she is going to Lazarus' tomb.

Instead, Mary goes to Jesus, falls at his feet weeping, and repeats the sentiments her sister expressed: "Lord, if you had been here, my brother would not have died." Moved at seeing Mary and the crowds weeping, Jesus groans, becomes troubled, and even gives way to tears. That touches the onlookers. But some ask: 'If Jesus could heal a man born blind, could he not prevent this one from dying?' —John 11:32, 37.

◇ When Jesus arrives near Bethany, what is the situation?

◇ What basis does Martha have for belief in a resurrection?

◇ How does Jesus indicate that he can do something about Lazarus' death?

LAZARUS IS RESURRECTED

JOHN 11:38-54

After Jesus meets Martha and then Mary near Bethany, they go to the memorial tomb of Lazarus. It is a cave with a stone covering the entrance. "Take the stone away," Jesus directs. Martha expresses concern, not understanding what Jesus intends to do. "Lord," she says, "by now he must smell, for it has been four days." But Jesus tells her: "Did I not tell you that if you would believe you would see the glory of God?" —John 11:39, 40.

So the stone is removed. Jesus then raises his eyes and prays: "Father, I thank you that you have heard me. True, I knew that you always hear me; but I spoke on account of the crowd standing around, so that they may believe that you sent me." Jesus' public prayer shows to ob-

servers that what he is about to do is by means of power from God. Then Jesus cries out with a loud voice: "Lazarus, come out!" And Lazarus does come out, with his hands and feet still bound with burial wrappings and his face covered with a cloth. "Free him and let him go," Jesus says.—John 11:41-44.

Many Jews who have come to comfort Mary and Martha see this miracle and put faith in Jesus. But others go off and tell the Pharisees what Jesus has done. The Pharisees and the chief priests hold a meeting of the Jewish high court, the Sanhedrin. That body includes the high priest, Caiaphas. Some of them lament: "What are we to do, for this man performs many signs? If we let him go on this way, they will all put faith in him, and the Romans will come and take away both our place and our nation." (John 11:47, 48) Though having heard eyewitness testimony that Jesus "performs many signs," these men are not rejoicing over what God is doing through him. Their prime concern is their own position and authority.

That Lazarus has been raised from the dead is a real blow to the Sadducees, who do not believe in the resurrection. Caiaphas, a Sadducee, now speaks up, saying: "You do not know anything at all, and you have not reasoned that it is to your benefit for one man to die in behalf of the people rather than for the whole nation

to be destroyed."—John 11:49, 50; Acts 5:17; 23:8.

In view of Caiaphas' sacred office, God causes him to say this—he does not do so "of his own originality." Caiaphas means that Jesus should be killed to prevent him from further undermining the authority and influence of the Jewish religious leaders. Yet, Caiaphas' prophecy points to the fact that by his death, Jesus would provide a ransom, not just for the Jews, but for all "the children of God who were scattered about."—John 11:51, 52.

Caiaphas succeeds in influencing the Sanhedrin to make plans to kill Jesus. Might Nicodemus, a member of the Sanhedrin who is friendly to Jesus, reveal these plans to him? In any event, Jesus leaves the immediate Jerusalem area, thus avoiding death before God's appointed time.

◊ How do those who see the resurrection of Lazarus respond to it?

◊ What reveals the wickedness of members of the Sanhedrin?

◊ Despite Caiaphas' intentions, what does God have him prophesy?

TEN LEPERS HEALED—ONE SHOWS GRATITUDE

LUKE 17:11-19

Frustrating the Sanhedrin's plans to kill him, Jesus travels to the city of Ephraim, somewhat northeast of Jerusalem. He stays there with his disciples, away from his enemies. (John 11:54) However, the time for the Passover of 33 C.E. is approaching, so Jesus is soon on the move again. He travels northward through Samaria and up into Galilee, his last visit to this area prior to his death.

Early in the trip, while Jesus is traveling from one village to another, he encounters ten men who have leprosy. In some of its forms, this disease can result in gradual loss of body tissue, such as that of the fingers, toes, or ears. (Numbers 12:10-12) God's Law requires that a leper call out "Unclean, unclean!" and that he live in isolation.—Leviticus 13:45, 46.

Accordingly, the ten lepers keep at a distance from Jesus. Yet, they cry out loudly: "Jesus, Instructor, have mercy on us!" On seeing the lepers, Jesus directs them: "Go and show yourselves to the priests." (Luke 17:13, 14) He thus shows respect for God's Law, which authorizes the priests to pronounce as cured lepers who have recovered from their illness. Then they can once again live among healthy people.—Leviticus 13:9-17.

The ten lepers have confidence in Jesus' miraculous powers. They head off to see the priests, even before they have been healed. While they are on the way, their faith in Jesus is rewarded. They begin to see and feel that they have been restored to health!

Nine of the cleansed lepers continue on their way. One does not. This man, a Samaritan, returns to look for Jesus. Why? The man is deeply grateful to Jesus for what has happened. The former leper is "glorifying God with a loud voice," realizing that God is actually responsible for his restored health. (Luke 17:15) When he finds Jesus, he falls down before him, thanking him.

To those around him, Jesus says: "All ten were cleansed, were they not? Where, then, are the other nine? Did no one else turn back to give glory to God except this man of another nation?" Then Jesus tells the Samaritan: "Get up and be on your way; your faith has made you well."—Luke 17:17-19.

By healing the ten lepers, Jesus shows that he has Jehovah God's backing. Now one of the ten is not only healed through Jesus' act but is likely on the way to life. We are not living at a time when God is using Jesus to perform such healings. However, by faith in Jesus, we can be on the way to life—everlasting life. Do we show that we are grateful, as that Samaritan man did?

◇ Frustrating plans to kill him, Jesus travels to where?

◇ Why do the ten lepers stand at a distance, and why does Jesus tell them to go to the priests?

◇ In light of what happened to the Samaritan, what lesson should we reflect on?

THE SON OF MAN WILL BE REVEALED

LUKE 17:20-37

Jesus is still either in Samaria or in Galilee. Pharisees now ask him about the arrival of the Kingdom, which they expect to be with pomp and ceremony. However, he says: "The Kingdom of God is not coming with striking observableness; nor will people say, 'See here!' or, 'There!' For look! the Kingdom of God is in your midst." —Luke 17:20, 21.

Some may conclude that Jesus is saying that the Kingdom reigns in the hearts of God's servants. However, that cannot be the case, for the Kingdom is not in the hearts of the Pharisees to whom Jesus is speaking. Yet, it is *in their midst* because the chosen King of God's Kingdom, Jesus, is right there among them.—Matthew 21:5.

Likely after the Pharisees leave, Jesus provides additional details for his disciples about the coming of the Kingdom. As to his presence in Kingdom power, he first warns: "Days will come when you will desire to see one of the days of the Son of man, but you will not see it." (Luke 17:22) Jesus is indicating that the reign of the Son of man in the Kingdom is to be in the future. Before that time arrives, some disciples might anxiously look for it, but they will have to continue waiting until it is God's appointed time for the Son of man to come.

Jesus continues: "People will say to you, 'See there!' or, 'See here!' Do not go out or chase af-ter them. For just as lightning flashes from one part of heaven to another part of heaven, so the Son of man will be in his day." (Luke 17:23, 24) How will Jesus' disciples be protected against chasing after false messiahs? Jesus says that the coming of the true Messiah will be as lightning seen over a wide area. The evidence of his presence in Kingdom power will be clearly visible to all observant onlookers.

Then Jesus makes comparisons with ancient events to show what the attitudes of people will be during that future period: "Just as it occurred in the days of Noah, so it will be in the days of the Son of man . . . Likewise, just as it occurred in the days of Lot: they were eating, they were drinking, they were buying, they were selling, they were planting, they were building. But on the day that Lot went out of Sodom, it rained fire and sulfur from heaven and destroyed them all. It will be the same on that day when the Son of man is revealed."—Luke 17:26-30.

Jesus is not saying that people in Noah's day and in Lot's day were destroyed because they pursued the normal activities of eating, drinking, buying, selling, planting, and building. Noah and Lot and their families did at least some of those things. But the other people were doing so without paying any attention to God's will and were ignoring the time in which they

lived. Hence, Jesus is admonishing his disciples to pay attention to God's will and to be actively involved in doing it. He is thus showing them the way to be preserved—that is, the way to keep living—when God brings destruction in the future.

The disciples will need to avoid becoming distracted by the things of the world around them, "the things behind." Jesus says: "On that day let the person who is on the housetop but whose belongings are in the house not come down to pick these up, and likewise, the person out in the field must not return to the things behind. Remember the wife of Lot." (Luke 17:31, 32) She became a pillar of salt.

Continuing his description of the situation existing when the Son of man will reign as King, Jesus tells his disciples: "In that night two people will be in one bed; the one will be taken along, but the other will be abandoned." (Luke 17:34) So some will gain salvation, but others will be abandoned, losing their life.

The disciples ask: "Where, Lord?" Jesus responds: "Where the body is, there also the eagles will be gathered together." (Luke 17:37) Yes, some will be like farsighted eagles. These disciples will gather to the true Christ, the Son of man. At that future time, Jesus will provide his disciples with lifesaving truth for those having faith.

◊ How is the Kingdom in the midst of the Pharisees?

◊ In what way will Christ's presence be like lightning?

◊ Why will Jesus' disciples need to be alert when the Son of man comes?

TWO GREAT NEEDS—PRAYER AND HUMILITY

LUKE 18:1-14

Jesus has already told his disciples an illustration about being persistent in prayer. (Luke 11:5-13) He may now be in Samaria or in Galilee, and he again emphasizes the need not to give up in praying. He does so with this further illustration:

"In a certain city there was a judge who had no fear of God and no respect for man. There was also a widow in that city who kept going to him and saying, 'See that I get justice from my

legal opponent.' Well, for a while he was unwilling, but afterward he said to himself, 'Although I do not fear God or respect any man, because this widow keeps making me trouble, I will see that she gets justice so that she will not keep coming and wearing me out with her demand.'" —Luke 18:2-5.

As to the application, Jesus says: "Hear what the judge, although unrighteous, said! Certainly, then, will not God cause justice to be done for his chosen ones who cry out to him day and night, while he is patient toward them?" (Luke 18:6, 7) What is Jesus thus indicating about his Father?

Jesus certainly does not mean that Jehovah God is in any way like the unrighteous judge. His point involves a contrast: If even an unrighteous human judge will respond to persistent entreaties, God unquestionably will do so. He is righteous and good and will answer if his people do not give up in praying. We can see that from what Jesus adds: "I tell you, [God] will cause justice to be done to them speedily." —Luke 18:8.

The lowly and the poor often do not receive justice, whereas the powerful and the rich often are favored. But that is not God's way. When the time is ripe, he will justly see to it that the wicked are punished and that his servants receive everlasting life.

Who have faith like that of the widow? How many truly believe that God will "cause justice to be done to them speedily"? Jesus has just illustrated the need to persist in prayer. Now, as to faith in the power of prayer, he asks: "When the Son of man arrives, will he really find this faith on the earth?" (Luke 18:8) The implication is that such faith may not be common when Christ arrives.

Some who are listening to Jesus feel self-assured in their faith. They trust in themselves that they are righteous, whereas they look down on others. To such ones, Jesus directs this illustration:

"Two men went up into the temple to pray, the one a Pharisee and the other a tax collector. The Pharisee stood and began to pray these things to himself, 'O God, I thank you that I am not like everyone else—extortioners, unrighteous, adulterers—or even like this tax collector. I fast twice a week; I give the tenth of all things I acquire.'" —Luke 18:10-12.

The Pharisees are known to make public displays of their seeming righteousness. They do so to impress others. The usual occasions for their self-imposed fasts are on Mondays and Thursdays, the days large markets are busy, when many will see them. And they scrupulously pay a tithe of even small plants. (Luke 11:42) A few months earlier, they expressed their contempt for the common people, saying: "This crowd who do not know the Law [according to the Pharisees' view] are accursed people."—John 7:49.

Jesus continues his illustration: "But the tax collector, standing at a distance, was not willing even to raise his eyes heavenward but kept beating his chest, saying, 'O God, be gracious to me, a sinner.'" Yes, the tax collector humbly acknowledges his shortcomings. Jesus concludes: "I tell you, this man went down to his home and was proved more righteous than that Pharisee. Because everyone who exalts himself will be humiliated, but whoever humbles himself will be exalted."—Luke 18:13, 14.

Thus Jesus makes clear the need to be humble. That is beneficial counsel for his disciples, who have been reared in a society in which the self-righteous Pharisees stress position and rank. And it is valuable counsel for all of Jesus' followers.

◊ Jesus makes what point in his illustration of the unrighteous judge who grants the widow's request?
◊ What faith will Jesus look for when he arrives?
◊ Jesus' followers need to avoid what attitude common among the Pharisees?

TEACHING ABOUT DIVORCE AND LOVE FOR CHILDREN

MATTHEW 19:1-15   MARK 10:1-16   LUKE 18:15-17

From Galilee, Jesus and his disciples cross the Jordan River and take the route southward through Perea. When Jesus was last in Perea, he had stated for the Pharisees the divine standard on divorce. (Luke 16:18) Now they raise that subject to test Jesus.

Moses wrote that a woman could be divorced over "something indecent" on her part. (Deuteronomy 24:1) There are differing views as to what constitutes grounds for divorce. Some believe that rather minor issues are included. So the Pharisees ask: "Is it lawful for a man to divorce his wife on every sort of grounds?"—Matthew 19:3.

Rather than appeal to human opinion, Jesus masterfully refers to God's design of marriage. "Have you not read that the one who created them from the beginning made them male and female and said: 'For this reason a man will leave his father and his mother and will stick to his wife, and the two will be one flesh'? So that they are no longer two, but one flesh. Therefore, what God has yoked together, let no man put apart." (Matthew 19:4-6) When God instituted marriage between Adam and Eve, he did not make provision for dissolving their marriage.

The Pharisees take issue with Jesus, saying: "Why, then, did Moses direct giving a certificate of dismissal and divorcing her?" (Matthew 19:7) Jesus tells them: "Out of regard for your hard-heartedness, Moses made the concession to you of divorcing your wives, but that has not been the case from the beginning." (Matthew 19:8) That "beginning" was not in Moses' day; it was when God originated marriage in Eden.

Then Jesus presents an important truth: "I say to you that whoever divorces his wife, ex-cept on the grounds of sexual immorality [Greek, *por·nei′a*], and marries another commits adultery." (Matthew 19:9) Sexual immorality is thus the only Scriptural grounds for divorce.

The disciples are moved to say: "If that is the situation of a man with his wife, it is not advisable to marry." (Matthew 19:10) Clearly, one contemplating marriage should consider it to be permanent!

Regarding singleness, Jesus explains that some are born eunuchs, being incapable of marital relations. Others are made eunuchs, becoming disabled sexually. Yet, some suppress their desire to enjoy sexual relations. They do so in order to focus more fully on matters relating to the Kingdom. "Let the one who can make room for [singleness] make room for it," Jesus urges his listeners.—Matthew 19:12.

People now begin to bring their young children to Jesus. However, the disciples scold the people, likely wanting to keep Jesus from being bothered. On seeing this, Jesus becomes indignant and says to them: "Let the young children come to me; do not try to stop them, for the Kingdom of God belongs to such ones. Truly I say to you, whoever does not receive the Kingdom of God like a young child will by no means enter into it."—Mark 10:14, 15; Luke 18:15.

What a fine lesson! To receive God's Kingdom, we must be meek and teachable, like young children. Jesus now shows his love for little ones by taking them into his arms and blessing them. And he has such tender love for all who "receive the Kingdom of God like a young child."—Luke 18:17.

◇ How do the Pharisees test Jesus on the subject of divorce?

◇ According to Jesus, what is the divine standard regarding divorce?

◇ Why might some disciples choose to remain single?

◇ Jesus teaches what lesson through his dealings with young children?

JESUS ANSWERS A RICH YOUNG RULER

MATTHEW 19:16-30 MARK 10:17-31 LUKE 18:18-30

Jesus is still traveling through Perea toward Jerusalem. A rich young man runs up to him and falls down on his knees before him. The man is "one of the rulers," perhaps serving as a presiding officer in a synagogue or as a member of the Sanhedrin. "Good Teacher," he inquires, "what must I do to inherit everlasting life?"—Luke 8: 41; 18:18; 24:20.

"Why do you call me good?" Jesus replies. "Nobody is good except one, God." Likely the young man uses "good" as a formalistic title, which is what the rabbis do. Although Jesus is good at teaching, he lets the man know that as a title, "Good" belongs only to God.

"If, though, you want to enter into life, observe the commandments continually," Jesus advises him. So the young man asks: "Which ones?" Jesus cites five of the Ten Commandments—about murder, adultery, stealing, bearing false witness, and honoring one's parents. Then he adds a more important commandment: "You must love your neighbor as yourself."—Matthew 19:17-19.

"I have kept all of these," the man answers. "What am I still lacking?" (Matthew 19:20) He may feel that he is lacking some good, heroic act that will qualify him for everlasting life. Sensing the earnestness of his request, Jesus 'feels love for him.' (Mark 10:21) However, the man has an obstacle before him.

The man is attached to his possessions, so Jesus says: "One thing is missing about you: Go, sell what things you have and give to the poor, and you will have treasure in heaven; and come be my follower." Yes, the man could distribute his money to the poor, who cannot repay him, and become a disciple of Jesus. But likely with pity, Jesus sees him rise and turn

away sad. The man's attachment to wealth, to his "many possessions," blinds him to true treasure. (Mark 10:21, 22) Jesus says: "How difficult it will be for those having money to make their way into the Kingdom of God!"—Luke 18:24.

The disciples are astounded by these words and by what Jesus next states: "It is easier, in fact, for a camel to get through the eye of a sewing needle than for a rich man to enter the Kingdom of God." That moves the disciples to ask: "Who possibly can be saved?" Is being saved so challenging that it is beyond a man's reach? Jesus looks straight at them and replies: "The things impossible with men are possible with God."—Luke 18:25-27.

Peter points out that they have made a choice different from that of the rich man, saying: "Look! We have left all things and followed you; what, then, will there be for us?" Jesus mentions the final outcome of their right choice: "In the re-creation, when the Son of man sits down on his glorious throne, you who have followed me will sit on 12 thrones, judging the 12 tribes of Israel."—Matthew 19:27, 28.

Clearly, Jesus has in mind the future time on earth when there will be a re-creation of conditions that existed in the garden of Eden. Peter and the other disciples will be rewarded by ruling with Jesus over that earthly Paradise, a reward truly worth any sacrifice they may make!

Yet the rewards are not all future. His disciples experience some right now. "There is no one who has left house or wife or brothers or parents or children for the sake of the Kingdom of God," Jesus states, "who will not get many times more in this period of time, and in the coming system of things, everlasting life." —Luke 18:29, 30.

Yes, wherever his disciples go, they can enjoy a brotherhood with fellow worshippers that is closer and more precious than that enjoyed with natural family members. Sadly, it seems that the rich young ruler is going to lose out on that blessing as well as the reward of life in God's heavenly Kingdom.

Jesus adds: "But many who are first will be last and the last first." (Matthew 19:30) What does he mean?

The rich young ruler is among the "first," being among the leaders of the Jews. As an observer of God's commandments, he shows much promise and much might be expected of him. Yet he is putting riches and possessions ahead of all else in life. In contrast, the common people of the land see in Jesus' teaching the truth and the way to life. They have been "last," so to speak, but they are now coming to be "first." They can look forward to sitting on thrones in heaven with Jesus and ruling over the Paradise earth.

◇ What kind of man approaches Jesus?
◇ Why does Jesus object to being called "good"?
◇ What rewards does Jesus promise his followers?
◇ How do the "first" become "last" and the "last," "first"?

ILLUSTRATION OF THE WORKERS IN THE VINEYARD

MATTHEW 20:1-16

Jesus has just told his listeners in Perea that "many who are first will be last and the last first." (Matthew 19:30) He underscores this statement with an illustration about workers in a vineyard:

"The Kingdom of the heavens is like the master of a house who went out early in the morning to hire workers for his vineyard. After he had agreed with the workers for a denarius a day, he sent them into his vineyard. Going out also about the third hour, he saw others standing unemployed in the marketplace; and to those he said, 'You too go into the vineyard, and I will give you whatever is fair.' So off they went. Again he went out about the sixth hour and the ninth hour and did likewise. Finally, about the 11th hour, he went out and found others standing around, and he said to them, 'Why have you been standing here all day unemployed?' They replied, 'Because nobody has hired us.' He said to them, 'You too go into the vineyard.'"—Matthew 20:1-7.

Jesus' listeners likely think of Jehovah God when they hear mention of "the Kingdom of the heavens" and "the master of a house." The Scriptures present Jehovah as the owner of a vineyard, which represented the nation of Israel. (Psalm 80:8, 9; Isaiah 5:3, 4) Those in the Law covenant are likened to workers in the vineyard. Jesus, though, is not illustrating the past. He is describing a situation existing in his time.

The religious leaders, like the Pharisees who recently tried to test him on the subject of divorce, are supposedly laboring continually in God's service. They are like full-time workers who expect full pay, the wage being a denarius for a day's work.

The priests and others in this group consider the common Jews as serving God to a lesser extent, like part-time laborers in God's vineyard. In Jesus' illustration, these are the men who are employed "about the third hour" (9:00 a.m.) or later in the workday—at the sixth, ninth, and finally the eleventh hour (5:00 p.m.).

The men and women who follow Jesus are viewed as "accursed people." (John 7:49) For most of their lives, they have been fishermen or other laborers. Then, in the fall of 29 C.E., "the master of the vineyard" sent Jesus to call these lowly people to labor for God as Christ's disciples. They are "the last" whom Jesus mentions, the 11th-hour vineyard workers.

Finishing his illustration, Jesus describes what occurs at the close of the workday: "When evening came, the master of the vineyard said to his man in charge, 'Call the workers and pay them their wages, starting with the last and ending with the first.' When the 11th-hour men came, they each received a denarius. So when the first came, they assumed that they would receive more, but they too were paid at the rate of a denarius. On receiving it, they began to complain against the master of the house and said, 'These last men put in one hour's work; still you made them equal to us who bore the burden of the day and the burning heat!' But he said in reply to one of them, 'Fellow, I do you no wrong. You agreed with me for a denarius, did you not? Take what is yours and go. I want to give to this last one the same as to you. Do I not have the right to do what I want with my own things? Or is your eye envious because I am good?' In this way, the last ones will be first, and the first ones last."—Matthew 20:8-16.

The disciples may wonder about that final part of Jesus' illustration. How will the Jew-

ish religious leaders, who imagine themselves "first," become "last"? And how will Jesus' disciples become "first"?

Jesus' disciples, whom the Pharisees and others view as "last," are in line to be "first," to receive full pay. With Jesus' death, earthly Jerusalem is to be cast off, whereupon God will choose a new nation, "the Israel of God." (Galatians 6:16; Matthew 23:38) John the Baptist pointed to such ones when he spoke about a coming baptism with holy spirit. Those who have been "last" are to be the first to receive that baptism and to be given the privilege of being witnesses of Jesus "to the most distant part of the earth." (Acts 1:5, 8; Matthew 3:11) To the extent that the disciples grasp the dramatic change Jesus is pointing to, they may foresee facing extreme displeasure from the religious leaders, who become "last."

◇ Why is it logical to understand Jehovah to be "the master of the vineyard," and who are "the workers" in it?

◇ What dramatic change is Jesus pointing to with this illustration?

◇ When does this change become evident?

THE APOSTLES AGAIN SEEK PROMINENCE

MATTHEW 20:17-28   MARK 10:32-45   LUKE 18:31-34

As Jesus and his disciples complete their journey southward in Perea toward Jerusalem, they cross the Jordan River near Jericho. Others are traveling with them for the Passover of 33 C.E.

Jesus is walking on ahead of the disciples, determined to be in the city on time for the Passover. But the disciples are afraid. Earlier, when Lazarus died and Jesus was about to go from Perea into Judea, Thomas told the others: "Let us also go, so that we may die with him." (John 11:16, 47-53) So going to Jerusalem is risky, and the disciples' fear is understandable.

To prepare them for what lies ahead, Jesus takes the apostles aside and tells them: "We are going up to Jerusalem, and the Son of man will be handed over to the chief priests and the scribes. They will condemn him to death and hand him over to men of the nations to be mocked and scourged and executed on a stake; and on the third day he will be raised up."—Matthew 20:18, 19.

This is the third time that Jesus has told his disciples about his death and resurrection. (Matthew 16:21; 17:22, 23) However, this time he says that he will be executed on a stake. They listen to him, yet they do not comprehend the meaning. Perhaps they are expecting the restoration on earth of the kingdom of Israel, wanting to enjoy glory and honor in an earthly kingdom with Christ.

The mother of the apostles James and John, who is apparently Salome, is among the travelers. Jesus has given these two apostles a name meaning "Sons of Thunder," no doubt because of their fiery disposition. (Mark 3:17; Luke 9:54) For some time, these two have had the ambition of being prominent in Christ's Kingdom. Their

mother is aware of that. She now approaches Jesus in their behalf, bows before him, and asks for a favor. Jesus replies: "What do you want?" She says: "Give the word that these two sons of mine may sit down, one at your right hand and one at your left, in your Kingdom."—Matthew 20:20, 21.

The request is really coming from James and John. Having just outlined the shame and humiliation he will experience, Jesus says to them: "You do not know what you are asking for. Can you drink the cup that I am about to drink?" They reply: "We can." (Matthew 20:22) Still, they likely do not really comprehend what this means for them.

Nevertheless, Jesus tells them: "You will indeed drink my cup, but to sit down at my right hand and at my left is not mine to give, but it belongs to those for whom it has been prepared by my Father."—Matthew 20:23.

On learning about James and John's request, the other ten apostles are indignant. Might James and John have been outspoken in the earlier argument among the apostles about who is the greatest? (Luke 9:46-48) Regardless, the present request reveals that the Twelve

have not applied the counsel Jesus has given about conducting oneself as a lesser one. Their desire for prominence persists.

Jesus decides to deal with this latest controversy and the ill will it is creating. He calls the Twelve together and counsels them lovingly, saying: "You know that those who appear to be ruling the nations lord it over them and their great ones wield authority over them. This must not be the way among you; but whoever wants to become great among you must be your minister, and whoever wants to be first among you must be the slave of all."—Mark 10: 42-44.

Jesus brings up the example they should imitate—his example. He explains: "The Son of man came, not to be ministered to, but to minister and to give his life as a ransom in exchange for many." (Matthew 20:28) For some three years, Jesus has been ministering in behalf of others. And he will yet do so to the extent of dying for mankind! The disciples need that same Christlike disposition of desiring to serve rather than to be served, to be a lesser one rather than to be in a position of prominence.

◇ What does Jesus do to prepare his disciples for what lies ahead?
◇ Two apostles make what request of Jesus, and how do the other apostles react?
◇ How does Jesus deal with his apostles' interest in being prominent?

JESUS HEALS BLIND MEN AND HELPS ZACCHAEUS

MATTHEW 20:29-34   MARK 10:46-52   LUKE 18:35–19:10

Jesus and those traveling with him arrive at Jericho, which is about a day's journey from Jerusalem. In a sense, Jericho is a double city, the older city being about a mile from the newer Roman city. As Jesus and the crowds make their way out of one of these cities and approach the other, two blind beggars hear the commotion. One of them is named Bartimaeus.

On hearing that Jesus is passing by, Bartimaeus and his companion begin shouting: "Lord, have mercy on us, Son of David!" (Matthew 20:30) Some in the crowd sternly tell them to be quiet, but the two cry out even louder. Hearing the disturbance, Jesus stops. He asks those with him to call whoever is shouting. They go to the beggars and say to one of them: "Take courage! Get up; he is calling you." (Mark 10:49) Excitedly, the blind man throws off his outer garment, leaps to his feet, and goes to Jesus.

"What do you want me to do for you?" Jesus asks. Both blind men plead: "Lord, let our eyes be opened." (Matthew 20:32, 33) Moved with pity, Jesus touches their eyes and, particularly to one of them, says: "Go. Your faith has made you well." (Mark 10:52) The two blind beggars receive sight, and doubtless both begin glorifying God. Seeing what has happened, the people also give praise to God. The formerly blind men now begin to follow Jesus.

There are tremendous crowds around Jesus as he passes through Jericho. Everyone wants to see the one who has healed the blind men. The people press in on Jesus from every direction; hence, some cannot even get a glimpse of him. That is true of Zacchaeus. He is chief over the tax collectors in and around Jericho. Because he is short, he cannot see what is going on. So Zacchaeus runs ahead and climbs a sycamore (or, fig-mulberry) tree along the route that Jesus is taking. From up there, Zacchaeus gets a good view of everything. As Jesus draws near and sees Zacchaeus up in the tree, he says: "Zacchaeus, hurry and get down, for today I must stay in your house." (Luke 19:5) Zacchaeus climbs down and hurries home to welcome his distinguished visitor.

When the people see what is happening, they begin to grumble. They feel that it is not right for Jesus to be the guest of a man whom they view as a sinner. Zacchaeus has become rich by dishonestly extorting money while he is collecting taxes.

As Jesus enters Zacchaeus' home, the people complain: "He went as a guest to the house of a man who is a sinner." However, Jesus sees in Zacchaeus the potential for repentance. And Jesus is not disappointed. Zacchaeus stands up and tells him: "Look! The half of my belongings, Lord, I am giving to the poor, and whatever I extorted from anyone, I am restoring four times over."—Luke 19:7, 8.

What a fine way for Zacchaeus to prove that his repentance is genuine! He can likely calculate from his tax records just how much he had received from various Jews, and he vows to make a fourfold restoration. That is even more than God's law requires. (Exodus 22:1; Leviticus 6:2-5) Moreover, Zacchaeus promises to take half of his belongings and give them to the poor.

Jesus is pleased with this evidence of Zacchaeus' repentance and tells him: "Today salvation has come to this house, because he too is a son of Abraham. For the Son of man came to seek and to save what was lost."—Luke 19:9, 10.

Recently, Jesus has focused on the situation of 'the lost' with his illustration about the lost son. (Luke 15:11-24) Now he has provided a real-life example of someone who was as good as lost but who has been found. The religious leaders and their followers may complain about Jesus and criticize him for giving attention to ones like Zacchaeus. Still, Jesus continues to look for and restore these lost sons of Abraham.

◊ Where, apparently, does Jesus meet two blind beggars, and what does he do for them?

◊ Who is Zacchaeus, and how does he prove his repentance?

◊ What lesson can be learned from Jesus' treatment of Zacchaeus?

HIS ILLUSTRATION OF TEN MINAS

LUKE 19:11-28

Though Jerusalem is Jesus' destination, he may still be at the home of Zacchaeus with his disciples. They believe that "the Kingdom of God" is soon to be set up with Jesus as King. (Luke 19:11) They misunderstand this matter, just as they fail to grasp that Jesus must die. So he gives an illustration to help them to see that the Kingdom is yet a long way off.

He says: "A man of noble birth traveled to a distant land to secure kingly power for himself and to return." (Luke 19:12) Such a trip would take time. Clearly Jesus is the "man of noble birth" who travels to a "distant land," to heaven, where his Father will give him kingly power.

In the illustration, before the "man of noble birth" departs, he calls ten slaves and gives each a silver mina, telling them: "Do business with these until I come." (Luke 19:13) Literal silver minas are valuable pieces of money. A mina amounts to the wages that an agricultural worker earns in over three months.

The disciples may discern that they are like the ten slaves in the illustration, for Jesus has already likened them to harvest workers. (Matthew 9:35-38) Of course, he has not asked them to bring in a harvest of grain. Rather, the harvest consists of other disciples who can find a place in the Kingdom of God. The disciples use what assets they have to produce more heirs of the Kingdom.

What more does Jesus reveal in this illustration? He says that citizens "hated [the man of noble birth] and sent out a body of ambassadors after him to say, 'We do not want this man to become king over us.'" (Luke 19:14) The disciples know that the Jews do not accept Jesus —some even want to kill him. After Jesus' death and departure to heaven, the Jews in general show their view of him by persecuting his disciples. These opposers make it clear that they do not want Jesus as King.—John 19:15, 16; Acts 4:13-18; 5:40.

As for the ten slaves, how do they use their minas until the "man of noble birth" receives "kingly power" and returns? Jesus relates: "When he eventually got back after having secured the kingly power, he summoned the slaves to whom he had given the money, in order to ascertain what they had gained by their business activity. So the first one came forward and said, 'Lord, your mina gained ten minas.' He said to him, 'Well done, good slave! Because in a very small matter you have proved yourself faithful, hold authority over ten cities.' Now the second came, saying, 'Your mina, Lord, made five minas.' He said to this one as well, 'You too be in charge of five cities.'"—Luke 19:15-19.

If the disciples perceive that they are like the slaves who use their assets to the full to make more disciples, they can rest assured that Jesus will be pleased. And they can trust that he will reward such diligence. Of course, not all of Jesus' disciples have the same circumstances in life nor the same opportunities or abilities. Yet Jesus, who receives "kingly power," will recognize and bless their loyal efforts at disciple-making.—Matthew 28:19, 20.

Note a contrast, though, as Jesus concludes his illustration: "But another [slave] came, saying, 'Lord, here is your mina that I kept hidden away in a cloth. You see, I was in fear of you, because you are a harsh man; you take what you did not deposit, and you reap what you did not sow.' He said to him, 'By your own words I judge you, wicked slave. You knew, did you, that I am a harsh man, taking what I did not depos-

it and reaping what I did not sow? So why did you not put my money in a bank? Then on my coming, I would have collected it with interest.' With that he said to those standing by, 'Take the mina from him and give it to the one who has the ten minas.'"—Luke 19:20-24.

For failing to work to increase the wealth of his master's kingdom, this slave experiences loss. The apostles are anticipating Jesus' reigning in the Kingdom of God. So from what he says about this last slave, they likely perceive that if they are not diligent, they will not find a place in that Kingdom.

Jesus' words must stimulate the loyal disciples to increased efforts. He concludes: "I say to you, to everyone who has, more will be given, but from the one who does not have, even what he has will be taken away." He adds that his enemies, who do not want him "to become king over them," will experience execution. Then Jesus resumes his trip up to Jerusalem.—Luke 19:26-28.

◇ What prompts Jesus' illustration of the minas?

◇ Who is the "man of noble birth," and what is the land to which he goes?

◇ Who are the slaves, and who are the citizens who show hatred?

◇ What is the difference between the slaves who are rewarded and the slave whose mina is taken away?

"YOUR KING IS
COMING TO YOU."
—MATTHEW 21:5

A MEAL AT SIMON'S HOUSE IN BETHANY

MATTHEW 26:6-13   MARK 14:3-9   JOHN 11:55–12:11

Leaving Jericho, Jesus heads for Bethany. The trip involves a climb of some 12 miles over difficult terrain. Jericho is about 820 feet *below* sea level, and Bethany is about 2,000 feet *above* sea level. Lazarus and his two sisters live in the little village of Bethany, which is about two miles from Jerusalem and on the eastern slope of the Mount of Olives.

Many Jews have already arrived in Jerusalem for the Passover. They have come early "to cleanse themselves ceremonially" in case they have touched a dead body or done something else that makes them unclean. (John 11:55; Numbers 9:6-10) Some of these who arrive early gather at the temple. They speculate on whether Jesus will come to the Passover.—John 11:56.

There is great controversy regarding Jesus. Some religious leaders want to seize him to put him to death. In fact, they have ordered that if any learn of Jesus' whereabouts, they are to report to them 'so that they can seize him.' (John 11:57) These leaders have already tried to kill Jesus after he resurrected Lazarus. (John 11:49-53) Understandably, some may doubt whether Jesus will appear in public at all.

Jesus arrives at Bethany on Friday, "six days before the Passover." (John 12:1) A new day (Sabbath, Nisan 8) begins at sundown. Thus, he has completed the trip before the Sabbath. He could not have traveled from Jericho on the Sabbath—from sundown Friday to sundown Saturday—for such travel is restricted by Jewish law. Jesus probably goes to Lazarus' home, as he has done before.

Simon, who also lives in Bethany, invites Jesus and his companions, including Lazarus, for a meal Saturday evening. Simon is called "the

leper," perhaps being a former leper whom Jesus had at some point healed. Reflecting her industrious character, Martha ministers to the guests. Mary is particularly attentive to Jesus, this time in a way that stirs controversy.

Mary opens an alabaster case, or small flask, that holds about "a pound of perfumed oil, genuine nard." (John 12:3) This oil is very precious, its value (300 denarii) being the equivalent of about a year's wages! Mary pours the oil on Jesus' head and on his feet and then wipes his feet with her hair. The aromatic scent fills the whole house.

The disciples are angry and ask: "Why has this perfumed oil been wasted?" (Mark 14:4) Judas Iscariot objects, saying: "Why was this perfumed oil not sold for 300 denarii and given to the poor?" (John 12:5) Judas is not really concerned about the poor. He has been steal-

ing from the money box he keeps for the disciples.

Jesus defends Mary, saying: "Why do you try to make trouble for the woman? She did a fine deed toward me. For you always have the poor with you, but you will not always have me. When she put this perfumed oil on my body, she did it to prepare me for burial. Truly I say to you, wherever this good news is preached in all the world, what this woman did will also be told in memory of her."—Matthew 26:10-13.

He has now been in Bethany for more than a day, and word of Jesus' presence has spread about. Many Jews come to Simon's house not only to see Jesus but also to see Lazarus, "whom [Jesus] had raised up from the dead." (John 12:9) The chief priests now take counsel to kill both Jesus and Lazarus. These religious leaders feel that Lazarus' being alive again is the reason why many people are putting faith in Jesus. How wicked these religious leaders are!

◇ What are the Jews at the temple discussing?
◇ Why must Jesus have arrived in Bethany on Friday rather than on Saturday?
◇ What is Mary doing that stirs controversy, and how does Jesus defend her?
◇ What shows the great wickedness of the chief priests?

THE KING ENTERS JERUSALEM ON A COLT

MATTHEW 21:1-11, 14-17   MARK 11:1-11   LUKE 19:29-44   JOHN 12:12-19

The next day, Sunday, Nisan 9, Jesus leaves Bethany with his disciples and heads to Jerusalem. As they approach Bethphage, on the Mount of Olives, Jesus tells two of his disciples:

"Go into the village that is within sight, and you will at once find a donkey tied and a colt with her. Untie them and bring them to me. If someone says anything to you, you must say, 'The Lord needs them.' At that he will immediately send them."—Matthew 21:2, 3.

The disciples fail to see that Jesus' instructions involve Bible prophecy. Later, however, they grasp the fulfillment of Zechariah's prophecy. He foretold that God's promised King would come into Jerusalem "humble and riding on a donkey, on a colt, the foal of a female donkey."—Zechariah 9:9.

When the disciples come to Bethphage and take the male colt and its mother, people standing nearby ask: "What are you doing untying the colt?" (Mark 11:5) But when they hear that the animals are for the Lord, they let the disciples bring them to Jesus. The disciples place their outer garments on the donkey and on its offspring, but Jesus mounts the colt.

The crowd increases as Jesus rides toward Jerusalem. Many spread their garments on the road. Others cut branches from the trees or "foliage from the fields" and spread them out. They cry: "Save, we pray! Blessed is the one who comes in Jehovah's name! Blessed is the coming Kingdom of our father David!" (Mark 11: 8-10) Pharisees in the crowd are upset over these proclamations. They tell Jesus: "Teacher, rebuke your disciples." Jesus replies: "I tell you, if these remained silent, the stones would cry out."—Luke 19:39, 40.

As Jesus views Jerusalem, he begins to weep and says: "If you, even you, had discerned on this day the things having to do with peace—but now they have been hidden from your eyes." Jerusalem will pay the price for willful disobedience. Jesus foretells: "Your enemies will build around you a fortification of pointed stakes and will encircle you and besiege you from every side. They will dash you and your children within you to the ground, and they will not leave a stone upon a stone in you." (Luke 19:42-44) True to Jesus' words, Jerusalem's destruction comes in the year 70 C.E.

When Jesus enters Jerusalem, 'the whole city is in an uproar, saying: "Who is this?"' And the crowds keep saying: "This is the prophet Jesus, from Nazareth of Galilee!" (Matthew 21: 10, 11) Those in the crowd who had seen Jesus resurrect Lazarus tell others about that miracle. The Pharisees lament that they are getting absolutely nowhere. They say to one another: "The whole world has gone after him."—John 12:18, 19.

As is his custom when visiting Jerusalem, Jesus goes to the temple to teach. There he cures the blind and the lame. When the chief priests and the scribes see what he is doing and hear the boys in the temple cry out, "Save, we pray, the Son of David!" they become angry. The religious leaders ask Jesus: "Do you hear what these are saying?" He replies: "Did you never read this, 'Out of the mouth of children and infants, you have brought forth praise'?"—Matthew 21:15, 16.

Jesus looks around upon the things in the temple. It is now late, so he leaves with the apostles. Before Nisan 10 begins, he travels back to Bethany, where he spends Sunday night.

◇ When and in what manner does Jesus enter Jerusalem as King?

◇ How does Jesus feel when he views Jerusalem, and what prophecy does he utter?

◇ What happens when Jesus goes to the temple?

THE TEMPLE CLEANSED AGAIN

MATTHEW 21:12, 13, 18, 19   MARK 11:12-18   LUKE 19:45-48   JOHN 12:20-27

Jesus and his disciples have spent three nights in Bethany since they arrived from Jericho. Now, early in the morning on Monday, Nisan 10, they are heading to Jerusalem. Jesus is hungry. So when he sees a fig tree, he walks toward it. Does it have figs?

It is now late March, but the season for figs is not until June. Still, the leaves are out, having sprouted early. Thus, Jesus feels that there might be early figs. He finds, though, that there are none. The leaves have given the tree a deceptive appearance. Jesus then says: "Let no one eat fruit from you ever again." (Mark 11:14) Immediately the tree starts to wither, the meaning of which is to be learned the next morning.

Before long, Jesus and his disciples reach Jerusalem. He goes to the temple, which he inspected the previous afternoon. Today he does more than make an inspection; he takes action similar to what he did three years earlier at the Passover of 30 C.E. (John 2:14-16) This time Jesus throws out "those selling and buying in the temple." He also overturns "the tables of the money changers and the benches of those selling doves." (Mark 11:15) He does not even let anyone carrying things to another part of the city take a shortcut through the temple courtyard.

Why is Jesus taking decisive action against those changing money and selling animals in the temple? He says: "Is it not written, 'My house will be called a house of prayer for all the nations'? But you have made it a cave of robbers." (Mark 11:17) His reason for calling these men robbers is that they demand exorbitant prices from those who have to buy animals needed for sacrifice. Jesus views their dealings as extortion, or robbery.

Of course, the chief priests, scribes, and principal ones of the people hear what Jesus has done, and they respond with renewed efforts to have him killed. However, they face a problem. They do not know how to do away with Jesus, because the people are flocking to hear him.

Not only natural Jews but also proselytes, converts to the Jews' religion, have come for the Passover. Among them are Greeks who have come to worship at the festival. These approach Philip, perhaps attracted by his Greek name, and ask to see Jesus. Philip may be unsure whether such a meeting is appropriate, so he confers with Andrew. The two take the matter to Jesus, who is apparently still at the temple.

Jesus knows that he is to die in a few days, so this is not the time to satisfy people's curiosity or to seek popularity. He responds to the two apostles with an illustration, saying: "The hour has come for the Son of man to be glorified. Most truly I say to you, unless a grain of wheat falls to the ground and dies, it remains just one grain; but if it dies, it then bears much fruit." —John 12:23, 24.

One grain of wheat might seem of little value. Yet, if it is put into the soil and "dies" as a seed, it can germinate and in time grow into a productive stalk with many grains. Similarly, Jesus is one perfect man. Still, by his being faithful to God till his death, he will become the means of imparting everlasting life to many who have a similar spirit of self-sacrifice. Thus, Jesus says: "Whoever is fond of his life destroys it, but whoever hates his life in this world will safeguard it for everlasting life." —John 12:25.

Jesus is not thinking of himself only, for he says: "If anyone would minister to me, let him

follow me, and where I am, there my minister will be also. If anyone would minister to me, the Father will honor him." (John 12:26) What a reward! Those honored by the Father will become Christ's associates in the Kingdom.

Bearing in mind the great suffering and agonizing death that awaits him, Jesus says: "Now I am troubled, and what should I say? Father, save me out of this hour." But Jesus does not want to avoid accomplishing God's will. He adds: "Nevertheless, this is why I have come to this hour." (John 12:27) Jesus is in agreement with all that God has purposed, including his own sacrificial death.

◇ Why does Jesus expect to find figs, though it is not yet the normal season for them?

◇ Why is it appropriate for Jesus to call those selling in the temple "robbers"?

◇ How can Jesus be compared to a grain of wheat, and how does he feel about the suffering and death that awaits him?

THE JEWS HEAR GOD'S VOICE—WILL THEY SHOW FAITH?

JOHN 12:28-50

At the temple on Monday, Nisan 10, Jesus is speaking about his approaching death. Concerned about how God's reputation will be affected, Jesus says: "Father, glorify your name." A mighty voice from the heavens responds: "I have glorified it and will glorify it again."—John 12:27, 28.

The people nearby are bewildered. Some think that they heard thunder. Others say: "An angel has spoken to him." (John 12:29) However, it is Jehovah whom they just heard speaking! And this is not the first time that humans have heard God's voice in connection with Jesus.

Three and a half years earlier, at Jesus' baptism, John the Baptist heard God say of Jesus: "This is my Son, the beloved, whom I have approved." Later, after the Passover of 32 C.E., Jesus was transfigured before James, John, and Peter. Those three men heard God declare: "This is my Son, the beloved, whom I have approved. Listen to him." (Matthew 3:17; 17:5) But now, this third time, Jehovah is speaking in a way that many can hear!

Jesus says: "This voice has occurred, not for my sake, but for your sakes." (John 12:30) It is proof that he truly is God's Son, the foretold Messiah.

Moreover, Jesus' faithful life course both exemplifies the way humans should live and confirms that Satan the Devil, the ruler of the world, deserves to be executed. Jesus says: "Now there is a judging of this world; now the ruler of this world will be cast out." Rather than being a defeat, Jesus' approaching death will be a victory. How so? He explains: "Yet I, if I am lifted up from the earth, will draw all sorts of men to myself." (John 12:31, 32) By means of his death on a stake, Jesus will draw others to himself, opening the way to everlasting life.

In response to Jesus' comment about being "lifted up," the crowd says: "We heard from the Law that the Christ remains forever. How can you say that the Son of man must be lifted up? Who is this Son of man?" (John 12:34) Despite all the evidence, including hearing God's own voice, most of them do not accept Jesus as the *true* Son of man, the promised Messiah.

As he has done before, Jesus speaks of himself as "the light." (John 8:12; 9:5) He urges the crowd: "The light will be among you a little while longer. Walk while you still have the light, so that darkness does not overpower you . . . While you have the light, exercise faith in the light, so that you may become sons of light." (John 12:35, 36) Then Jesus withdraws, because Nisan 10 is not the day for him to die. Passover Nisan 14 is when he is to be "lifted up"—nailed to a stake.—Galatians 3:13.

Looking back on Jesus' ministry, it is clear that prophecy was being fulfilled when the Jews did not put faith in him. Isaiah foretold that the eyes of people would be blinded and their hearts would be hard so that they would not turn around to be healed. (Isaiah 6:10; John 12:40) Yes, most of the Jews stubbornly reject the evidence that Jesus is their promised Deliverer, the way to life.

Nicodemus, Joseph of Arimathea, and many other rulers "actually put faith" in Jesus. But will they act in faith, or will they hold back, either because they fear being expelled from the synagogue or because they 'love the glory of men'? —John 12:42, 43.

Jesus himself explains what putting faith in him involves: "Whoever puts faith in me puts faith not only in me but also in him who sent me; and whoever sees me sees also the One who sent me." The truths that God instructed Jesus to teach and that Jesus continues to proclaim are vital, so much so that he can say: "Whoever disregards me and does not receive my sayings has one to judge him. The word that I have spoken is what will judge him on the last day." —John 12:44, 45, 48.

Jesus then concludes: "I have not spoken of my own initiative, but the Father who sent me has himself given me a commandment about what to say and what to speak. And I know that his commandment means everlasting life." (John 12:49, 50) Jesus knows that shortly he will pour out his own lifeblood in sacrifice for humans who exercise faith in him.—Romans 5: 8, 9.

◇ With regard to Jesus, on what three occasions has God's voice been heard?

◇ What rulers put faith in Jesus, but why might they not confess him openly?

◇ On what basis will people be judged "on the last day"?

A FIG TREE IS USED TO TEACH A LESSON ABOUT FAITH

MATTHEW 21:19-27 MARK 11:19-33 LUKE 20:1-8

Leaving Jerusalem on Monday afternoon, Jesus returns to Bethany on the eastern slope of the Mount of Olives. He likely spends the night at the home of his friends Lazarus, Mary, and Martha.

Now it is the morning of Nisan 11. Jesus and his disciples are on the road again, heading back to Jerusalem where he will be at the temple for the last time. And it is the final day of his public ministry before he celebrates the Passover, institutes the Memorial of his death, and then faces trial and execution.

En route from Bethany over the Mount of Olives toward Jerusalem, Peter notices the tree that Jesus cursed the previous morning. "Rabbi, see!" he exclaims, "the fig tree that you cursed has withered."—Mark 11:21.

But why did Jesus cause the tree to wither? He reveals the reason in his response: "Truly I say to you, if you have faith and do not doubt, not only will you do what I did to the fig tree, but even if you say to this mountain, 'Be lifted up and thrown into the sea,' it will happen. And all the things you ask in prayer, having faith, you will receive." (Matthew 21:21, 22) He is thus repeating the point he made earlier about faith being able to move a mountain. —Matthew 17:20.

So by causing the tree to wither, Jesus provides an object lesson on the need to have faith in God. He states: "All the things you pray and ask for, have faith that you have received them, and you will have them." (Mark 11:24) What an important lesson for all of Jesus' followers! It is especially appropriate for the apostles in view of the difficult tests they will soon face. There is yet another connection between the withering of the fig tree and the quality of faith.

Like this fig tree, the nation of Israel has a deceptive appearance. The people of this nation are in a covenant relationship with God, and they might outwardly appear to observe his Law. However, the nation as a whole has proved to be both lacking faith and barren of good fruitage. They even reject God's own Son! Hence, by causing the unproductive fig tree to wither, Jesus demonstrates what the end will be for this fruitless, faithless nation.

Shortly, Jesus and his disciples enter Jerusalem. As is his custom, Jesus goes to the temple and begins teaching. The chief priests and elders of the people, likely having in mind what Jesus did the day before to the money changers, challenge him: "By what authority do you do these things? Or who gave you this authority to do these things?"—Mark 11:28.

Jesus replies: "I will ask you one question. Answer me, and I will tell you by what authority I do these things. Was the baptism by John from heaven or from men? Answer me." Now his opponents are the ones being challenged. The priests and elders consult one another about how to answer: "If we say, 'From heaven,' he will say, 'Why, then, did you not believe him?' But dare we say, 'From men'?" They reason this way because they are in fear of the crowd, "for these all held that John had really been a prophet." —Mark 11:29-32.

Those opposing Jesus cannot come up with an appropriate answer. So they reply: "We do not know." Jesus, in turn, says: "Neither am I telling you by what authority I do these things." —Mark 11:33.

◇ Why is Nisan 11 significant?

◇ Jesus teaches what lessons with the fig tree that he caused to wither?

◇ How does Jesus confound those who ask by what authority he does things?

TWO ILLUSTRATIONS ABOUT VINEYARDS

MATTHEW 21:28-46   MARK 12:1-12   LUKE 20:9-19

At the temple, Jesus has just confounded the chief priests and the elders of the people, who challenged him as to the authority by which he is doing things. Jesus' reply silences them. Then he gives an illustration that exposes what kind of people they really are.

Jesus relates: "A man had two children. Going up to the first, he said, 'Child, go work today in the vineyard.' In answer this one said, 'I will not,' but afterward, he felt regret and went out. Approaching the second, he said the same. This one replied, 'I will, Sir,' but did not go out. Which of the two did the will of his father?" (Matthew 21:28-31) The answer is obvious—the first son is the one who in the end did his father's will.

So Jesus tells his opposers: "Truly I say to you that the tax collectors and the prostitutes are going ahead of you into the Kingdom of God." The tax collectors and the prostitutes initially would not serve God. However, like the first son, they later repented and now are serving him. In contrast, the religious leaders are like the second son, professing to serve God but really failing to do so. Jesus notes: "John [the Baptist] came to you in a way of righteousness, but you did not believe him. However, the tax collectors and the prostitutes believed him, and even when you saw this, you did not feel regret afterward so as to believe him."—Matthew 21:31, 32.

Jesus follows up that illustration with another. This time, Jesus shows that the religious leaders' failure goes beyond neglecting to serve God. They are actually wicked. "A man planted a vineyard," Jesus relates, "and put a fence around it and dug a vat for the winepress and erected a tower; then he leased it to cultivators and traveled abroad. In due sea-

son he sent a slave to the cultivators to collect some of the fruits of the vineyard from them. But they took him, beat him, and sent him away empty-handed. Again he sent another slave to them, and that one they struck on the head and dishonored. And he sent another, and that one they killed, and many others, some of whom they beat and some of whom they killed."—Mark 12:1-5.

Will those hearing Jesus understand the illustration? Well, they may remember Isaiah's words of criticism: "The vineyard of Jehovah of armies is the house of Israel; the men of Judah are the plantation he was fond of. He kept hoping for justice, but look! there was injustice." (Isaiah 5:7) Jesus' illustration is similar. The landowner is Jehovah, and the vineyard is the nation of Israel, fenced in and protected by God's Law. Jehovah sent prophets to instruct his people and help them produce good fruitage.

However, "the cultivators" mistreated and killed the "slaves" sent to them. Jesus explains: "One more [the owner of the vineyard] had, a beloved son. He sent him to them last, saying, 'They will respect my son.' But those cultivators said among themselves, 'This is the heir. Come, let us kill him, and the inheritance will be ours.' So they took him and killed him."—Mark 12:6-8.

Now Jesus asks: "What will the owner of the vineyard do?" (Mark 12:9) The religious leaders answer: "Because they are evil, he will bring a terrible destruction on them and will lease the vineyard to other cultivators, who will give him the fruits when they become due."—Matthew 21:41.

They thus unwittingly proclaim judgment upon themselves, for they are among "the cultivators" of Jehovah's "vineyard," the nation of

Israel. The fruitage that Jehovah rightly expects from such cultivators includes faith in his Son, the Messiah. Jesus looks straight at the religious leaders and says: "Did you never read this scripture: 'The stone that the builders rejected, this has become the chief cornerstone. This has come from Jehovah, and it is marvelous in our eyes'?" (Mark 12:10, 11) Then Jesus drives home his point: "This is why I say to you, the Kingdom of God will be taken from you and be given to a nation producing its fruits."—Matthew 21:43.

The scribes and chief priests recognize that Jesus "told this illustration with them in mind." (Luke 20:19) More than ever, they want to kill him, the rightful "heir." But they fear the crowds, who consider Jesus a prophet, so they do not try to kill him right then.

◇ Whom do the two sons in Jesus' illustration represent?

◇ In the second illustration, who are represented by the "landowner," "the vineyard," "the cultivators," the "slaves," and the "heir"?

◇ What does the future hold for "the cultivators"?

A KING CALLS THOSE INVITED TO A MARRIAGE FEAST

MATTHEW 22:1-14

As Jesus' ministry draws to an end, he continues to use illustrations to expose the scribes and the chief priests. Hence, they want to kill him. (Luke 20:19) But Jesus is not finished exposing them. He relates another illustration:

"The Kingdom of the heavens may be likened to a king who made a marriage feast for his son. And he sent his slaves to call those invited to the marriage feast, but they were unwilling to come." (Matthew 22:2, 3) Jesus introduces his illustration by mentioning "the Kingdom of the heavens." Logically, then, the "king" must be Jehovah God. What of the king's son and those invited to the marriage feast? Again, it is not difficult to identify the king's son as Jehovah's Son, who is there presenting the illustration, and to grasp that those invited are the ones who will be with the Son in the Kingdom of the heavens.

Who are the first ones to be invited? Well, to whom have Jesus and the apostles been preaching about the Kingdom? It has been to the Jews. (Matthew 10:6, 7; 15:24) This nation accepted the Law covenant in 1513 B.C.E., thereby coming first in line to make up "a kingdom of priests." (Exodus 19:5-8) But when would they actually be called to "the marriage feast"? Logically, that invitation went out in 29 C.E. when Jesus began preaching about the Kingdom of the heavens.

And how did most Israelites respond to the invitation? As Jesus said, "they were unwilling to come." The majority of the religious leaders and the people did not accept him as the Messiah and as God's designated King.

Jesus indicates, though, that the Jews were to have another opportunity: "Again [the king] sent other slaves, saying, 'Tell those invited: "Look! I have prepared my dinner, my bulls and fattened animals are slaughtered, and everything is ready. Come to the marriage feast."'" But unconcerned they went off, one to his own

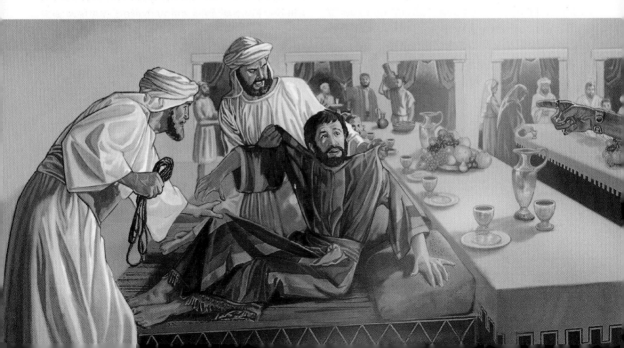

field, another to his business; but the rest, seizing his slaves, treated them insolently and killed them." (Matthew 22:4-6) That corresponds to what would occur once the Christian congregation was established. At that time, the Jews still had the opportunity to be in the Kingdom, yet most spurned this call, even abusing 'the king's slaves.'—Acts 4:13-18; 7:54, 58.

With what outcome for the nation? Jesus relates: "The king grew wrathful and sent his armies and killed those murderers and burned their city." (Matthew 22:7) The Jews experienced that in 70 C.E. when the Romans destroyed "their city," Jerusalem.

Does their refusing the king's call mean that no one else would be invited? Not according to Jesus' illustration. He goes on to say: "Then [the king] said to his slaves, 'The marriage feast is ready, but those invited were not worthy. Therefore, go to the roads leading out of the city, and invite anyone you find to the marriage feast.' Accordingly, those slaves went out to the roads and gathered all they found, both wicked and good; and the room for the wedding ceremonies was filled with those dining."—Matthew 22:8-10.

Significantly, the apostle Peter would later begin helping Gentiles—ones who were not Jews by birth or conversion—to become true Christians. In 36 C.E., Roman army officer Cornelius and his family received God's spirit, coming in line for a place in the Kingdom of the heavens that Jesus mentioned.—Acts 10:1, 34-48.

Jesus indicates that not all who come to the feast will finally prove acceptable to "the king." He says: "When the king came in to inspect the guests, he caught sight of a man not wearing a marriage garment. So he said to him, 'Fellow, how did you get in here without a marriage garment?' He was speechless. Then the king said to his servants, 'Bind him hand and foot and throw him into the darkness outside. There is where his weeping and the gnashing of his teeth will be.' For there are many invited, but few chosen."—Matthew 22:11-14.

The religious leaders hearing Jesus may not understand the meaning or implications of all that he is saying. Nevertheless, they are displeased and more determined than ever to rid themselves of the one causing them such embarrassment.

◇ In Jesus' illustration, who is "the king," who is "his son," and who are those first invited to the wedding feast?

◇ When is the call extended to the Jews, and who afterward are invited?

◇ What is indicated by the fact that many are called but few are chosen?

JESUS THWARTS ATTEMPTS TO ENTRAP HIM

MATTHEW 22:15-40   MARK 12:13-34   LUKE 20:20-40

Jesus' religious enemies are upset. He has just related illustrations that expose their wickedness. The Pharisees now conspire to ensnare him. They try to get him to say something for which he can be turned over to the Roman governor, and they pay some of their disciples to entrap him.—Luke 6:7.

"Teacher," these say, "we know you speak and teach correctly and show no partiality, but you teach the way of God in line with truth: Is it lawful for us to pay head tax to Caesar or not?" (Luke 20:21, 22) Jesus is not fooled by their flattery, for behind it is hypocrisy and cunning. If he says, 'No, it is not right to pay this tax,' he can be accused of sedition against Rome. But if he says, 'Yes, pay this tax,' the people, chafing at being subject to Rome, may misunderstand and turn on him. So how does he answer?

Jesus responds: "Why do you put me to the test, hypocrites? Show me the tax coin." They bring a denarius, whereupon he asks: "Whose image and inscription is this?" "Caesar's," they reply. Then Jesus gives the masterful direction: "Pay back, therefore, Caesar's things to Caesar, but God's things to God."—Matthew 22:18-21.

The men are amazed at Jesus' words. Silenced by his skillful reply, they leave. But the day is not over, nor are the efforts to entrap

him. After the Pharisees' failed attempt, leaders of another religious group approach Jesus.

Sadducees, who say that there is no resurrection, bring up a question involving the resurrection and brother-in-law marriage. They ask: "Teacher, Moses said: 'If any man dies without having children, his brother must marry his wife and raise up offspring for his brother.' Now there were seven brothers with us. The first married and died, and having no offspring, he left his wife for his brother. The same thing happened with the second and the third, through all seven. Last of all, the woman died. So in the resurrection, of the seven, whose wife will she be? For they all had her as a wife."—Matthew 22: 24-28.

Drawing on the writings of Moses, which the Sadducees accept, Jesus replies: "Is not this why you are mistaken, because you know neither the Scriptures nor the power of God? For when they rise from the dead, neither do men marry nor are women given in marriage, but they are as angels in the heavens. But concerning the dead being raised up, have you not read in the book of Moses, in the account about the thornbush, that God said to him: 'I am the God of Abraham and God of Isaac and God of Jacob'? He is a God, not of the dead, but of the living. You are very much mistaken." (Mark 12: 24-27; Exodus 3:1-6) The crowds are astounded by that answer.

Jesus has silenced both the Pharisees and the Sadducees, so now a coalition of these religious opposers comes to test him further. One scribe asks: "Teacher, which is the greatest commandment in the Law?"—Matthew 22:36.

Jesus answers: "The first is, 'Hear, O Israel, Jehovah our God is one Jehovah, and you must love Jehovah your God with your whole heart and with your whole soul and with your whole mind and with your whole strength.' The second is this, 'You must love your neighbor as yourself.' There is no other commandment greater than these."—Mark 12:29-31.

At hearing the answer, the scribe responds: "Teacher, you spoke well, in line with truth, 'He is One, and there is no other besides him'; and to love him with one's whole heart, with one's whole understanding, and with one's whole strength and to love one's neighbor as oneself is worth far more than all the whole burnt offerings and sacrifices." Seeing that the scribe has answered intelligently, Jesus tells him: "You are not far from the Kingdom of God."—Mark 12: 32-34.

For three days (Nisan 9, 10, and 11) Jesus has been teaching in the temple. Some people, such as this scribe, have listened to him with pleasure. But not the religious leaders, who now lack "the courage to question him anymore."

◊ The Pharisees make what attempt to entrap Jesus, and with what result?
◊ When the Sadducees try to ensnare him, how does Jesus foil their attempt?
◊ In answering a scribe's question, what does Jesus stress as very important?

DENOUNCING RELIGIOUS OPPOSERS

MATTHEW 22:41–23:24   MARK 12:35-40   LUKE 20:41-47

Religious opposers fail to discredit Jesus or to entrap him and turn him over to the Romans. (Luke 20:20) Now, while still at the temple on Nisan 11, Jesus turns the tables on them and shows his true identity. Taking the initiative, he asks them: "What do you think about the Christ? Whose son is he?" (Matthew 22:42) It is well-known that the Christ, or Messiah, is to be in David's line. That is the answer that they give. —Matthew 9:27; 12:23; John 7:42.

Jesus asks: "How is it, then, that David under inspiration calls him Lord, saying, 'Jehovah said to my Lord: "Sit at my right hand until I put your enemies beneath your feet"'? If, then, David calls him Lord, how is he his son?"—Matthew 22:43-45.

The Pharisees remain silent, for they are hoping for a human descendant of David who might liberate them from Roman domination. But drawing on David's words recorded at Psalm 110:1, 2, Jesus establishes that the Messiah is to be more than a human ruler. He is David's Lord, and after sitting at God's right hand, he will exercise power. Jesus' reply silences his opposers.

The disciples and many others have been listening. Now Jesus addresses them, warning about the scribes and the Pharisees. Those men have "seated themselves in the seat of Moses" to teach God's Law. Jesus instructs his listeners: "All the things they tell you, do and observe, but do not do according to their deeds, for they say but they do not practice what they say."—Matthew 23:2, 3.

Jesus then gives examples of their hypocrisy, saying: "They broaden the scripture-containing cases that they wear as safeguards." Some Jews wore on the forehead or on the arm these relatively small cases containing short passages from the Law. The Pharisees enlarge theirs to give the impression that they are zealous about the Law. Also, they "lengthen the fringes of their garments." The Israelites were to make fringes on their garments, but the Pharisees make sure that their fringes are quite long. (Numbers 15:38-40) They do all of this "to be seen by men."—Matthew 23:5.

Even Jesus' disciples could be affected by a desire for prominence, so he counsels them: "Do not you be called Rabbi, for one is your Teacher, and all of you are brothers. Moreover, do not call anyone your father on earth, for one is your Father, the heavenly One. Neither be called leaders, for your Leader is one, the Christ." How, then, should the disciples view themselves and act? Jesus tells them: "The greatest one among you must be your minister. Whoever exalts himself will be humbled, and whoever humbles himself will be exalted." —Matthew 23:8-12.

Next, Jesus pronounces a series of woes on the hypocritical scribes and Pharisees: "Woe to you, scribes and Pharisees, hypocrites! because you shut up the Kingdom of the heavens before men; for you yourselves do not go in, neither do you permit those on their way in to go in."—Matthew 23:13.

Jesus condemns the Pharisees' lack of spiritual values, as shown by the arbitrary distinctions they make. For example, they say: "If anyone swears by the temple, it is nothing; but if anyone swears by the gold of the temple, he is under obligation." They thus show their moral blindness, for they put more emphasis on the gold of the temple than on the spiritual value

of Jehovah's place of worship. And they "have disregarded the weightier matters of the Law, namely, justice and mercy and faithfulness." —Matthew 23:16, 23; Luke 11:42.

Jesus calls these Pharisees "blind guides, who strain out the gnat but gulp down the camel!" (Matthew 23:24) They strain a gnat from their wine because that insect is ceremonially unclean. Yet, the way they disregard weightier matters of the Law is like swallowing a camel, also a ceremonially unclean animal, only far larger.—Leviticus 11:4, 21-24.

◊ When Jesus questions the Pharisees about what David said as recorded in Psalm 110, why are they silent?

◊ Why do the Pharisees enlarge their scripture-containing cases and lengthen the fringes on their garments?

◊ What counsel does Jesus give his disciples?

JESUS' FINAL DAY AT THE TEMPLE

MATTHEW 23:25–24:2   MARK 12:41–13:2   LUKE 21:1-6

During Jesus' last appearance at the temple, he continues to expose the hypocrisy of the scribes and Pharisees, openly calling them hypocrites. He uses illustrative language, saying: "You cleanse the outside of the cup and of the dish, but inside they are full of greediness and self-indulgence. Blind Pharisee, cleanse first the inside of the cup and of the dish, so that the outside of it may also become clean." (Matthew 23:25, 26) While the Pharisees are scrupulous when it comes to ceremonial cleanness and outward appearance, they are neglecting the inner person and are failing to purify their figurative heart.

Their hypocrisy is also manifest in their willingness to build and decorate tombs for the prophets. Yet, as Jesus mentions, they "are sons of those who murdered the prophets." (Matthew 23:31) This they have proved in their efforts to kill Jesus.—John 5:18; 7:1, 25.

Jesus then points to what awaits these religious leaders if they do not repent: "Serpents, offspring of vipers, how will you flee from the judgment of Gehenna?" (Matthew 23:33) The nearby Valley of Hinnom is used for burning garbage, a graphic image of the permanent destruction awaiting the wicked scribes and Pharisees.

Jesus' disciples will represent him as "prophets and wise men and public instructors." How will they be treated? Addressing the religious leaders, Jesus says: "Some of [my disciples] you will kill and execute on stakes, and some of them you will scourge in your synagogues and persecute from city to city, so that there may come upon you all the righteous blood spilled on earth, from the blood of righteous Abel to the blood of Zechariah . . . whom you mur-

dered." He warns: "Truly I say to you, all these things will come upon this generation." (Matthew 23:34-36) That proves to be the case in 70 C.E. when the Roman armies destroy Jerusalem and many thousands of Jews perish.

Contemplating this frightful situation distresses Jesus. He says with sadness: "Jerusalem, Jerusalem, the killer of the prophets and stoner of those sent to her—how often I wanted to gather your children together the way a hen gathers her chicks under her wings! But you did not want it. Look! Your house is abandoned to you." (Matthew 23:37, 38) Those hearing these words must wonder what "house" he means. Could he possibly be referring to the magnificent temple there in Jerusalem, which God seems to be protecting?

Then Jesus adds: "I say to you, you will by no means see me from now until you say, 'Blessed is the one who comes in Jehovah's name!'" (Matthew 23:39) He is quoting from the prophetic words of Psalm 118:26: "Blessed is the one who comes in the name of Jehovah; we bless you from the house of Jehovah." Clearly, once this material temple is destroyed, no one will be coming to it in God's name.

Jesus now moves to a section of the temple where there are trumpet-shaped treasury chests. People can put contributions in the small openings at the top. Jesus sees various Jews doing just that, the rich "dropping in many coins" as gifts. Then Jesus observes a poor widow who drops in "two small coins of very little value." (Mark 12:41, 42) No doubt Jesus knows how pleased God is with her gift.

Calling his disciples over, Jesus says: "Truly I say to you that this poor widow put in more than all the others who put money into the trea-

• JESUS FURTHER CONDEMNS THE RELIGIOUS LEADERS
• THE TEMPLE WILL BE DESTROYED
• A POOR WIDOW CONTRIBUTES TWO SMALL COINS

110

sury chests." How is that so? He explains: "They all put in out of their surplus, but she, out of her want, put in everything she had, all she had to live on." (Mark 12:43, 44) How she differs in thought and deed from the religious leaders!

As Nisan 11 progresses, Jesus leaves the temple for the last time. One of his disciples exclaims: "Teacher, see! what wonderful stones and buildings!" (Mark 13:1) Indeed, some of the stones in the temple's walls are extremely large, contributing to the impression of its strength

and permanence. It certainly seems strange, then, that Jesus says: "Do you see these great buildings? By no means will a stone be left here upon a stone and not be thrown down."—Mark 13:2.

After saying these things, Jesus and his apostles cross the Kidron Valley and climb to a spot on the Mount of Olives. At one point he is with four of the apostles—Peter, Andrew, James, and John. From that position, they can gaze down on the magnificent temple.

◊ What does Jesus do during his final visit to the temple?
◊ Jesus foretells what future for the temple?
◊ Why does Jesus say that the widow contributed more than the rich?

It is Tuesday afternoon, and Nisan 11 is drawing to a close. Also ending are days of intense activity here on earth for Jesus. By day he has been teaching in the temple, and by night he has lodged outside the city. There has been great interest among the people, who "would come to him early in the morning to hear him in the temple." (Luke 21:37, 38) Now that is past, and Jesus is seated on the Mount of Olives with four apostles—Peter, Andrew, James, and John.

These four have come to him privately. They are concerned about the temple because Jesus has just foretold that not a stone of it will be left upon a stone. They have more on their minds, though. Jesus had earlier urged them: "Keep ready, because at an hour that you do not think likely, the Son of man is coming." (Luke 12:40) He had also spoken about the "day when the Son of man is revealed." (Luke 17:30) Are those comments somehow related to what he just said about the temple? The apostles are very curious. "Tell us," they say, "when will these things be, and what will be the sign of your presence and of the conclusion of the system of things?"—Matthew 24:3.

They may have in mind the end of the very temple that they can see not far away. Also, they ask about the presence of the Son of man. They may recall that Jesus gave an illustration about "a man of noble birth" who 'traveled to secure kingly power and then to return.' (Luke 19:11, 12) And, finally, they wonder what "the conclusion of the system of things" will involve.

In his detailed response, Jesus provides a sign that identifies when the existing Jewish system of things, including its temple, will end. But he provides more. This sign will help Christians in the future to know when they are living during his "presence" and near the end of the entire system of things on earth.

As the years go by, the apostles observe Jesus' prophecy being fulfilled. Yes, many things that he foretold start to occur in their lifetime. Thus, alert Christians who are living 37 years later, in 70 C.E., are not caught unawares by the approaching destruction of the Jewish system with its temple. However, not all that Jesus foretells actually takes place in the period leading up to and including 70 C.E. Hence, what will yet mark his presence in Kingdom power? Jesus reveals the answer to the apostles.

Jesus foretells that there will be "wars and reports of wars" and that "nation will rise against nation and kingdom against kingdom." (Matthew 24:6, 7) He also says that "there will be great earthquakes, and in one place after another food shortages and pestilences." (Luke 21:11) Jesus warns his disciples: "People will lay their hands on you and persecute you." (Luke 21:12) False prophets will arise and mislead many. Lawlessness will increase, and the love of the greater number will grow cold. Additionally, he says that the "good news of the Kingdom will be preached in all the inhabited earth for a witness to all the nations, and then the end will come."—Matthew 24:14.

◇ What prompts the apostles to ask about future events, but what else do they apparently have in mind?

◇ When does Jesus' prophecy start to be fulfilled, and how?

◇ What are some conditions that are to mark Christ's presence?

Although Jesus' prophecy is fulfilled in some respects prior to and during the destruction of Jerusalem by the Romans, might Jesus be including a later, larger fulfillment? Do you see the evidence that Jesus' momentous prophecy has been undergoing its major fulfillment in modern times?

One thing that Jesus includes in the sign of his presence is the appearance of "the disgusting thing that causes desolation." (Matthew 24:15) In 66 C.E., this disgusting thing appears in the form of the "encamped armies" of Rome, with their idolatrous standards, or ensigns. The Romans surround Jerusalem and undermine some of its walls. (Luke 21:20) Thus, "the disgusting thing" is standing where it ought not, in what the Jews consider "a holy place."

Jesus further foretells: "There will be great tribulation such as has not occurred since the world's beginning until now, no, nor will occur again." In 70 C.E., the Romans destroy Jerusalem. That destructive conquest of the Jews' 'holy city,' including its temple, proves to be a great tribulation, with many thousands being killed. (Matthew 4:5; 24:21) It is far greater than any destruction the city and the Jewish people have ever experienced, and it brings to an end the organized system of worship that the Jews had followed for centuries. Accordingly, any later, larger fulfillment of Jesus' prophetic words is certain to be horrific.

CONFIDENCE DURING THE FORETOLD DAYS

Jesus' discussion with his apostles regarding the sign of his presence in Kingdom power and of the end of the system of things is far from over. He now warns them about chasing after "false Christs and false prophets." Attempts will be made, he says, "to mislead, if possible, even the chosen ones." (Matthew 24:24) But these chosen ones will not be misled. False Christs can make only a visible appearance. In contrast, Jesus' presence will not be visible.

Referring to a larger tribulation that would break out at the end of the present system of things, Jesus says: "The sun will be darkened, and the moon will not give its light, and the stars will fall from heaven, and the powers of the heavens will be shaken." (Matthew 24:29) The apostles hearing those chilling words do not know exactly what will occur, but it certainly will be awesome.

How will these shocking events affect mankind? Jesus says: "People will become faint out of fear and expectation of the things coming upon the inhabited earth, for the powers of the heavens will be shaken." (Luke 21:26) Indeed, Jesus is describing what will be the darkest period of human existence.

Encouragingly, Jesus makes it clear to the apostles that not all will be lamenting when 'the Son of man comes with power and great glory.' (Matthew 24:30) He had already indicated that God will intervene "on account of the chosen ones." (Matthew 24:22) So how should such faithful disciples react to the shocking developments that Jesus is outlining? Jesus encourages his followers: "As these things start to occur, stand up straight and lift up your heads, because your deliverance is getting near." —Luke 21:28.

How, though, would Jesus' disciples who are living during this foretold period be able to determine the nearness of the end? Jesus gives an illustration about a fig tree: "Just as soon as its young branch grows tender and sprouts its leaves, you know that summer is near. Likewise also you, when you see all these things, know that he is near at the doors. Truly I say to you that this generation will by no means pass away until all these things happen."—Matthew 24:32-34.

young child not aware
but nature is do see
it coming

Thus, when his disciples see the many different features of the sign being fulfilled, they should realize that the end is near. Admonishing the disciples who will be alive during that momentous period, Jesus says:

"Concerning that day and hour nobody knows, neither the angels of the heavens nor the Son, but only the Father. For just as the days of Noah were, so the presence of the Son of man will be. For as they were in those days before the Flood, eating and drinking, men marrying and women being given in marriage, until the day that Noah entered into the ark, and they took no note until the Flood came and swept them all away, so the presence of the Son of man will be." (Matthew 24:36-39) The event that Jesus uses as a parallel—the historic Flood of Noah's day—had a global impact. *covid 19*

The apostles listening to Jesus on the Mount of Olives must undoubtedly recognize the need to keep alert. Jesus says: "Pay attention to yourselves that your hearts never become weighed down with overeating and heavy drinking and anxieties of life, and suddenly that day be instantly upon you as a snare. For it will come upon all those dwelling on the face of the whole earth, Keep awake, then, all the time making supplication that you may succeed in escaping all these things that must occur and in standing before the Son of man."—Luke 21: 34-36.

Jesus is once again showing that what he is foretelling is not of limited scope. He is not prophesying about events that would occur in a few decades and that would affect only the city of Jerusalem or the Jewish nation. No, he is pointing to developments that "will come upon all those dwelling on the face of the whole earth."

He says that his disciples will need to keep alert, to be on the watch, and to be ready. Jesus underscores this warning with another illustration: "Know one thing: If the householder had known in what watch the thief was coming, he would have kept awake and not allowed his house to be broken into. On this account, you too prove yourselves ready, because the Son of man is coming at an hour that you do not think to be it."—Matthew 24:43, 44.

Jesus goes on to give his disciples reason for optimism. He assures them that when his prophecy is being fulfilled, there will be a "slave" who is alert and active. Jesus draws on a situation that the apostles can readily picture: "Who really is the faithful and discreet slave whom his master appointed over his domestics, to give them their food at the proper time? Happy is that slave if his master on coming finds him doing so! Truly I say to you, he will appoint him over all his belongings." If, though, the "slave" develops an evil attitude and mistreats others, the master will "punish him with the greatest severity."—Matthew 24: 45-51; compare Luke 12:45, 46.

However, Jesus is not saying that a group of his followers will develop an evil disposition. What, then, is the lesson that Jesus wants to impress upon his disciples? He wants them to stay alert and active, as he makes clear in yet another illustration.

◇ How does a "disgusting thing" appear, and what events follow its appearance?
◇ How will people react when they witness the fulfillment of Jesus' prophecy?
◇ Jesus gives what illustration to help his disciples discern when the end is near?
◇ What indicates that the fulfillment of Jesus' prophecy is global? *Lk 21 : effect all dwelling on face of earth*
◇ What admonition does Jesus provide for his disciples living near the end of the system of things?

A LESSON IN VIGILANCE—THE VIRGINS

MATTHEW 25:1-13

Jesus has been answering his apostles' question regarding the sign of his presence and of the conclusion of the system of things. With this in mind, he now gives them wise admonition by means of an additional illustration. Its fulfillment would be observable by those living during his presence.

He introduces the illustration, saying: "The Kingdom of the heavens may be likened to ten virgins who took their lamps and went out to meet the bridegroom. Five of them were foolish, and five were discreet."—Matthew 25:1, 2.

Jesus does not mean that half of his disciples who inherit the Kingdom of the heavens are foolish and the other half are discreet. Rather, he is making the point that in connection with the Kingdom, each of his disciples has the capacity to choose to be vigilant or to be distracted. Jesus has no doubt, though, that each of his servants can remain faithful and receive his Father's blessings.

In the illustration, all ten virgins go out to welcome the bridegroom and to join the wedding procession. When he arrives, the virgins will light the route with their lamps, honoring him as he brings his bride to the house prepared for her. How do things work out, though?

Jesus explains: "The foolish took their lamps but took no oil with them, whereas the discreet

took oil in their flasks along with their lamps. While the bridegroom was delaying, they all became drowsy and fell asleep." (Matthew 25:3-5) The bridegroom does not arrive as soon as expected. There seems to be a long delay, during which the virgins fall asleep. The apostles may recall what Jesus related about a man of noble birth who went away and "eventually got back after having secured the kingly power."—Luke 19:11-15.

In the illustration of the ten virgins, Jesus describes what happens when the bridegroom finally arrives: "Right in the middle of the night there was a shout: 'Here is the bridegroom! Go out to meet him.'" (Matthew 25:6) What is the situation of the virgins as to their preparedness and vigilance?

Jesus continues: "Then all those virgins got up and put their lamps in order. The foolish said to the discreet, 'Give us some of your oil, because our lamps are about to go out.' The discreet answered, saying: 'Perhaps there may not be enough for both us and you. Go instead to those who sell it, and buy some for yourselves.'"—Matthew 25:7-9.

So the five foolish virgins are not vigilant and are not prepared for the arrival of the bridegroom. They lack sufficient oil for their lamps and need to try to find some. Jesus relates: "While they were going off to buy it, the bridegroom came. The virgins who were ready went in with him to the marriage feast, and the door was shut. Afterward, the rest of the virgins also came, saying, 'Sir, Sir, open to us!' In answer he said, 'I tell you the truth, I do not know you.'" (Matthew 25:10-12) What a sad outcome for not remaining prepared and vigilant!

The apostles can see that the bridegroom whom Jesus mentions refers to himself. Earlier he had even likened himself to a bridegroom. (Luke 5:34, 35) And the wise virgins? When speaking about the "little flock," who would be given the Kingdom, Jesus used the words: "Be dressed and ready and have your lamps burning." (Luke 12:32, 35) So in this illustration about the virgins, the apostles can grasp that Jesus is referring to ones such as themselves. Hence, what is the message that Jesus is conveying with this illustration?

Jesus does not leave any doubt about that. He concludes his illustration by saying: "Keep on the watch, therefore, because you know neither the day nor the hour."—Matthew 25:13.

Clearly, Jesus is admonishing his faithful followers that in connection with his presence, they will need to "keep on the watch." He will be coming, and they need to be prepared and vigilant—like the five discreet virgins—in order not to lose sight of their precious hope and miss out on the reward that can be theirs.

◇ How do the five discreet virgins differ from the five foolish ones as respects vigilance and preparedness?

◇ To whom does the bridegroom refer, and to whom do the virgins refer?

◇ What message is Jesus conveying with the illustration of the ten virgins?

Never has faithful & discreet slave not shared spiritual
enlightment with others — at that point its too late

A LESSON IN DILIGENCE—THE TALENTS

MATTHEW 25:14-30

While still with his four apostles on the Mount of Olives, Jesus tells them another illustration. A few days earlier, while he was at Jericho, he gave the illustration of the minas to show that the Kingdom was yet far off in the future. The illustration he now relates has a number of similar features. It is part of his answer to the question about his presence and the conclusion of the system of things. It highlights that his disciples must be diligent with what he entrusts to them.

Jesus begins: "It is just like a man about to travel abroad who summoned his slaves and entrusted his belongings to them." (Matthew 25:14) Given that Jesus had already likened himself to a man who traveled abroad "to secure kingly power for himself," the apostles could easily see that Jesus is the "man" being spoken of now.—Luke 19:12.

Before the man in the illustration travels abroad, he commits to his slaves valuable belongings. During the three and a half years of his ministry, Jesus focused on preaching the good news of God's Kingdom, and he trained his disciples to do this work. Now he is going away, confident that they will carry on doing what he trained them to do.—Matthew 10:7; Luke 10:1, 8, 9; compare John 4:38; 14:12.

In the illustration, how does the man distribute his belongings? Jesus relates: "He gave five talents to one, two to another, and one to still another, to each according to his own ability, and he went abroad." (Matthew 25:15) What will these slaves do with what is entrusted to them? Will they be diligent in using them in their master's interests? Jesus tells the apostles:

"Immediately the one who received the five talents went and did business with them and gained five more. Likewise, the one who received the two gained two more. But the slave who received just one went off and dug in the ground and hid his master's money." (Matthew 25:16-18) What will happen when the master returns?

"After a long time," Jesus continues, "the master of those slaves came and settled accounts with them." (Matthew 25:19) The first two did all they could, "each according to his own ability." Each slave was diligent, hardworking, and productive with what had been entrusted to him. The one who received five talents doubled that, as did the one who received two talents. (Back then, a worker would have to labor about 19 years to earn the equivalent of one talent.) The master has the same commendation for each of them: "Well done, good and faithful slave! You were faithful over a few things. I will appoint you over many

things. Enter into the joy of your master."—Matthew 25:21.

It is different, though, with the slave who received one talent. He says: "Master, I knew you to be a demanding man, reaping where you did not sow and gathering where you did not winnow. So I grew afraid and went and hid your talent in the ground. Here, you have what is yours." (Matthew 25:24, 25) He has not even deposited the money with bankers so as to accumulate at least some profit for his master. He has, in effect, worked against his master's interests.

Fittingly, the master designates him a "wicked and sluggish slave." What he had is taken away and given to the slave who is willing to apply himself diligently. The master sets out his standard: "To everyone who has, more will be given, and he will have an abundance. But the one who does not have, even what he has will be taken away from him."—Matthew 25:26, 29.

Jesus' disciples have much to think about, even in connection with this one illustration. They can see that what Jesus is entrusting to them—the precious privilege of making disciples—is of great value. And he expects them to be diligent in using this privilege. Jesus does not think that they all must do the same in carrying out the preaching work that he has charged them to do. As illustrated, each should do all that he can "according to his own ability." This by no means implies that Jesus will be pleased if one is "sluggish" and fails to do his best in promoting the Master's belongings.

How pleased the apostles must be, though, with the assurance: "To everyone who has, more will be given"!

◇ In the illustration of the talents, who is like the master, and who are like the slaves?

◇ What lessons does Jesus teach his disciples?

CHRIST IN POWER JUDGES THE SHEEP AND THE GOATS

shepard would seperate the sheep fm. the more aggressive goats

On the Mount of Olives, Jesus has just related the illustrations of the ten virgins and of the talents. How does he end his answer to the apostles' question regarding the sign of his presence and of the conclusion of the system of things? He does so with a final illustration, one about sheep and goats.

Jesus begins by establishing its setting, telling them: "When the Son of man comes in his glory, and all the angels with him, then he will sit down on his glorious throne." (Matthew 25:31) He leaves no doubt that he, Jesus, is the central figure in this illustration. He often called himself "the Son of man."—Matthew 8:20; 9:6; 20:18, 28. *Son of a human - occurs 80 x's*

When will this illustration find fulfillment? It is when Jesus "comes in his glory" with the angels and sits down "on his glorious throne." He had already spoken about "the Son of man coming on the clouds of heaven with power and great glory" and with his angels. When would that be? "Immediately after the tribulation." (Matthew 24:29-31; Mark 13:26, 27; Luke 21:27) So this illustration is to find fulfillment at Jesus' future coming in glory. What will he then do?

Jesus explains: "When the Son of man comes . . . , all the nations will be gathered before him, and he will separate people one from another, just as a shepherd separates the sheep from the goats. And he will put the sheep on his right hand, but the goats on his left."—Matthew 25:31-33.

Regarding the sheep, separated to the favored side, Jesus says: "Then the King will say to those on his right: 'Come, you who have been blessed by my Father, inherit the Kingdom prepared for you from the founding of the world.'"

Attitude that big sheep have towards the brothers

(Matthew 25:34) Why do the sheep receive the King's favor?

The King explains: "I became hungry and you gave me something to eat; I was thirsty and you gave me something to drink. I was a stranger and you received me hospitably; naked and you clothed me. I fell sick and you looked after me. I was in prison and you visited me." When these sheep, "the righteous ones," ask in what way they did those good things, he answers: "To the extent that you did it to one of the least of these my brothers, you did it to me." (Matthew 25:35, 36, 40, 46) They do not do these good deeds in heaven, for there are no sick or hungry ones there. These must be deeds done for Christ's brothers on earth.

What of the goats, who are put on the left side? Jesus says: "Then [the King] will say to those on his left: 'Go away from me, you who have been cursed, into the everlasting fire prepared for the Devil and his angels. For I became hungry, but you gave me nothing to eat; and I was thirsty, but you gave me nothing to drink. I was a stranger, but you did not receive me hospitably; naked, but you did not clothe me; sick and in prison, but you did not look after me.'" (Matthew 25:41-43) This judgment is merited because the goats failed to treat Christ's brothers on earth kindly, as they should have done.

The apostles learn that this future time of

judgment is to have permanent—everlasting—consequences. Jesus tells them: "Then [the King] will [say]: 'Truly I say to you, to the extent that you did not do it to one of these least ones, you did not do it to me.' These will depart into everlasting cutting-off, but the righteous ones into everlasting life."—Matthew 25: 45, 46.

Jesus' response to the apostles' question provides much for his followers to think about, helping them to examine their attitudes and deeds.

*preaching work
financial support
obeying anointed*

⬦ In Jesus' illustration of the sheep and the goats, who is "the King," and when is the illustration to be fulfilled?

⬦ Why will the sheep be judged as meriting Jesus' favor?

⬦ On what basis will some people be judged as goats, and what future will the sheep and the goats have?

JESUS' FINAL PASSOVER APPROACHES

MATTHEW 26:1-5, 14-19 MARK 14:1, 2, 10-16 LUKE 22:1-13

Jesus finishes teaching the four apostles on the Mount of Olives, answering their question about his future presence and the conclusion of the system of things.

What a busy day Nisan 11 has been! It is perhaps while they are returning to Bethany for the night when Jesus tells the apostles: "You know that two days from now the Passover takes place, and the Son of man will be handed over to be executed on the stake."—Matthew 26:2.

Jesus apparently spends the next day, Wednesday, quietly with his apostles. On Tuesday, he had rebuked the religious leaders and exposed them publicly. They are seeking to kill him. Hence, he does not openly show himself on Nisan 12 so that nothing will prevent his celebrating the Passover with his apostles after sunset the next evening, as Nisan 14 begins.

But the chief priests and the older men of the people are not remaining quiet before the Passover. They gather in the courtyard of the high priest, Caiaphas. Why? They are upset because Jesus has been exposing them. Now they conspire together "to seize Jesus by cunning and to kill him." How and when will they do so? They say: "Not at the festival, so that there may not be an uproar among the people." (Matthew 26: 4, 5) They are in fear because Jesus enjoys the favor of many.

Meanwhile, the religious leaders receive a visitor. To their surprise, it is one of Jesus' own apostles, Judas Iscariot. Satan has implanted in him the idea of betraying his Master! Judas asks them: "What will you give me to betray him to you?" (Matthew 26:15) Delighted at this, they "agree to give him silver money." (Luke

22:5) How much? They gladly consent to give him 30 silver pieces. It is significant that the price of a slave is 30 shekels. (Exodus 21:32) The religious leaders thus show contempt for Jesus, that he is of little value. Judas now starts "looking for a good opportunity to betray him to them without a crowd around."—Luke 22:6.

Nisan 13 begins at sundown Wednesday, and this is the sixth and last night Jesus spends in Bethany. The next day, final preparations will need to be made for the Passover. A lamb must be obtained so that it can be slaughtered and roasted whole after Nisan 14 begins. Where will they have the meal, and who will prepare it? Jesus has not provided such details. Thus, Judas cannot pass them on to the chief priests.

Probably early Thursday afternoon, Jesus dispatches Peter and John from Bethany, saying: "Go and get the Passover ready for us to eat." They respond: "Where do you want us to get it ready?" Jesus explains: "When you enter into the city, a man carrying an earthenware water jar will meet you. Follow him into the house that he enters. And say to the landlord of the house, 'The Teacher says to you: "Where is the guest room where I may eat the Passover with my disciples?"' And that man will show you a large, furnished upper room. Get it ready there."—Luke 22:8-12.

No doubt the landlord is a disciple of Jesus. He may anticipate Jesus' request to use his house for this occasion. When the two apostles get to Jerusalem, they find everything just as Jesus had told them. So they see to it that the lamb is ready and that the other arrangements for the Passover meal are in place to care for the needs of the 13—Jesus and his 12 apostles.

◇ What does Jesus apparently do Wednesday, Nisan 12, and why?

◇ Why do the religious leaders meet, and why does Judas go to them?

◇ Whom does Jesus send into Jerusalem on Thursday, and what do they do?

TEACHING HUMILITY AT THE LAST PASSOVER

MATTHEW 26:20 MARK 14:17 LUKE 22:14-18 JOHN 13:1-17

At Jesus' direction, Peter and John have already arrived in Jerusalem to prepare for the Passover. Later Jesus and the ten other apostles head there. It is afternoon, and the sun is sinking in the western sky as Jesus and his party descend the Mount of Olives. This is Jesus' last daytime view from here until after his resurrection.

Soon Jesus and his party reach the city and make their way to the home where they will have the Passover meal. They climb the stairs to the large upper room. There they find that all preparations have been made for their private meal. Jesus has looked forward to this occasion, for he says: "I have greatly desired to eat this Passover with you before I suffer."—Luke 22:15.

Many years earlier, the custom of passing a number of cups of wine among the Passover participants was introduced. Now, after accepting one of the cups, Jesus gives thanks and says: "Take this and pass it from one to the other among yourselves, for I tell you, from now on, I will not drink again from the product of the vine until the Kingdom of God comes." (Luke 22: 17, 18) It should be clear that his death is close.

At some point during the Passover meal, something unusual occurs. Jesus gets up, sets aside his outer garments, and picks up a towel. Then he puts water in a basin that is at hand. Ordinarily, a host would see to it that his guests' feet were washed, perhaps by a servant. (Luke 7:44) On this occasion no host is present, so Jesus performs this personal service. Any of the apostles could have taken the opportunity to do it, but not one of them does. Is it because some rivalry still exists among them? Whatever the case, they are embarrassed to have Jesus wash their feet.

When Jesus comes to Peter, he protests: "You will certainly never wash my feet." Jesus replies: "Unless I wash you, you have no share with me." Peter responds with feeling: "Lord, wash not only my feet but also my hands and my head." How surprised he must be, then, at Jesus' answer: "Whoever has bathed does not need to have more than his feet washed, but is completely clean. And you men are clean, but not all of you."—John 13:8-10.

Jesus washes the feet of all 12, including the feet of Judas Iscariot. After putting his outer garments on and reclining at the table again,

Jesus asks: "Do you understand what I have done to you? You address me as 'Teacher' and 'Lord,' and you are correct, for I am such. Therefore, if I, the Lord and Teacher, washed your feet, you also should wash the feet of one another. For I set the pattern for you, that just as I did to you, you should also do. Most truly I say to you, a slave is not greater than his master, nor is one who is sent greater than the one who sent him. If you know these things, happy you are if you do them."—John 13:12-17.

What a beautiful lesson in humble service! Jesus' followers should not seek the first place, thinking that they are important and should be served. Rather, they should follow Jesus' example, not by any ritual of foot washing, but by being willing to serve with humility and without partiality.

a pattern of humility

◊ During the Passover meal, what does Jesus tell the apostles that indicates his death is close?

◊ Why is it unusual that Jesus washes the apostles' feet?

◊ By performing the menial service of washing his apostles' feet, what lesson is Jesus providing?

THE LORD'S EVENING MEAL *similarly committed suicide*

MATTHEW 26:21-29   MARK 14:18-25   LUKE 22:19-23   JOHN 13:18-30

1 Earlier this evening Jesus taught his apostles a lesson in humility by washing their feet. Now, apparently after the Passover meal, he quotes David's prophetic words: "The man at peace with me, one whom I trusted, who was eating my bread, has lifted his heel against me." Then he explains: "One of you will betray me."—Psalm 41:9; John 13:18, 21.

2 The apostles look at one another, and each asks: "Lord, it is not I, is it?" Even Judas Iscariot does so. Peter urges John, who is next to Jesus at the table, to find out who it is. So John leans close to Jesus and asks: "Lord, who is it?" —Matthew 26:22; John 13:25.

3 Jesus answers: "It is the one to whom I will give the piece of bread that I dip." Dipping some bread in a dish on the table, Jesus hands it to Judas, saying: "The Son of man is going away,

not predestined to do it

just as it is written about him, but woe to that man through whom the Son of man is betrayed! It would have been better for that man if he had not been born." (John 13:26; Matthew 26:24) Satan then enters Judas. This man, already corrupt, now gives himself over to do the Devil's will and thus becomes "the son of destruction." —John 6:64, 70; 12:4; 17:12.

4 Jesus tells Judas: "What you are doing, do it more quickly." The other apostles imagine that Judas, who is holding the money box, is being told: "'Buy what we need for the festival,' or that he should give something to the poor." (John 13: 27-30) Instead, Judas goes off to betray Jesus.

5 On this same evening as the Passover meal, Jesus introduces an entirely new type of meal. He takes a loaf, says a prayer of thanks, breaks it, and gives it to his apostles to eat. He says:

Satan entered into him ~ pt of no return

270

"This means my body, which is to be given in your behalf. Keep doing this in remembrance of me." (Luke 22:19) The piece of bread is passed around, and the apostles eat of it.

Now Jesus takes a cup of wine, says a prayer of thanks over it, and passes it to them. Each drinks from the cup, about which Jesus says: "This cup means the new covenant by virtue of my blood, which is to be poured out in your behalf."—Luke 22:20. *post passover*

Thus Jesus arranges for a memorial of his death that his followers are to hold each year on Nisan 14. It will call to mind what Jesus and his Father have done to enable men of faith to escape from the condemnation of sin and death. Even more so than did the Passover for the Jews, it highlights true liberation for believing mankind.

Jesus says that his blood "is to be poured out in behalf of many for forgiveness of sins." Among the many to gain such forgiveness are his faithful apostles and others like them. They are the ones who will be with him in the Kingdom of his Father.—Matthew 26:28, 29.

◇ What Bible prophecy does Jesus quote about a companion, and how does he apply it?

◇ Jesus tells Judas to do what, but how do the other apostles understand Jesus' direction?

◇ What new event does Jesus introduce, and what purpose does it serve?

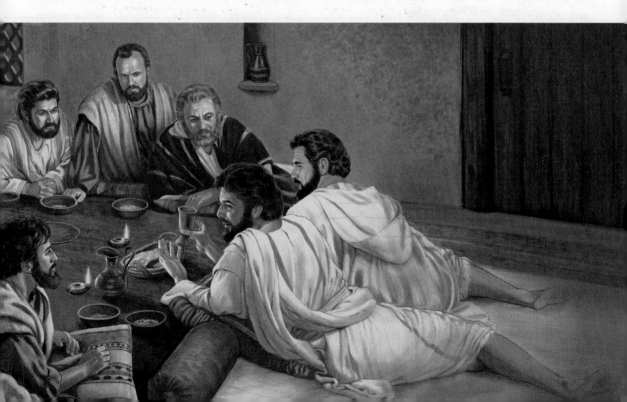

A DISPUTE OVER GREATNESS

MATTHEW 26:31-35   MARK 14:27-31   LUKE 22:24-38   JOHN 13:31-38

[handwritten: All Sp Inspired harmony in God's word is "truly marvellous"]

During his last evening with his apostles, Jesus has provided them with a fine lesson in humble service by washing their feet. Why is that fitting? Because of a weakness they have shown. They are devoted to God, yet they still are concerned about which of them is greatest. (Mark 9:33, 34; 10:35-37) That weakness resurfaces this evening. *[handwritten: grant us to sit dn at rt hand + left in glory]*

2 The apostles become involved in "a heated dispute among them over which one of them was considered to be the greatest." (Luke 22:24) How saddened Jesus must be to see them bickering again! What does he do?

3 Rather than scolding the apostles for their attitude and behavior, Jesus patiently reasons with them: "The kings of the nations lord it over them, and those having authority over them are called Benefactors. You, though, are not to be that way. . . . For which one is greater, the one dining or the one serving?" Then, reminding them of the example that he has constantly set for them, Jesus says: "But I am among you as the one serving."—Luke 22:25-27.

4 Despite their imperfections, the apostles have stuck with Jesus through many challenging situations. So he says: "I make a covenant with you, just as my Father has made a covenant with me, for a kingdom." (Luke 22:29) These men are Jesus' loyal followers. He assures them that by means of a covenant between him and them, they will be in the Kingdom and share in his royal dominion.

5 Although the apostles have this marvelous prospect, they are still in the flesh and are still imperfect. Jesus tells them: "Satan has demanded to have all of you to sift as wheat," which scatters as it is sifted. (Luke 22:31) He also warns: "All of you will be stumbled in con-

nection with me on this night, for it is written: 'I will strike the shepherd, and the sheep of the flock will be scattered about.'"—Matthew 26:31; Zechariah 13:7.

6 Peter confidently objects: "Although all the others are stumbled in connection with you, I will never be stumbled!" (Matthew 26:33) Jesus tells Peter that before a rooster crows twice that night, Peter will disown him. However, Jesus adds: "I have made supplication for you that your faith may not give out; and you, once you have returned, strengthen your brothers." (Luke 22:32) Yet Peter boldly affirms: "Even if I should have to die with you, I will by no means disown you." (Matthew 26:35) The other apostles say the same thing.

7 Jesus tells his disciples: "I am with you a little longer. You will look for me; and just as I said to the Jews, 'Where I go you cannot come,' I now say it also to you." Then he adds: "I am giving you a new commandment, that you love one another; just as I have loved you, you also love one another. By this all will know that you are my disciples—if you have love among yourselves."—John 13:33-35.

8 At hearing Jesus say that he is to be with them just a little longer, Peter asks: "Lord, where are you going?" Jesus replies: "Where I am going, you cannot follow me now, but you will follow later." Puzzled, Peter says: "Lord, why is it I cannot follow you now? I will surrender my life in your behalf."—John 13:36, 37.

9 Jesus now refers to the time when he sent the apostles out on a preaching tour of Galilee without a money bag or a food pouch. (Matthew 10:5, 9, 10) He asks: "You did not lack anything, did you?" They reply: "No!" But what should they do in the days ahead? Jesus directs them: "Let the

one who has a money bag take it, likewise a food pouch, and let the one who has no sword sell his outer garment and buy one. For I tell you that what is written must be accomplished in me, namely, 'He was counted with lawless ones.' For this is being fulfilled concerning me."—Luke 22:35-37.

Jesus is pointing to the time when he will be nailed to a stake alongside evildoers, or lawless ones. Thereafter his followers will face severe persecution. They feel that they are prepared and say: "Lord, look! here are two swords." He answers: "It is enough." (Luke 22:38) That they have two swords with them will soon afford Jesus an opportunity to teach another important lesson.

◇ Why are the apostles arguing, and how does Jesus deal with the situation?
◇ What is to be accomplished by the covenant that Jesus makes with his faithful disciples?
◇ How does Jesus respond to Peter's display of confidence?

JESUS—THE WAY, THE TRUTH, THE LIFE

JOHN 14:1-31

lived in harmony with the truth & fulfilled scores of prophecy

↳ by ransom we can gain "real life" "everlasting life"

Still in the upper room with the apostles after the memorial meal, Jesus encourages them: "Do not let your hearts be troubled. Exercise faith in God; exercise faith also in me."—John 13:36; 14:1. *↱ you'll follow later*

Jesus gives the faithful apostles reason not to be troubled over his departure: "In the house of my Father are many dwelling places. . . . If I go my way and prepare a place for you, I will come again and will receive you home to myself, so that where I am you also may be." The apostles, however, do not grasp that he is speaking about going to heaven. Thomas asks: "Lord, we do not know where you are going. How can we know the way?"—John 14: 2-5.

"I am the way and the truth and the life," Jesus answers. Only by accepting him and his teachings and imitating his life course can one enter the heavenly house of his Father. Jesus says: "No one comes to the Father except through me."—John 14:6.

↳ for humans to be reconciled to God

Philip, listening intently, requests: "Lord, show us the Father, and it is enough for us." Philip seems to want some manifestation of God, like the visions that Moses, Elijah, and Isaiah received. However, the apostles have something better than such visions. Jesus highlights that, replying: "Even after I have been with you men for such a long time, Philip, have you not come to know me? Whoever has seen me has seen the Father also." Jesus perfectly reflects the Father's personality; hence, living with and observing Jesus is like seeing the Father. Of course, the Father is superior to the Son, for Jesus points out: "The things I say to you I do not speak of my own originality." (John 14:8-10) The apostles can see that Jesus is giving all credit for his teachings to his Father.

Jesus' apostles have seen him do wonderful works and have heard him proclaim the good news about the Kingdom of God. Now he tells them: "Whoever exercises faith in me will also do the works that I do; and he will do works greater than these." (John 14:12) Jesus is not saying that they will perform greater miracles than he did. They will, though, carry out their ministry for a much longer time, over a much greater area, and to far more people.

Jesus' departure will not leave them abandoned, for he promises: "If you ask anything in my name, I will do it." Moreover, he says: "I will ask the Father and he will give you another helper to be with you forever, the spirit of the truth." (John 14:14, 16, 17) He guarantees them that they will receive the holy spirit, this other helper. That happens on the day of Pentecost.

"In a little while," Jesus says, "the world will see me no more, but you will see me, because I live and you will live." (John 14:19) Not only will Jesus appear to them in bodily form after his resurrection but he will, in time, resurrect them to be with him in heaven as spirit creatures.

Now Jesus states a simple truth: "Whoever has my commandments and observes them is the one who loves me. In turn, whoever loves me will be loved by my Father, and I will love him and will clearly show myself to him." At this the apostle Judas, who is also called Thaddaeus, asks: "Lord, what has happened that you intend to show yourself clearly to us and not to the world?" Jesus replies: "If anyone loves me, he will observe my word, and my Father will love him . . . Whoever does not love me does not observe my words." (John 14:21-24) Unlike his followers, the world does not recognize Jesus as the way, the truth, and the life.

Jesus is going away, so how will his disciples be able to recall all that he taught them? Jesus explains: "The helper, the holy spirit, which the Father will send in my name, that one will teach you all things and bring back to your minds all the things I told you." The apostles have seen how powerfully the holy spirit can work, so this assurance is comforting. Jesus adds: "I leave you peace; I give you my peace. . . . Do not let your hearts be troubled nor let them shrink out of fear." (John 14:26, 27) The disciples have reason, then, not to be troubled—they will have direction and protection from Jesus' Father.

Evidence of God's protection will soon be seen. Jesus says: "The ruler of the world is coming, and he has no hold on me." (John 14:30) The Devil was able to enter into Judas and get a hold on him. But there is no sinful weakness in Jesus that Satan can play on to turn him against God. Nor will the Devil be able to restrain Jesus in death. Why not? Jesus states: "I am doing just as the Father has commanded me to do." He is certain that his Father will resurrect him.—John 14:31.

◇ Where is Jesus going, and what assurance does Thomas receive regarding the way there?
◇ What does Philip apparently want Jesus to provide?
◇ How will Jesus' followers do greater works than he is doing?
◇ Why is it reassuring that the Father is greater than Jesus?

BEARING FRUIT AS BRANCHES AND BEING JESUS' FRIENDS

JOHN 15:1-27

degenerate shoots of a foreign vine

Jesus has been encouraging his faithful apostles in a heart-to-heart talk. It is late, perhaps past midnight. Jesus now presents a motivating illustration:

"I am the true vine, and my Father is the cultivator," he begins. (John 15:1) His illustration resembles what had been said centuries earlier about the nation of Israel, which was called Jehovah's vine. (Jeremiah 2:21; Hosea 10:1, 2) However, Jehovah is casting off that nation. (Matthew 23:37, 38) So Jesus is introducing a new thought. He is the vine that his Father has been cultivating since anointing Jesus with holy spirit in 29 C.E. But Jesus shows that the vine symbolizes more than just him, saying:

"[My Father] takes away every branch in me not bearing fruit, and he cleans every one bearing fruit, so that it may bear more fruit. . . . Just as the branch cannot bear fruit by itself unless it remains in the vine, neither can you unless you remain in union with me. I am the vine; you are the branches."—John 15:2-5.

Jesus has promised his faithful disciples that after he goes away, he would send a helper, the holy spirit. Fifty-one days later, when the apostles and others receive that spirit, they become branches of the vine. And all the "branches" would have to remain united with Jesus. To accomplish what?

He explains: "Whoever remains in union with me and I in union with him, this one bears much fruit; for apart from me you can do nothing at all." These "branches"—his faithful followers—would bear much fruit, imitating Jesus' qualities, actively speaking to others about God's Kingdom, and making more disciples. What if one does not remain in union with Jesus and does not bear fruit? Jesus explains: "If

anyone does not remain in union with me, he is thrown out." On the other hand, Jesus says: "If you remain in union with me and my sayings remain in you, ask whatever you wish and it will take place for you."—John 15:5-7.

Now Jesus returns to what he has mentioned twice—keeping his commandments. (John 14:15, 21) He describes a key way for disciples to prove that they are doing so: "If you observe my commandments, you will remain in my love, just as I have observed the commandments of the Father and remain in his love." However, more is involved than loving Jehovah God and his Son. Jesus says: "This is my commandment, that you love one another just as I have loved you. No one has love greater than this, that someone should surrender his life in behalf of his friends. You are my friends if you do what I am commanding you."—John 15:10-14.

In a few hours, Jesus will demonstrate his love by giving his life for all who exercise faith in him. His example should move his followers to have similar self-sacrificing love for one another. This love will identify them, as Jesus stated earlier: "By this all will know that you are my disciples—if you have love among yourselves." —John 13:35.

The apostles should take note of Jesus' calling them "friends." He relates why they are such: "I have called you friends, because I have made known to you all the things I have heard from my Father." What a precious relationship to have—to be intimate friends of Jesus and to know what the Father told him! In order to enjoy this relationship, though, they must "keep bearing fruit." If they do, Jesus says, "no matter what you ask the Father in my name he [will] give it to you."—John 15:15, 16.

The love among these "branches," his disciples, will help them to endure what is to come. He warns them that the world will hate them, yet he offers this comfort: "If the world hates you, you know that it has hated me before it hated you. If you were part of the world, the world would be fond of what is its own. Now because you are no part of the world, . . . for this reason the world hates you."—John 15:18, 19.

Explaining further why the world will hate them, Jesus adds: "They will do all these things against you on account of my name, because they do not know the One who sent me." Jesus says that his miraculous works, in effect, convict those who hate him: "If I had not done among them the works that no one else did, they would have no sin; but now they have both seen me and hated me as well as my Father." Actually, their hatred fulfills prophecy.—John 15:21, 24, 25; Psalm 35:19; 69:4.

Again, Jesus promises to send the helper, the holy spirit. That powerful force is available for all his followers and is able to help them to bear fruit, "to bear witness."—John 15:27.

◊ Who is the cultivator, who is the vine, and who are the branches in Jesus' illustration?

◊ What fruit does God desire from the branches?

◊ How can Jesus' disciples be his friends, and what will help them to face up to the world's hatred?

"TAKE COURAGE! I HAVE CONQUERED THE WORLD"

JOHN 16:1-33

Simon Peter asks - Lord where are you going? - 0 follow untill later

Jesus and the apostles are poised to leave the upper room where they held the Passover meal. Having given them considerable admonition, Jesus adds: "I have said these things to you so that you may not be stumbled." Why was such a warning appropriate? He tells them: "Men will expel you from the synagogue. In fact, the hour is coming when everyone who kills you will think he has offered a sacred service to God."—John 16:1, 2.

That may be troubling news for the apostles. Although Jesus had said earlier that the world would hate them, he had not directly told them that they would be killed. Why not? "I did not tell you these things at first, because I was with you," he says. (John 16:4) Now he is forearming them before he departs. This may help them to avoid being stumbled later.

Jesus continues: "I am going to the One who sent me; yet not one of you asks me, 'Where are you going?'" Earlier that evening they had inquired about where he was going. (John 13:36; 14:5; 16:5) But now, shaken by what he said about persecution, they are absorbed in their own grief. Thus they fail to ask further about the glory that awaits him or what that would mean for true worshippers. Jesus observes: "Because I have told you these things, grief has filled your hearts."—John 16:6.

Then Jesus explains: "It is for your benefit that I am going away. For if I do not go away, the helper will not come to you; but if I do go, I will send him to you." (John 16:7) Only by Jesus' dying and going to heaven can his disciples receive the holy spirit, which he can send as a helper to his people anywhere on earth.

The holy spirit "will give the world convincing evidence concerning sin and concerning righteousness and concerning judgment." (John 16:8) Yes, the world's failure to exercise faith in God's Son will be exposed. Jesus' ascension to heaven will provide convincing evidence of his righteousness and will demonstrate why Satan, "the ruler of this world," merits adverse judgment.—John 16:11.

"I still have many things to say to you," Jesus continues, "but you are not able to bear them now." When he pours out the holy spirit, it will guide them to an understanding of "all the truth," and they will be able to live by that truth. —John 16:12, 13.

The apostles are puzzled by Jesus' further statement: "In a little while you will see me no longer, and again, in a little while you will see me." They ask one another what he means. Jesus realizes that they want to question him about this, so he explains: "Most truly I say to you, you will weep and wail, but the world will rejoice; you will be grieved, but your grief will be turned into joy." (John 16:16, 20) When Jesus is killed the next afternoon, the religious leaders rejoice, but the disciples grieve. Then their grief changes into joy when Jesus is resurrected! And their joy continues when he pours out upon them God's holy spirit.

Comparing the apostles' situation to that of a woman during birth pangs, Jesus says: "When a woman is giving birth, she has grief because her hour has come, but when she has given birth to the child, she remembers the tribulation no more because of the joy that a man has been born into the world." Jesus encourages his apostles, saying: "You also, now you have grief; but I will see you again, and your hearts will rejoice, and no one will take away your joy."—John 16:21, 22.

Up to this time, the apostles have never made requests in Jesus' name. He now says: "In that day you will make request of the Father in my name." Why are they to do so? Not because the Father is reluctant to respond. In fact, Jesus says: "The Father himself has affection for you, because you have had affection for me . . . as God's representative."—John 16:26, 27.

Jesus' encouraging words to the apostles may have emboldened them to affirm: "By this we believe that you came from God." That conviction will soon be tested. In fact, Jesus describes what is just ahead: "Look! The hour is coming, indeed, it has come, when each one of you will be scattered to his own house and you will leave me alone." Yet he assures them: "I have said these things to you so that by means of me you may have peace. In the world you will have tribulation, but take courage! I have conquered the world." (John 16:30-33) No, Jesus is not abandoning them. He is sure that they too can be world conquerors, just as he is, by their faithfully accomplishing God's will despite the attempts of Satan and his world to break their integrity.

◊ The apostles are troubled when Jesus gives what warning? *They may face death*
◊ Why do the apostles fail to ask Jesus any further questions?
◊ How does Jesus illustrate the apostles' change from grief to joy?

JESUS' CONCLUDING PRAYER IN THE UPPER ROOM

JOHN 17:1-26

Moved by deep love for his apostles, Jesus has been preparing them for his imminent departure. He now raises his eyes to heaven and prays to his Father: "Glorify your son so that your son may glorify you, just as you have given him authority over all flesh, so that he may give everlasting life to all those whom you have given to him."—John 17:1, 2.

Clearly, Jesus recognizes that giving God glory is of prime importance. But how comforting is the prospect that Jesus mentions—everlasting life! Having received "authority over all flesh," Jesus can offer the benefits of his ransom to all mankind. Yet, only some will be so blessed. Why only some? Because Jesus will impart the benefits of his ransom only to those who act in accord with what Jesus next mentions: "This means everlasting life, their coming to know you, the only true God, and the one whom you sent, Jesus Christ."—John 17:3.

A person must come to know both the Father and the Son intimately, having a close bond with them. He must feel as they do about matters. Further, he must strive to imitate their matchless qualities in dealing with others. And he must appreciate that humans' receiving everlasting life is secondary to the glorification of God. Jesus now returns to this theme:

"I have glorified you on the earth, having finished the work you have given me to do. So now, Father, glorify me at your side with the glory that I had alongside you before the world was." (John 17:4, 5) Yes, Jesus asks to be restored to heavenly glory by means of a resurrection.

However, Jesus has not forgotten what he has accomplished in his ministry. He prays: "I have made your name manifest to the men whom you gave me out of the world. They were yours, and you gave them to me, and they have observed your word." (John 17:6) Jesus did more than pronounce God's name, Jehovah, in his ministry. He helped his apostles to come to know what the name represents—God's qualities and his way of dealing with humans.

The apostles have come to know Jehovah, the role of his Son, and the things Jesus has taught. Jesus humbly says: "I have given them the sayings that you gave me, and they have accepted them and have certainly come to know that I came as your representative, and they have believed that you sent me."—John 17:8.

Jesus then acknowledges the distinction between his followers and the world of mankind in general: "I make request, not concerning the world, but concerning those whom you have given me, because they are yours . . . Holy Father, watch over them on account of your own name, which you have given me, so that they may be one just as we are one. . . . I have protected them, and not one of them is destroyed except the son of destruction," namely, Judas Iscariot, who is on his mission to betray Jesus. —John 17:9-12.

"The world has hated them," Jesus continues to pray. "I do not request that you take them out of the world, but that you watch over them because of the wicked one. They are no part of the world, just as I am no part of the world." (John 17:14-16) The apostles and other disciples are in the world, human society ruled by Satan, but they must remain separate from it and its badness. How?

They must keep themselves holy, set apart to serve God, by applying the truths found in the Hebrew Scriptures and the truths that Jesus himself has taught. Jesus prays: "Sanctify them by means of the truth; your word is truth." (John 17:17) In time, some of the apostles will write inspired books that will also be part of "the truth" that can help to sanctify a person.

But there will in time be others who will accept "the truth." Jesus thus prays "not concerning these only [those who are there], but also concerning those putting faith in [him] through their word." What does Jesus request for all of them? "That they may all be one, just as you, Father, are in union with me and I am in union with you, that they also may be in union with us." (John 17:20, 21) Jesus and his Father are not literally one person. They are one in that they are in agreement on all things. Jesus prays that his followers enjoy this same oneness.

Shortly before this, Jesus had told Peter and the others that he was going his way to prepare a place for them, meaning a place in heaven. (John 14:2, 3) Jesus now returns to that idea in prayer: "Father, I want those whom you have given me to be with me where I am, in order that they may look upon my glory that you have given me, because you loved me before the founding of the world." (John 17:24) He thus confirms that long ago—before Adam and Eve conceived offspring—God loved his only-begotten Son, who became Jesus Christ.

Concluding his prayer, Jesus reemphasizes both his Father's name and God's love for the apostles and for others who will yet accept "the truth," saying: "I have made your name known to them and will make it known, so that the love with which you loved me may be in them and I in union with them."—John 17:26.

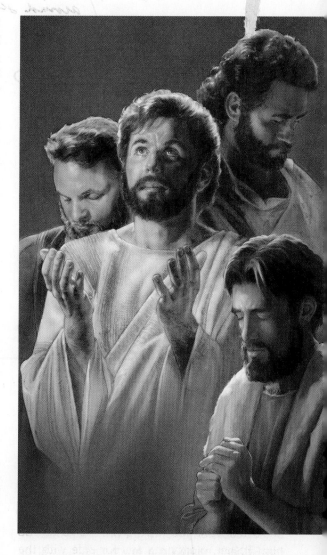

◇ What does coming to know God and his Son mean?

◇ In what ways has Jesus made God's name manifest?

◇ How are God, his Son, and all true worshippers one?

PRAYING WHEN DEEPLY GRIEVED

MATTHEW 26:30, 36-46   MARK 14:26, 32-42   LUKE 22:39-46   JOHN 18:1

vs 34   ? local - Romans cut da all trees around Jerusalem in 70 CE.

Jesus finishes praying with his faithful apostles. Then, 'after singing praises, they go out to the Mount of Olives.' (Mark 14:26) They head eastward to a garden called Gethsemane, where Jesus is accustomed to going.

Once they arrive at this pleasant spot among the olive trees, Jesus leaves eight of the apostles behind. Perhaps they remain near the garden's entrance, for he tells them: "Sit down here while I go over there and pray." Taking along three apostles—Peter, James, and John—Jesus goes farther into the garden. He becomes greatly troubled and tells the three: "I am deeply grieved, even to death. Stay here and keep on the watch with me."—Matthew 26:36-38.

sons of Zeb

Going some distance away from them, Jesus 'falls to the ground and begins praying.' What is he praying to God about at this intense moment? He prays: "Father, all things are possible for you; remove this cup from me. Yet, not what I want, but what you want." (Mark 14:35, 36) What does he mean? Is he backing away from his role as Ransomer? No!

Jesus has observed from heaven the extreme suffering of others put to death by the Romans. Now as a human, who has tender feelings and who can feel pain, Jesus is not looking forward to what awaits him. More important, though, he is in agony because he senses that his dying like a despicable criminal might bring reproach on his Father's name. In a few hours, he will be hanged on a stake as if he were a blasphemer against God.

After praying at length, Jesus returns and finds the three apostles sleeping. He says to Peter: "Could you not so much as keep on the watch for one hour with me? Keep on the watch and pray continually, so that you may not enter into temptation." Jesus realizes that the apostles too have been under stress, and it is late. He adds: "The spirit, of course, is eager, but the flesh is weak."—Matthew 26:40, 41.

Then Jesus goes off a second time and asks that God remove from him "this cup." On returning, he once again finds the three apostles asleep, when they should have been praying that they not enter into temptation. When Jesus speaks to them, they do "not know what to answer him." (Mark 14:40) A third time Jesus goes off, and he bends down on his knees to pray.

Jesus is deeply concerned about the reproach that his death as a criminal will bring on his Father's name. Jehovah is hearing his Son's prayers, though, and at one point God sends an angel to strengthen him. Even so, Jesus does not stop supplicating his Father, but he keeps "praying more earnestly." The emotional stress is enormous. What a weight is on Jesus' shoulders! His own eternal life and that of believing

HIS SWEAT IS AS DROPS OF BLOOD

Physician Luke does not explain how Jesus' sweat "became as drops of blood." (Luke 22:44) Luke may have been speaking illustratively, that the sweat resembled blood dripping from a wound. An alternate idea was offered by Dr. William D. Edwards in *The Journal of the American Medical Association* (JAMA): "Although this is a very rare phenomenon, bloody sweat (hematidrosis . . .) may occur in highly emotional states . . . As a result of hemorrhage into the sweat glands, the skin becomes fragile and tender."

figure of speech for God's will or assigned portion

humans is at stake. In fact, his 'sweat becomes as drops of blood falling to the ground.'—Luke 22:44.

When Jesus returns the third time to his apostles, he again finds them sleeping. "At such a time as this," he says, "you are sleeping and resting! Look! The hour has drawn near for the Son of man to be betrayed into the hands of sinners. Get up, let us go. Look! My betrayer has drawn near."—Matthew 26:45, 46.

◇ After leaving the upper room, where does Jesus lead the apostles?

◇ What are three apostles doing while Jesus prays?

◇ That Jesus' sweat becomes as drops of blood indicates what about his feelings?

CHRIST IS BETRAYED AND ARRESTED

MATTHEW 26:47-56   MARK 14:43-52   LUKE 22:47-53   JOHN 18:2-12

It is well past midnight. The priests have agreed to pay Judas 30 pieces of silver to betray Jesus. So Judas leads a large crowd of chief priests and Pharisees, seeking to find Jesus. They are accompanied by a detachment of armed Roman soldiers with a military commander.

Evidently, when Jesus dismissed him from the Passover meal, Judas went directly to the chief priests. (John 13:27) They assembled their own officers as well as a band of soldiers. Judas may have led them first to the room where Jesus and his apostles had celebrated the Passover. But now the mob has crossed the Kidron Valley and is headed for the garden. In addition to weapons, they are carrying lamps and torches, determined to find Jesus.

As Judas leads the procession up the Mount of Olives, he feels sure that he knows where to find Jesus. During the past week, as Jesus and the apostles traveled back and forth between Bethany and Jerusalem, they often stopped in the garden of Gethsemane. But now it is night, and Jesus may be in the shadows of the olive trees in the garden. So how will the soldiers, who may not have seen Jesus before, be able to identify him? To help them, Judas will provide a sign. He says: "Whoever it is I kiss, he is the one; take him into custody, and lead him away under guard."—Mark 14:44.

Leading the crowd into the garden, Judas sees Jesus with his apostles and goes straight up to him. "Greetings, Rabbi!" Judas says, and he kisses Jesus very tenderly. "Fellow, for what purpose are you present?" Jesus responds. (Matthew 26:49, 50) Answering his own question, Jesus says: "Judas, are you betraying the Son of man with a kiss?" (Luke 22:48) But that is enough of his betrayer!

Jesus now steps into the light of the torches and lamps and asks: "Whom are you looking for?" From the mob comes the answer: "Jesus the Nazarene." Jesus courageously says: "I am he." (John 18:4, 5) Not knowing what to expect, the men fall to the ground.

Rather than seizing that moment to flee into the night, Jesus again asks whom they are seeking. When they again say, "Jesus the Nazarene," he calmly continues: "I told you that I am he. So if you are looking for me, let these men go." Even at this crucial moment, Jesus recalls what he said earlier, that he would not lose a single one. (John 6:39; 17:12) Jesus has kept his faithful apostles and not one has been lost "except the son of destruction"—Judas. (John 18:7-9) Thus he now asks that his loyal followers be let go.

As the soldiers stand and move toward Jesus, the apostles realize what is happening. "Lord, should we strike with the sword?" they ask. (Luke 22:49) Before Jesus can reply, Peter wields one of the two swords that the apostles have at hand. He attacks Malchus, a slave of the high priest, cutting off his right ear.

Jesus touches the ear of Malchus, healing the wound. He then teaches an important lesson, commanding Peter: "Return your sword to its place, for all those who take up the sword will perish by the sword." Jesus is willing to be arrested, for he explains: "How would the Scriptures be fulfilled that say it must take place this way?" (Matthew 26:52, 54) He adds: "Should I not drink the cup that the Father has given me?" (John 18:11) Jesus agrees with God's will for him, even to the point of dying.

Jesus asks the crowd: "Did you come out to arrest me with swords and clubs as against a robber? Day after day I used to sit in the temple teaching, and yet you did not take me into custody. But all of this has taken place for the writings of the prophets to be fulfilled."—Matthew 26:55, 56.

The soldier band, the military commander, and the officers of the Jews seize Jesus and bind him. Seeing this, the apostles flee. However, "a certain young man"—perhaps the disciple Mark—remains among the crowd so as to follow Jesus. (Mark 14:51) This young man is recognized, and the crowd attempts to seize him, which forces him to leave behind his linen garment as he gets away.

◇ Why does Judas look for Jesus in the garden of Gethsemane?

◇ Trying to defend Jesus, what does Peter do, but what does Jesus say about this?

◇ How does Jesus reveal that he is in agreement with God's will for him?

◇ When the apostles abandon Jesus, who remains, and what happens then?

JESUS IS TAKEN TO ANNAS, THEN TO CAIAPHAS

MATTHEW 26:57-68   MARK 14:53-65   LUKE 22:54, 63-65   JOHN 18:13, 14, 19-24

Once Jesus is bound like a common criminal, he is led to Annas, who was the high priest when young Jesus amazed the teachers at the temple. (Luke 2:42, 47) Some of Annas' sons later served as high priest, and now his son-in-law Caiaphas holds that position.

While Jesus is at the home of Annas, Caiaphas has time to assemble the Sanhedrin. That court of 71 members includes the high priest and others who had held that office.

Annas questions Jesus "about his disciples and about his teaching." Jesus replies simply: "I have spoken to the world publicly. I always taught in a synagogue and in the temple, where all the Jews come together, and I said nothing in secret. Why do you question me? Question those who have heard what I told them."—John 18:19-21.

An officer standing there slaps Jesus in the face and says reprovingly: "Is that the way you answer the chief priest?" But Jesus, knowing that he has done no wrong, responds: "If I said something wrong, bear witness about the wrong; but if what I said was right, why do you hit me?" (John 18:22, 23) Annas then has Jesus taken away to his son-in-law Caiaphas.

By now those composing the whole Sanhedrin—the current high priest, the elders of the

people, and the scribes—have assembled. They meet at the home of Caiaphas. It is illegal to hold such a trial on the night of Passover, but this does not deter them from pursuing their wicked purpose.

This is hardly an unbiased group. After Jesus resurrected Lazarus, the Sanhedrin decided that Jesus should die. (John 11:47-53) And just days ago the religious authorities conspired to seize Jesus and kill him. (Matthew 26:3, 4) Yes, even before his trial begins, Jesus is as good as condemned to death!

In addition to meeting illegally, the chief priests and others of the Sanhedrin are attempting to find witnesses who will give false evidence to build the case against Jesus. They find many, but these cannot agree as to their testimony. Finally, two come forward and claim: "We heard him say, 'I will throw down this temple that was made with hands, and in three days I will build another not made with hands.'" (Mark 14:58) Yet even these men do not fully agree.

Caiaphas asks Jesus: "Do you say nothing in reply? What is it these men are testifying against you?" (Mark 14:60) Jesus remains silent in the face of this false charge made by witnesses whose stories disagree. So High Priest Caiaphas switches to a different tactic.

Caiaphas knows that the Jews are sensitive about anyone claiming to be the Son of God. Earlier, when Jesus had called God his Father, the Jews wanted to kill him because they claimed that he was "making himself equal to God." (John 5:17, 18; 10:31-39) Aware of such sentiments, Caiaphas now craftily demands of Jesus: "I put you under oath by the living God to tell us whether you are the Christ, the Son of God!" (Matthew 26:63) Of course, Jesus has acknowledged being the Son of God. (John 3:18; 5:25; 11:4) If he does not do so now, that could be construed as denying that he is God's Son and the Christ. So Jesus says: "I am; and you will see the Son of man sitting at the right hand of power and coming with the clouds of heaven."—Mark 14:62.

At this, Caiaphas with great drama rips his garments and exclaims: "He has blasphemed! What further need do we have of witnesses? See! Now you have heard the blasphemy. What is your opinion?" The Sanhedrin hand down the unjust judgment: "He deserves to die."—Matthew 26:65, 66.

Then they begin to mock Jesus and hit him with their fists. Others slap his face and spit into it. After they cover his whole face and slap him, they say sarcastically: "Prophesy! Who is it that struck you?" (Luke 22:64) Here is the Son of God being treated abusively at an illegal nighttime trial!

◇ Where is Jesus led first, and what happens to him there?

◇ Where is Jesus next taken, and how is Caiaphas able to get the Sanhedrin to proclaim that Jesus deserves to die?

◇ What abusive behavior occurs during the trial?

DENIALS AT THE HOUSE OF CAIAPHAS

MATTHEW 26:69-75   MARK 14:66-72   LUKE 22:54-62   JOHN 18:15-18, 25-27

John does not refer to himself in his gospel account

Upon Jesus' being arrested in the garden of Gethsemane, the apostles abandon him, fleeing in fear. However, two of them stop their flight. They are Peter "as well as another disciple," evidently the apostle John. (John 18:15; 19:35; 21:24) They may catch up with Jesus as he is taken to the home of Annas. When Annas sends Jesus to High Priest Caiaphas, Peter and John follow at a distance. They are likely torn between fear for their own lives and concern for what will happen to their Master.

John is known to the high priest and is thus able to gain entrance into the courtyard at Caiaphas' house. Peter remains outside at the door until John returns and speaks to a servant girl who is acting as doorkeeper. Then Peter is allowed to enter. *by now it verb ends it*

It is cold this night, so those in the courtyard have a charcoal fire burning. Peter sits with them to keep warm as he waits "to see the outcome" of Jesus' trial. (Matthew 26:58) Now, in the light of the fire, the doorkeeper who let Peter in gets a better look at him. "You are not also one of this man's disciples, are you?" she demands. (John 18:17) And she is not alone in recognizing Peter and accusing him of being with Jesus.—Matthew 26:69, 71-73; Mark 14:70. *twice*

This greatly upsets Peter. He is trying to be inconspicuous, even withdrawing to the entryway. So Peter denies that he was with Jesus, at one point saying: "Neither do I know him nor do I understand what you are talking about." (Mark 14:67, 68) He also starts to "curse and swear," meaning that he is willing to take an oath that

his words are true and to face calamity if they are not.—Matthew 26:74.

Meanwhile, Jesus' trial is in progress, apparently in a part of Caiaphas' house that is above the courtyard. Peter and the others waiting below may see the comings and goings of various witnesses who are brought in to testify.

Peter's Galilean accent is an indication that his denial is false. Moreover, one in the group is related to Malchus, whose ear Peter cut off. So the charge is leveled against Peter: "I saw you in the garden with him, did I not?" When Peter denies this for a third time, a rooster crows, as was foretold.—John 13:38; 18:26, 27.

At that point, Jesus apparently is on a balcony overlooking the courtyard. The Lord turns and looks straight at Peter, which must pierce Peter to the core. He recalls what Jesus said only a few hours earlier in the upper room. Imagine how Peter feels as the realization of what he has done crashes down on him! Peter goes outside and weeps bitterly.—Luke 22:61, 62.

How could this happen? How could Peter—who was so certain of his spiritual strength and loyalty—deny his Master? Truth is being distorted, and Jesus is being depicted as a vile criminal. When Peter could have stood up for an innocent man, he turned his back on the very One who has "sayings of everlasting life."—John 6:68.

Peter's tragic experience shows that even a person of faith and devotion can be thrown off balance if he is not properly prepared for unexpected trials or temptations. May what Peter went through serve as a warning to all of God's servants!

◊ How do Peter and John gain entrance to the courtyard at Caiaphas' house?

◊ While Peter and John are in the courtyard, what is going on in the house?

◊ What does it mean that Peter curses and swears?

◊ Peter's experience contains what serious lesson?

TRIED BY THE SANHEDRIN, THEN ON TO PILATE

MATTHEW 27:1-11   MARK 15:1   LUKE 22:66–23:3   JOHN 18:28-35

The night is drawing to a close when Peter denies Jesus for the third time. The members of the Sanhedrin have finished with their mock trial and have dispersed. Come dawn Friday morning, they reconvene, likely to give some cloak of legality to the illegal night trial. Jesus is brought before them.

Again the court demands: "If you are the Christ, tell us." Jesus answers: "Even if I told you, you would not believe it at all. Moreover, if I questioned you, you would not answer." However, Jesus courageously indicates to them his identity as the one foretold at Daniel 7:13. He says: "From now on the Son of man will be seated at the powerful right hand of God."—Luke 22: 67-69; Matthew 26:63.

They persist: "Are you, therefore, the Son of God?" Jesus replies: "You yourselves are saying that I am." This seems to justify killing Jesus on the charge of blasphemy. "Why do we need further testimony?" they ask. (Luke 22:70, 71; Mark 14:64) So they bind Jesus and lead him away to Roman Governor Pontius Pilate.

Judas Iscariot may see Jesus being taken to Pilate. When Judas realizes that Jesus has been condemned, he feels a certain remorse and despair. However, rather than turning to God in true repentance, he goes to give back the 30 pieces of silver. Judas tells the chief priests: "I sinned when I betrayed innocent blood." But he gets the heartless reply: "What is that to us? You must see to it!"—Matthew 27:4.

Judas throws the 30 silver pieces into the temple and then adds to his wrongs by attempting self-murder. As Judas tries to hang himself, apparently the branch to which he ties the rope breaks. His body drops to the rocks below, where it bursts apart.—Acts 1:17, 18.

It is still early in the morning when Jesus is taken to the palace of Pontius Pilate. But

the Jews taking him there refuse to enter. They think that such contact with Gentiles will defile them. That would disqualify them from eating the meal on Nisan 15, the first day of the Festival of Unleavened Bread, which is viewed as part of the Passover period.

Pilate comes out and asks them: "What accusation do you bring against this man?" They respond: "If this man were not a wrongdoer, we would not have handed him over to you." Pilate may feel that they are trying to pressure him, so he says: "Take him yourselves and judge him according to your law." The Jews reveal their murderous intent, replying: "It is not lawful for us to kill anyone."—John 18:29-31.

Actually, if they kill Jesus during the Passover festival, it will likely cause a public uproar. Yet if they can get the Romans to execute Jesus on a political charge, which the Romans are authorized to do, it will tend to absolve these Jews of responsibility before the people.

The religious leaders do not tell Pilate that they had condemned Jesus for blasphemy. Now they trump up different charges: "We found this man [1] subverting our nation, [2] forbidding the paying of taxes to Caesar, and [3] saying he himself is Christ a king."—Luke 23:2.

As a representative of Rome, Pilate has reason for concern about the charge that Jesus is claiming to be a king. So Pilate reenters the palace, calls Jesus to him, and asks: "Are you the King of the Jews?" In other words, 'Have you broken the law of the empire by declaring yourself to be a king in opposition to Caesar?' Perhaps to find out how much Pilate already has heard about him, Jesus says: "Are you asking this of your own originality, or did others tell you about me?"—John 18:33, 34.

Professing ignorance of the facts about Jesus but desiring to learn them, Pilate replies: "I am not a Jew, am I?" He adds: "Your own nation and the chief priests handed you over to me. What did you do?"—John 18:35.

Jesus does not attempt to dodge the central issue—kingship. He answers in a way that no doubt greatly surprises Governor Pilate.

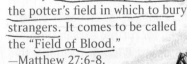

THE FIELD OF BLOOD The chief priests are not sure what to do with the silver pieces that Judas throws into the temple. "It is not lawful to put them into the sacred treasury," they say, "because they are the price of blood." So they use the money to purchase the potter's field in which to bury strangers. It comes to be called the "Field of Blood."—Matthew 27:6-8.

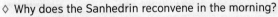

◇ Why does the Sanhedrin reconvene in the morning?

◇ How does Judas die, and what happens to the 30 pieces of silver?

◇ On what charges do the Jews want Pilate to have Jesus killed?

FOUND INNOCENT BY BOTH PILATE AND HEROD

MATTHEW 27:12-14, 18, 19   MARK 15:2-5   LUKE 23:4-16   JOHN 18:36-38

Jesus does not try to conceal from Pilate that he really is a king. Still, his Kingdom is no threat to Rome. "My Kingdom is no part of this world," Jesus says. "If my Kingdom were part of this world, my attendants would have fought that I should not be handed over to the Jews. But as it is, my Kingdom is not from this source." (John 18:36) Yes, Jesus has a Kingdom, but it is not of this world.

Pilate does not leave the issue at that. He asks: "Well, then, are you a king?" Jesus lets Pilate know that he has drawn the right conclusion, answering: "You yourself are saying that I am a king. For this I have been born, and for this I have come into the world, that I should bear witness to the truth. Everyone who is on the side of the truth listens to my voice."—John 18:37.

Jesus had earlier told Thomas: "I am the way and the truth and the life." Now even Pilate hears that the purpose of Jesus' being sent to earth is to bear witness to "the truth," specifically the truth about his Kingdom. Jesus is determined to be faithful to that truth even if it costs him his life. Pilate asks: "What is truth?" but he does not wait for further explanation. He feels that he has heard enough to judge this man.—John 14:6; 18:38.

Pilate returns to the crowd waiting outside the palace. Jesus apparently is at his side when he tells the chief priests and those with them: "I find no crime in this man." Angered by that decision, the crowd insists: "He stirs up the people by teaching throughout all Judea, starting from Galilee even to here."—Luke 23: 4, 5.

The Jews' unreasoning fanaticism must amaze Pilate. As the chief priests and older men continue shouting, Pilate asks Jesus: "Do you not hear how many things they are testifying against you?" (Matthew 27:13) Jesus makes no attempt to answer. His calm in the face of the wild accusations surprises Pilate.

The Jews indicated that Jesus had 'started from Galilee.' Pursuing that clue, Pilate learns that Jesus is, in fact, a Galilean. This gives Pilate an idea of how he might escape responsibility for judging Jesus. Herod Antipas (the son of Herod the Great) is the ruler of Galilee, and he is in Jerusalem this Passover season. So Pilate sends Jesus to Herod. It was Herod Antipas who had John the Baptist beheaded. Later, at hearing that Jesus was performing miraculous works, Herod was concerned that Jesus might be John raised from the dead.—Luke 9: 7-9.

Herod now rejoices at the prospect of seeing Jesus. This is not because he wants to help Jesus or wishes to make any real attempt to learn whether there are valid charges against him. Herod is simply curious, and he is "hoping to see some sign performed by him." (Luke 23:8) However, Jesus does not satisfy Herod's curiosity. In fact, as Herod questions him, Jesus says not a word. Disappointed, both Herod and his soldiers treat Jesus "with contempt." (Luke 23: 11) They clothe him with a splendid garment and mock him. Then Herod sends Jesus back to Pilate. Herod and Pilate had been enemies, but now they become good friends.

When Jesus returns, Pilate calls together the chief priests, the Jewish rulers, and the people and says: "I examined him in front of you but found in this man no grounds for the charges you are bringing against him. In fact, neither did Herod, for he sent him back to us, and look!

he has done nothing deserving of death. I will therefore punish him and release him."—Luke 23:14-16.

Pilate is eager to free Jesus, for he realizes that it is out of envy that the priests have handed him over. As Pilate tries to release Jesus, he receives further motivation to do so.

While he is on his judgment seat, his wife sends him the message: "Have nothing to do with that righteous man, for I suffered a lot today in a dream [evidently of divine origin] because of him."—Matthew 27:19.

How can Pilate release this innocent man, as he should?

◇ How does Jesus tell "the truth" regarding his kingship?

◇ Pilate reaches what conclusion about Jesus, how do the people respond, and what does Pilate do?

◇ Why is Herod Antipas pleased to see Jesus, and what does he do with him?

◇ Why does Pilate want to free Jesus?

PILATE PROCLAIMS: "LOOK! THE MAN!"

MATTHEW 27:15-17, 20-30   MARK 15:6-19   LUKE 23:18-25   JOHN 18:39–19:5

Pilate told the crowd seeking Jesus' death: "I . . . found in this man no grounds for the charges you are bringing against him. In fact, neither did Herod." (Luke 23:14, 15) Now, trying to spare Jesus, Pilate uses another approach, saying to the people: "You have a custom that I should release a man to you at the Passover. So do you want me to release to you the King of the Jews?"—John 18:39.

Pilate is aware of a prisoner named Barabbas, who is known as a robber, a seditionist, and a murderer. So Pilate asks: "Which one do you want me to release to you, Barabbas or Jesus the so-called Christ?" Having been stirred up by the chief priests, the people ask that Barabbas be released, not Jesus. Pilate asks again: "Which of the two do you want me to release to you?" The crowd shouts: "Barabbas"!—Matthew 27:17, 21.

Dismayed, Pilate asks: "What, then, should I do with Jesus the so-called Christ?" The people roar: "To the stake with him!" (Matthew 27:22) To their shame, they are demanding the death of an innocent man. Pilate pleads: "Why? What bad thing did this man do? I found in him nothing deserving of death; I will therefore punish him and release him."—Luke 23:22.

Despite Pilate's repeated efforts, the enraged crowd yells in unison: "To the stake with him!" (Matthew 27:23) The religious leaders have worked the crowd into such a frenzy that they want blood! And it is not the blood of some criminal, some murderer. It is the blood of an innocent man who five days before was welcomed into Jerusalem as King. If Jesus' disciples are present, they remain silent and inconspicuous.

Pilate sees that his appeals are doing no good. An uproar is arising, so he takes some water and washes his hands before the eyes of the crowd. He tells them: "I am innocent of the blood of this man. You yourselves must see to it." Even that does not put the people off. Rather, they say: "Let his blood come upon us and upon our children."—Matthew 27:24, 25.

The governor wishes to satisfy them more than he wishes to do what he knows is right. So in accord with their demand, Pilate releases Barabbas to the mob. He has Jesus stripped and then scourged.

After this torturous beating, the soldiers take

SCOURGING Dr. William D. Edwards in *The Journal of the American Medical Association* describes the Roman practice of scourging:

"The usual instrument was a short whip (flagrum or flagellum) with several single or braided leather thongs of variable lengths, in which small iron balls or sharp pieces of sheep bones were tied at intervals. . . . As the Roman soldiers repeatedly struck the victim's back with full force, the iron balls would cause deep contusions, and the leather thongs and sheep bones would cut into the skin and subcutaneous tissues. Then, as the flogging continued, the lacerations would tear into the underlying skeletal muscles and produce quivering ribbons of bleeding flesh."

Jesus into the governor's palace. The body of troops gather and heap further abuse on him. They braid a crown of thorns and push it down on his head. The soldiers also put a reed in Jesus' right hand and put a scarlet-colored robe on him, such as is worn by royalty. They say with scorn: "Greetings, you King of the Jews!" (Matthew 27:28, 29) More than that, they spit on Jesus and keep slapping his face. Taking the sturdy reed from him, they hit him on the head with it, driving deeper into his scalp the sharp thorns of his humiliating "crown."

Jesus' remarkable dignity and strength through all of this so impresses Pilate that he makes another attempt to absolve himself, saying: "See! I bring him outside to you in order for you to know that I find no fault in him." Could Pilate think that bringing Jesus out now, bruised and bleeding, would move the crowds to relent? As Jesus stands before the heartless mob, Pilate proclaims: "Look! The man!"—John 19:4, 5.

Though battered and wounded, Jesus displays a quiet dignity and calm that even Pilate must acknowledge, for his words seem to mingle respect with pity.

◇ How does Pilate attempt to have Jesus released and thereby absolve himself of responsibility?

◇ What is involved in being scourged?

◇ After Jesus is scourged, how is he further mistreated?

JESUS IS HANDED OVER AND LED AWAY TO DIE

MATTHEW 27:31, 32   MARK 15:20, 21   LUKE 23:24-31   JOHN 19:6-17

Despite Jesus' having been viciously abused and ridiculed, Pilate's efforts to release him do not move the chief priests and their accomplices. They want nothing to prevent having Jesus put to death. They keep shouting: "To the stake with him! To the stake with him!" Pilate responds: "Take him yourselves and execute him, for I do not find any fault in him." —John 19:6.

The Jews do not convince Pilate that Jesus is worthy of death on a political charge, but what about a religious one? They fall back on the charge of blasphemy that was raised at Jesus' trial before the Sanhedrin. "We have a law," they say, "and according to the law he ought to die, because he made himself God's son." (John 19:7) This is a new charge for Pilate.

He goes back into his palace and tries to find a way to release this man who has borne up under severe treatment and about whom Pilate's own wife had a dream. (Matthew 27:19) What of this new charge that the Jews are making—that the prisoner is "God's son"? Pilate knows that Jesus is from Galilee. (Luke 23:5-7) Yet he asks Jesus: "Where are you from?" (John 19:9) Could Pilate be wondering whether Jesus might have lived before and, in some sense, be of divine origin?

Pilate had heard directly from Jesus that he is a king but that his Kingdom is no part of this world. Not needing to elaborate on what he earlier said, Jesus remains silent. His refusal to reply stings Pilate's pride, and he indignantly says to Jesus: "Are you refusing to speak to me? Do you not know that I have authority to release you and I have authority to execute you?"—John 19:10.

Jesus says simply: "You would have no authority over me at all unless it had been granted to you from above. This is why the man who handed me over to you has greater sin." (John 19:11) Jesus likely does not have in mind one specific individual. Rather, he means that Caiaphas, his accomplices, and Judas Iscariot bear a heavier responsibility than Pilate does.

Impressed by Jesus' comportment and words, and increasingly fearful that Jesus may be of divine origin, Pilate tries again to release him. However, the Jews bring up another fear that Pilate must have. They threaten: "If you release this man, you are not a friend of Caesar. Everyone who makes himself a king speaks against Caesar."—John 19:12.

The governor brings Jesus outside once more and, sitting on the judgment seat, tells the people: "See! Your king!" The Jews will not relent, though. "Take him away! Take him away! To the stake with him!" they shout. Pilate pleads: "Shall I execute your king?" The Jews have long chafed under Roman rule; still, the chief priests boldly assert: "We have no king but Caesar." —John 19:14, 15.

Cowardly caving in under the Jews' relentless demands, Pilate hands Jesus over to be executed. The soldiers strip the scarlet-colored cloak off Jesus and put on his outer garments. As Jesus is led off, he must bear his own torture stake.

It is now well into the morning of Friday, Nisan 14. Jesus has been awake since early Thursday morning and has suffered one agonizing experience after another. As he struggles under the weight of the stake, Jesus' strength gives out. So the soldiers force a passerby, Simon from Cyrene in Africa, to carry the stake to the place of execution. Many people follow, some

beating themselves in grief and bewailing what is happening.

Jesus says to the grieving women: "Daughters of Jerusalem, stop weeping for me. Weep instead for yourselves and for your children; for look! days are coming when people will say, 'Happy are the barren women, the wombs that did not give birth and the breasts that did not nurse!' Then they will start saying to the mountains, 'Fall over us!' and to the hills, 'Cover us over!' If they do these things when the tree is moist, what will occur when it is withered?" —Luke 23:28-31.

Jesus is referring to the Jewish nation. It is like a dying tree that still has some moisture left, for Jesus is present and so are a number of Jews who believe in him. When these are taken out from the nation, only a spiritually withered national organization will remain, being like a dead tree. There will be intense weeping when the Roman armies act as God's executioners against that nation!

◇ The religious leaders make what charge against Jesus?
◇ Why does Pilate grow fearful?
◇ How do the chief priests get Pilate to have Jesus executed?
◇ What does Jesus mean by referring to the tree as "moist" and then "withered"?

AN INNOCENT KING SUFFERS ON THE STAKE

MATTHEW 27:33-44   MARK 15:22-32   LUKE 23:32-43   JOHN 19:17-24

Jesus is led to a location not far from the city where he and two robbers are to be executed. The place is called Golgotha, or Skull Place, and is a spot that is visible "from a distance."—Mark 15:40.

The three condemned men are stripped of their garments. Then wine drugged with myrrh and bitter gall is provided. Apparently, women of Jerusalem have prepared the mixture, and the Romans do not deny this pain-dulling potion to those being put to death. Upon tasting it, though, Jesus refuses to drink any. Why? He wants to have full possession of all his senses during this major test; he wants to be conscious and faithful to death.

Jesus is stretched out on the stake. (Mark 15: 25) The soldiers pound nails into his hands and his feet, piercing flesh and ligaments, causing intense pain. As the stake is swung upright, the pain is even more excruciating as the weight of Jesus' body tears at his wounds. Yet, Jesus does not berate the soldiers. He prays: "Father, forgive them, for they do not know what they are doing."—Luke 23:34.

The Romans customarily post a sign stating the crime of the condemned criminal. This time, Pilate has posted a sign that reads: "Jesus the Nazarene the King of the Jews." It is written in Hebrew, Latin, and Greek, so most everyone can read it. Pilate's act reflects his disdain for the Jews who insisted on Jesus' death. The dismayed chief priests protest: "Do not write, 'The King of the Jews,' but that he said, 'I am King of the Jews.'" However, not wanting to be their pawn once again, Pilate answers: "What I have written, I have written."—John 19:19-22.

The enraged priests repeat the false testimony that was given earlier at the Sanhedrin trials.

Not surprisingly, passersby wag their heads in mockery and say abusively: "Ha! You who would throw down the temple and build it in three days, save yourself by coming down off the torture stake." Similarly, the chief priests and scribes say to one another: "Let the Christ, the King of Israel, now come down off the torture stake, so that we may see and believe." (Mark 15:29-32) Even the condemned robbers on Jesus' left and right reproach him, though he is the only one truly innocent.

The four Roman soldiers also make fun of Jesus. They may have been drinking sour wine, so now in mockery they apparently hold some of it before Jesus, who obviously cannot reach out and take any. The Romans tauntingly allude to the sign above Jesus' head and say: "If you are the King of the Jews, save yourself." (Luke 23: 36, 37) Think of it! The man who has proved to be the way, the truth, and the life is now being subjected to undeserved abuse and ridicule. Yet he resolutely suffers it all, without reproaching

• JESUS IS NAILED TO A TORTURE STAKE
• THE SIGN OVER JESUS' HEAD PROVOKES MOCKERY
• JESUS OFFERS HOPE OF LIFE IN PARADISE ON EARTH

131

the Jews who are watching, the Roman soldiers mocking him, or the two condemned criminals hanging on stakes alongside him.

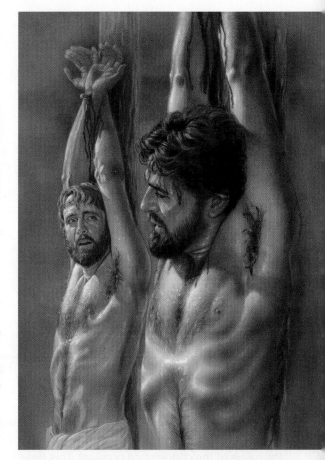

The four soldiers have taken Jesus' outer garments and divided them into four parts. They cast lots to see who gets which piece. Jesus' inner garment, though, is of superior quality, "without a seam, being woven from top to bottom." The soldiers reason: "Let us not tear it, but let us cast lots over it to decide whose it will be." They thus fulfill the scripture that says: "They divided my garments among themselves, and they cast lots for my clothing."—John 19: 23, 24; Psalm 22:18.

In time, one of the criminals realizes that Jesus truly must be a king. He rebukes his companion with the words: "Do you not fear God at all, now that you have received the same judgment? And we rightly so, for we are getting back what we deserve for the things we did; but this man did nothing wrong." Then he beseeches Jesus: "Remember me when you get into your Kingdom."—Luke 23:40-42.

Jesus replies: "Truly I tell you today, you will be with me," not in the Kingdom, but "in Paradise." (Luke 23:43) This promise differs from what Jesus has told his apostles, namely, that they would sit on thrones with him in the Kingdom. (Matthew 19:28; Luke 22:29, 30) However, this Jewish criminal may have heard about the earthly Paradise that Jehovah had originally provided as a home for Adam, Eve, and their descendants. Now this robber can die with that hope before him.

◇ Why does Jesus refuse to drink the wine offered to him?

◇ What sign is posted over Jesus' head, and how do the Jews react to it?

◇ How is prophecy fulfilled in what is done with Jesus' garments?

◇ What prospect does Jesus hold out to one of the criminals?

"CERTAINLY THIS MAN WAS GOD'S SON"

MATTHEW 27:45-56   MARK 15:33-41   LUKE 23:44-49   JOHN 19:25-30

It is now "the sixth hour," or noon. A strange darkness falls "over all the land until the ninth hour," three o'clock in the afternoon. (Mark 15:33) This eerie darkness is not caused by a solar eclipse. Those occur at the time of the new moon, but this is Passover season, when the moon is full. And this darkness lasts much longer than the few minutes of an eclipse. So God has caused this darkness!

Imagine the effect this must have on those mocking Jesus. During this dark period, four women approach the torture stake. They are Jesus' mother, Salome, Mary Magdalene, and Mary the mother of the apostle James the Less.

The apostle John is with Jesus' grieving mother "by the torture stake." Mary watches the son she bore and nurtured as he hangs there in agony. For her, it is like being pierced by "a long sword." (John 19:25; Luke 2:35) Despite his intense pain, however, Jesus thinks of her welfare. He makes the effort to nod toward John and say to his mother: "Woman, see! Your son!" Then, nodding toward Mary, he tells John: "See! Your mother!"—John 19:26, 27.

Jesus is entrusting the care of his mother, who is evidently now a widow, to the apostle whom he especially loves. Jesus is aware that his half brothers, Mary's other sons, have not as yet put faith in him. So he is making provision for his mother's physical care as well as for her spiritual needs. What a fine example!

About the time the darkness ends, Jesus says: "I am thirsty." In this he is fulfilling the scriptures. (John 19:28; Psalm 22:15) Jesus senses that his Father has, as it were, withdrawn his protection so that his Son's integrity might be tested to the limit. Christ calls out in what may be Aramaic of a Galilean dialect: *"Eli, Eli, lama sabachthani?"* which means, "My God, my God, why have you forsaken me?" Some standing nearby misunderstand him and exclaim: "See! He is calling Elijah." One of them runs and, placing a sponge soaked with sour wine on the end of a reed, gives Jesus a drink. But others say: "Let him be! Let us see whether Elijah comes to take him down."—Mark 15:34-36.

Jesus then cries out: "It has been accomplished!" (John 19:30) Yes, he has accomplished all that his Father sent him to earth to do. Finally, Jesus says: "Father, into your hands I entrust my spirit." (Luke 23:46) Jesus thus commits to Jehovah his life force, confident that God will restore it to him. With undiminished trust in God, Christ bows his head and dies.

At that, a violent earthquake occurs, splitting rocks. It is so powerful that tombs outside Jerusalem break open and corpses are thrown out of them. Passersby who see the dead bodies exposed enter "the holy city" and report what they just witnessed.—Matthew 12:11; 27:51-53.

"TO THE STAKE" Jesus' enemies yelled: "To the stake with him!" (John 19:15) The basic Greek word for "stake" used in the Gospel accounts is *stau·ros'.* The book *History of the Cross* reports: "*Stauros* means 'an upright pale,' a strong stake, such as farmers drive into the ground to make their fences or palisades—no more, no less."

When Jesus dies, the long, heavy curtain that divides the Holy from the Most Holy in God's temple is ripped in two, from top to bottom. The astonishing event is a manifestation of God's wrath against those who killed his Son and signifies that the way into the Most Holy, heaven itself, is now possible.—Hebrews 9:2, 3; 10:19, 20.

Understandably, the people become very afraid. The army officer in charge at the execution proclaims: "Certainly this man was God's Son." (Mark 15:39) He may have been there at Jesus' trial before Pilate when the issue of divine sonship was discussed. Now he is convinced that Jesus is righteous and is, in fact, the Son of God.

Others, overcome by these unusual events, head to their homes, "beating their chests" as a gesture of their intense grief and shame. (Luke 23:48) Among those observing at a distance are many female disciples who at times traveled with Jesus. They too are deeply moved by all these momentous events.

◇ Why can a solar eclipse not be the cause of the three hours of darkness?

◇ Jesus provides what fine example as to caring for aged parents?

◇ What does the earthquake cause, and what is signified by the temple curtain's being ripped in two?

◇ How do Jesus' death and surrounding events affect those present?

JESUS' BODY IS PREPARED AND BURIED

MATTHEW 27:57–28:2   MARK 15:42–16:4   LUKE 23:50–24:3   JOHN 19:31–20:1

It is getting late on Friday afternoon, Nisan 14. At sundown, the Sabbath of Nisan 15 will begin. Jesus is already dead, but the two robbers alongside him are still alive. According to the Law, dead bodies "should not remain all night on the stake" but, rather, should be buried "on that day."—Deuteronomy 21:22, 23.

Furthermore, Friday afternoon is called Preparation because people prepare meals and complete any other tasks that cannot wait until after the Sabbath. At sunset, a double, or "great," Sabbath will begin. (John 19:31) This is so because Nisan 15 will be the first day of the seven-day Festival of Unleavened Bread,

the first day of which is always a Sabbath. (Leviticus 23:5, 6) This time that first day coincides with the weekly Sabbath, the seventh day.

So the Jews ask Pilate to hasten the death of Jesus and the two robbers alongside him. How? By having their legs broken. That will make it impossible for them to use their legs to raise their bodies so as to breathe. The soldiers come and break the legs of the two robbers. But Jesus appears to be dead, and thus they do not break his legs. This fulfills Psalm 34:20: "He is guarding all his bones; not one of them has been broken."

To remove any doubt that Jesus is truly dead, a soldier jabs a spear into his side, piercing the

region of his heart. 'Immediately blood and water come out.' (John 19:34) This fulfills another scripture: "They will look to the one whom they pierced."—Zechariah 12:10.

Joseph from the city of Arimathea, "a rich man" and reputable member of the Sanhedrin, is also present at the execution. (Matthew 27: 57) He is described as "a good and righteous man," who is "waiting for the Kingdom of God." In fact, as "a disciple of Jesus but a secret one because of his fear of the Jews," he did not support the court's judgment of Jesus. (Luke 23:50; Mark 15:43; John 19:38) Joseph takes courage and asks Pilate for Jesus' body. Pilate summons the army officer in charge, who confirms that Jesus is dead. Thereupon, Pilate grants Joseph's request.

Joseph buys clean, fine linen and takes Jesus' body down from the stake. He wraps the corpse in the linen in preparation for burial. Nicodemus, "who had come to [Jesus] in the night the first time," helps with the preparation. (John 19:39) He brings about a hundred Roman pounds (72 modern pounds) of a costly mixture of myrrh and aloes. Jesus' body is wrapped in bandages containing these spices, according to the Jews' burial custom.

Joseph owns an unused tomb carved in rock nearby, and Jesus' body is laid in it. Then a large stone is rolled in front of the tomb. This is hastily done, before the Sabbath begins. Mary Magdalene and Mary the mother of James the Less may have been helping with the preparation of Jesus' body. They now hurry home "to prepare spices and perfumed oils" to treat Jesus' body further after the Sabbath.—Luke 23:56.

The next day, the Sabbath, the chief priests and Pharisees go to Pilate and say: "We recall what that impostor said while he was still alive, 'After three days I am to be raised up.' Therefore, command that the grave be made secure until the third day, so that his disciples may not come and steal him and say to the people, 'He was raised up from the dead!' Then this last deception will be worse than the first." Pilate replies: "You may have a guard. Go make it as secure as you know how."—Matthew 27:63-65.

Very early Sunday morning, Mary Magdalene, Mary the mother of James, and other women bring spices to the tomb to treat Jesus' body. They say to one another: "Who will roll the stone away from the entrance of the tomb for us?" (Mark 16:3) But an earthquake has occurred. Moreover, God's angel has rolled the stone away, the guards are gone, and the tomb appears empty!

◊ Why is Friday called Preparation, and why is this a "great" Sabbath?

◊ What do Joseph and Nicodemus have to do with Jesus' burial, and what is their relationship to Jesus?

◊ What do the priests want done, but what occurs early Sunday morning?

AN EMPTY TOMB—JESUS IS ALIVE!

MATTHEW 28:3-15   MARK 16:5-8   LUKE 24:4-12   JOHN 20:2-18

What a shock it is for the women to discover what appears to be an empty burial place! Mary Magdalene runs off to "Simon Peter and to the other disciple, for whom Jesus had affection" —the apostle John. (John 20:2) However, the other women at the tomb see an angel. And inside the memorial tomb is another angel, who is "clothed in a white robe."—Mark 16:5.

One of the angels tells them: "Do not be afraid, for I know that you are looking for Jesus who was executed on the stake. He is not here, for he was raised up, just as he said. Come, see the place where he was lying. Then go quickly and tell his disciples that he was raised up from the dead, for look! he is going ahead of you into Galilee." (Matthew 28:5-7) So "trembling and overwhelmed with emotion," the women run to report to the disciples.—Mark 16:8.

By now, Mary has found Peter and John. Breathlessly, she reports: "They have taken away the Lord out of the tomb, and we do not know where they have laid him." (John 20:2) Peter and John take off running. John is faster and reaches the tomb first. He peers into it and sees the bandages, but he remains outside.

When Peter arrives, he goes right in. He sees the linen cloths and the cloth used to wrap Jesus' head. John now enters, and he believes Mary's report. Despite what Jesus said earlier, neither of them understands that he has been raised up. (Matthew 16:21) Puzzled, they head home. But Mary, who has come back to the tomb, remains there.

Meanwhile, the other women are on their way to tell the disciples that Jesus has been raised. While they are running to do so, Jesus meets

them and says: "Good day!" They fall at his feet and 'do obeisance to him.' Then Jesus says: "Have no fear! Go, report to my brothers so that they may go to Galilee, and there they will see me."—Matthew 28:9, 10.

Earlier, when the earthquake occurred and the angels appeared, the soldiers at the tomb "trembled and became as dead men." After recovering, they entered the city and "reported to the chief priests all the things that had happened." The priests then consulted with elders of the Jews. The decision was made to bribe the soldiers to hide the matter and to claim: "His disciples came in the night and stole him while we were sleeping."—Matthew 28:4, 11, 13.

Roman soldiers can be put to death if they fall asleep at their post, so the priests promise: "If this [their lie about having been asleep] gets to the governor's ears, we will explain the matter to him and you will not need to worry." (Matthew 28:14) The soldiers take the bribe and do what the priests say. Thus the false story of Jesus' body being stolen spreads widely among the Jews.

Mary Magdalene is still grieving at the tomb. Stooping forward to look into it, she sees two angels in white! One sits at the head of where Jesus' body had been lying and the other at the foot. "Woman, why are you weeping?" they ask. Mary answers: "They have taken my Lord away, and I do not know where they have laid him." Turning around, Mary sees someone else. He repeats the angels' question and adds: "Whom are you looking for?" Thinking that he is the gardener, she says: "Sir, if you have carried him off, tell me where you have laid him, and I will take him away."—John 20:13-15.

Actually, Mary is speaking to the resurrected Jesus, but at the moment she does not recognize him. However, when he says, "Mary!" she knows that it is Jesus, recognizing him by the familiar way he speaks to her. *"Rabboni!"* (meaning, "Teacher!"), Mary exclaims joyfully. Yet, afraid that he is about to ascend to heaven, she grabs hold of him. Hence, Jesus urges her: "Stop clinging to me, for I have not yet ascended to the Father. But go to my brothers and say to them, 'I am ascending to my Father and your Father and to my God and your God.'" —John 20:16, 17.

Mary runs to the place where the apostles and other disciples are gathered. She tells them: "I have seen the Lord!" adding her account to what they have heard from the other women. (John 20:18) Yet, the reports 'seem like nonsense to them.'—Luke 24:11.

◇ After Mary Magdalene finds the tomb empty, what experiences do she and the other women have?

◇ How do Peter and John react at finding the tomb empty?

◇ Whom do the other women encounter on their way to the disciples, and what happens when Mary Magdalene is again at the tomb?

◇ How do the disciples respond to the reports they get?

THE RESURRECTED JESUS APPEARS TO MANY

LUKE 24:13-49 JOHN 20:19-29

On Sunday, Nisan 16, the disciples are in low spirits. They do not grasp the meaning of the empty tomb. (Matthew 28:9, 10; Luke 24:11) Later in the day, Cleopas and another disciple leave Jerusalem for Emmaus, which is about seven miles away.

As they walk, they discuss what has occurred. Then a stranger joins them. He asks: "What are these matters that you are debating between yourselves as you walk along?" Cleopas replies: "Are you a stranger dwelling alone in Jerusalem, and do not know the things that have occurred there during these days?" The stranger asks: "What things?"—Luke 24:17-19.

"The things concerning Jesus the Nazarene," they say. "We were hoping that this man was the one who was going to deliver Israel."—Luke 24:19-21.

Cleopas and his companion go on to relate things that happened that very day. They say that some women who went to the tomb where Jesus was buried found it empty and that these women were eyewitnesses to a supernatural event—the appearance of angels who said that Jesus is alive. They report that others also went to the tomb and "found it just as the women had said."—Luke 24:24.

The two disciples are clearly bewildered as to the meaning of what has occurred. The stranger responds with authority to correct their wrong thinking, which is affecting their hearts: "O senseless ones and slow of heart to believe all the things the prophets have spoken! Was it not necessary for the Christ to suffer these things and to enter into his glory?" (Luke 24: 25, 26) He goes on to interpret for them many Scriptural passages pertaining to the Christ.

Finally the three arrive near Emmaus. The two disciples want to hear more, so they urge the stranger: "Stay with us, because it is almost evening and the day is nearly over." He agrees to stay, and they have a meal. As the stranger says a prayer, breaks bread, and hands it to them, they recognize him, but then he disappears. (Luke 24:29-31) Now they know for sure that Jesus is alive!

The two disciples excitedly comment on what they experienced: "Were not our hearts burning within us as he was speaking to us on the road, as he was fully opening up the Scriptures to us?" (Luke 24:32) They hurry back to Jerusalem, where they find the apostles and others with them. Before Cleopas and his companion can give a report, they hear others say: "For a fact the Lord was raised up, and he appeared to Simon!" (Luke 24:34) Then the two tell how Jesus appeared to them. Yes, they too are eyewitnesses.

Now all are shocked—Jesus appears in the room! This seems unbelievable because they locked the doors out of fear of the Jews. Still, Jesus is standing right in their midst. He calmly says: "May you have peace." But they are frightened. As they did once before, they are 'imagining that they are seeing a spirit.'—Luke 24:36, 37; Matthew 14:25-27.

To prove that he is no apparition or something they merely imagine but, rather, that he does have a fleshly body, Jesus shows them his hands and feet and says: "Why are you troubled, and why have doubts come up in your hearts? See my hands and my feet, that it is I myself; touch me and see, for a spirit does not have flesh and bones just as you see that I have." (Luke 24:36-39) They are overjoyed and amazed but still somewhat reluctant to believe.

Further attempting to help them to see that he is real, he asks: "Do you have something there to eat?" He accepts a piece of broiled fish and eats it. Then he says: "These are my words that I spoke to you while I was yet with you [before my death], that all the things written about me in the Law of Moses and in the Prophets and Psalms must be fulfilled."—Luke 24:41-44.

Jesus had helped Cleopas and his companion to understand the Scriptures, and he does so now for all those gathered there: "This is what is written: that the Christ would suffer and rise from among the dead on the third day, and on the basis of his name, repentance for forgiveness of sins would be preached in all the nations—starting out from Jerusalem. You are to be witnesses of these things."—Luke 24: 46-48.

For some reason the apostle Thomas is not present. In the following days, others joyfully tell him: "We have seen the Lord!" Thomas responds: "Unless I see in his hands the print of the nails and stick my finger into the print of the nails and stick my hand into his side, I will never believe it."—John 20:25.

Eight days later, the disciples are again meeting behind locked doors, but this time Thomas is present. Jesus appears in their midst in a materialized body and greets them: "May you have peace." Turning to Thomas, Jesus says: "Put your finger here, and see my hands, and take your hand and stick it into my side, and stop doubting but believe." Thomas exclaims: "My Lord and my God!" (John 20:26-28) Yes, he now has no doubts that Jesus is alive as a divine being who is Jehovah God's representative.

"Because you have seen me, have you believed?" Jesus says. "Happy are those who have not seen and yet believe."—John 20:29.

◊ A stranger makes what inquiry of two disciples going to Emmaus?

◊ Why do the hearts of the disciples soon burn within them?

◊ When Cleopas and his companion return to Jerusalem, what exciting report do they hear, and what then happens?

◊ How is Thomas finally convinced that Jesus is alive?

ON THE SHORE OF THE SEA OF GALILEE

JOHN 21:1-25

On his final evening with the apostles, Jesus had told them: "After I have been raised up, I will go ahead of you into Galilee." (Matthew 26:32; 28:7, 10) Now many of his followers make that trip, but what should they do in Galilee?

At one point, Peter tells six of the apostles: "I am going fishing." All six respond: "We are coming with you." (John 21:3) The whole night, they do not catch anything. As it is getting light, Jesus appears on the beach, but they do not realize who it is. Jesus calls out: "Children, you do not have anything to eat, do you?" They answer: "No!" Jesus tells them: "Cast the net on the right side of the boat and you will find some." (John 21:5, 6) They catch so many fish that they cannot even draw in their net.

"It is the Lord!" John tells Peter. (John 21:7) Quickly, Peter girds on his outer garment, which he was not wearing while fishing. He plunges into the sea and swims about a hundred yards to shore. The others in the boat follow slowly, dragging the net full of fish.

Getting to shore, they see "a charcoal fire with fish lying on it and bread." Jesus says: "Bring some of the fish you just now caught." Peter pulls in the net, which contains 153 large fish! "Come, have your breakfast," Jesus says. None of them have the courage to ask, "Who are you?" because they realize that it is Jesus. (John 21:10-12) This is his third appearance to the disciples as a group.

Jesus gives each of them some bread and fish to eat. Then, likely looking toward the catch of fish, he asks: "Simon son of John, do you love me more than these?" Is Peter more attached to the fishing business than to the work that Jesus wants him to do? Peter replies: "Yes, Lord, you know I have affection for you."

So Jesus urges him: "Feed my lambs."—John 21:15.

Again, Jesus asks: "Simon son of John, do you love me?" Perhaps puzzled, Peter answers earnestly: "Yes, Lord, you know I have affection for you." Jesus' response is similar: "Shepherd my little sheep."—John 21:16.

The third time, Jesus asks: "Simon son of John, do you have affection for me?" Now Peter may be wondering whether Jesus doubts his loyalty. Peter says emphatically: "Lord, you are aware of all things; you know that I have affection for you." Once again Jesus highlights what Peter must do: "Feed my little sheep." (John 21:17) Yes, those taking the lead need to minister to those drawn into God's sheepfold.

Jesus was bound and executed because he did the work that God commissioned him to do. He now reveals that Peter will have a similar end. "When you were younger," Jesus says, "you used to clothe yourself and walk about where you wanted. But when you grow old, you will stretch out your hands and another man will clothe you and carry you where you do not wish." Yet Jesus urges him: "Continue following me."—John 21:18, 19.

Peter sees the apostle John and asks: "Lord, what about this man?" Yes, what does the future hold for the apostle for whom Jesus has special affection? Jesus answers: "If it is my will for him to remain until I come, of what concern is that to you?" (John 21:21-23) Peter needs to follow Jesus without worrying about what others do. Still, Jesus is indicating that John will outlive the other apostles and will be given a vision of Jesus' coming in Kingdom power.

Of course, there are other things that Jesus did, more than many scrolls can contain.

◇ What shows that the apostles are uncertain about what to do in Galilee?

◇ How are the apostles able to recognize Jesus at the Sea of Galilee?

◇ Jesus emphasizes that those taking the lead need to do what?

◇ How does Jesus indicate the manner in which Peter will die?

HUNDREDS SEE HIM PRIOR TO PENTECOST

MATTHEW 28:16-20   LUKE 24:50-52   ACTS 1:1-12; 2:1-4

After Jesus' resurrection, he arranges for his 11 apostles to meet him at a mountain in Galilee. Other disciples are there too, about 500 of them, some of whom initially have doubts. (Matthew 28:17; 1 Corinthians 15:6) But what Jesus now says helps to convince each one of them that he truly is alive.

Jesus explains that God has given him all authority in heaven and on earth. "Go, therefore," Jesus urges them, "and make disciples of people of all the nations, baptizing them in the name of the Father and of the Son and of the holy spirit, teaching them to observe all the things I have commanded you." (Matthew 28:18-20) Yes, not only is Jesus alive but he is still interested in having the good news preached.

All of Jesus' followers—men, women, and children—receive this same commission to make disciples. Opposers may try to stop their preaching and teaching, yet Jesus assures them: "All authority has been given me in heaven and on the earth." What does that mean for his followers? He tells them: "Look! I am with you all the days until the conclusion of the system of things." Jesus does not say that all who share in preaching the good news will be enabled to do miraculous works. Still, they will have the backing of holy spirit.

Altogether, Jesus appears to his disciples "throughout 40 days" after his resurrection. He materializes various bodies and shows "himself alive to them by many convincing proofs," instructing them "about the Kingdom of God." —Acts 1:3; 1 Corinthians 15:7.

Evidently while the apostles are still in Galilee, Jesus directs them to return to Jerusalem. When meeting with them in the city, he says: "Do not leave Jerusalem, but keep waiting for what the Father has promised, about which you heard from me; for John, indeed, baptized with water, but you will be baptized with holy spirit not many days after this."—Acts 1:4, 5.

Later Jesus meets again with his apostles. He leads "them out as far as Bethany," which is on the eastern slope of the Mount of Olives. (Luke 24:50) Despite everything that Jesus has told them about his departure, they still believe that in some way his Kingdom will be on earth.—Luke 22:16, 18, 30; John 14:2, 3.

The apostles ask Jesus: "Lord, are you restoring the kingdom to Israel at this time?" He simply replies: "It does not belong to you to know the times or seasons that the Father has placed in his own jurisdiction." Then, stressing again the work they must do, he says: "You will receive power when the holy spirit comes upon you, and you will be witnesses of me in Jerusalem, in all Judea and Samaria, and to the most distant part of the earth."—Acts 1:6-8.

The apostles are on the Mount of Olives with the resurrected Jesus when he begins to rise heavenward. Soon a cloud obscures him from their sight. After his resurrection, Jesus had materialized fleshly bodies. But now Jesus dematerializes the body he used on this occasion, and he ascends to heaven as a spirit creature. (1 Corinthians 15:44, 50; 1 Peter 3:18) As the faithful apostles are gazing after him, "two men in white garments" appear beside them. These are materialized angels, who ask: "Men of Galilee, why do you stand looking into the sky? This Jesus who was taken up from you into the sky will come in the same manner as you have seen him going into the sky."—Acts 1:10, 11.

Jesus left the earth without public fanfare, his faithful followers being the only observers.

He will return "in the same manner"—without public fanfare, with only his faithful followers discerning his presence in Kingdom power. ✳

The apostles return to Jerusalem. During the following days, they gather with other disciples, including "Mary the mother of Jesus and . . . his brothers." (Acts 1:14) This group persist in prayer. One subject of prayer is the choosing of a disciple to replace Judas Iscariot and thus restore the apostolic number to 12. (Matthew 19: 28) They want a disciple who has witnessed Jesus' activities and his resurrection. For the last time mentioned in the Bible, lots are cast to determine God's will. (Psalm 109:8; Proverbs 16: 33) Matthias, who may have been one of the 70 whom Jesus sent out, is selected and "counted along with the 11 apostles."—Acts 1:26.

Ten days after Jesus ascended to heaven, the Jewish Festival of Pentecost 33 C.E. takes place. About 120 of the disciples are assembled in an upper room in Jerusalem. Suddenly, a noise just like that of a rushing stiff breeze fills the whole house. Tongues as if of fire become visible, one upon each of those present. The disciples all begin to speak in different languages. This is the outpouring of the holy spirit that Jesus had promised!—John 14:26.

◇ Who are present when Jesus gives instructions at a mountain in Galilee, and what does he say?

◇ For how long after his resurrection does Jesus appear to his disciples, and what does he do?

◇ Given how he departs, in what manner is Jesus to return?

◇ What occurs at Pentecost 33 C.E.?

CHRIST AT GOD'S RIGHT HAND

ACTS 7:56

Ten days after Jesus ascended heavenward, the outpouring of holy spirit on the day of Pentecost provided evidence that he was, in fact, in heaven. And additional evidence of that was forthcoming. Just before the disciple Stephen was stoned for his faithful witnessing, he exclaimed: "Look! I see the heavens opened up and the Son of man standing at God's right hand."—Acts 7:56.

While with his Father in heaven, Jesus would await a specific command foretold in God's Word. David wrote under inspiration: "Jehovah declared to my Lord [Jesus]: 'Sit at my right hand *until* I place your enemies as a stool for your feet.'" When the period of waiting was completed, he would "go subduing in the midst of [his] enemies." (Psalm 110:1, 2) But what would Jesus do from heaven while awaiting the time to take action against his enemies?

At Pentecost 33 C.E., the Christian congregation came to be. From heaven, Jesus began to rule, or reign, over his spirit-anointed disciples. (Colossians 1:13) He guided them in their preaching and prepared them for their future role. What role? Those proving faithful to death would eventually be resurrected and would serve as associate kings with Jesus in the Kingdom.

An outstanding example of one who would be a future king was Saul, better known by his Roman name Paul. He was a Jew who had long been zealous for God's Law, but he was so misguided by Jewish religious leaders that he even approved of the stoning of Stephen. Then, "breathing threat and murder against the disciples of the Lord," Saul headed to Damascus. He was authorized by High Priest Caiaphas to arrest Jesus' disciples and bring them back to Je-

rusalem. (Acts 7:58; 9:1) However, while Saul was en route, a bright light flashed around him and he fell to the ground.

"Saul, Saul, why are you persecuting me?" a voice from an invisible source called out. "Who are you, Lord?" Saul asked. "I am Jesus, whom you are persecuting," came the reply.—Acts 9: 4, 5.

Jesus told Saul to enter Damascus and await further instructions, but he had to be led to the city because the miraculous light had blinded him. In a separate vision, Jesus appeared to Ananias, one of his disciples living in Damascus. Jesus told Ananias to go to a certain address to find Saul. Ananias was apprehensive about doing so, but Jesus assured him: "This man is a chosen vessel to me to bear my name to the nations as well as to kings and the sons of Israel." Saul recovered his sight, and there in Damascus "he began to preach about Jesus, that this one is the Son of God."—Acts 9:15, 20.

With Jesus' support, Paul and other evangelizers carried on the preaching work that Jesus had started. God blessed them with outstanding success. About 25 years after Jesus appeared to him on the road to Damascus, Paul wrote that the good news had been "preached in all creation under heaven."—Colossians 1:23.

Years later, Jesus gave his beloved apostle John a series of visions, which are found in the Bible book of Revelation. Through these visions, John, in effect, lived to see Jesus return in Kingdom power. (John 21:22) "By inspiration [John] came to be in the Lord's day." (Revelation 1:10) When would that be?

A careful study of Bible prophecy reveals that "the Lord's day" began in modern times. In 1914, what became known as World War I broke out. And the decades since then have been marked by more wars, plagues, starvation, earthquakes, and other evidences marking a large-scale fulfillment of "the sign" that Jesus gave his apostles about his "presence" and "the end." (Matthew 24:3, 7, 8, 14) The preaching of the good news of the Kingdom is now being done, not just in the area of the Roman Empire, but globally.

John was inspired to describe what this means: "Now have come to pass the salvation and the power and the Kingdom of our God and the authority of his Christ." (Revelation 12:10) Yes, the Kingdom of God in heaven, which Jesus so widely proclaimed, is a reality!

That is wonderful news for all loyal disciples of Jesus. They can take to heart John's words: "On this account be glad, you heavens and you who reside in them! Woe for the earth and for the sea, because the Devil has come down to you, having great anger, knowing that he has a short period of time."—Revelation 12:12.

Thus, Jesus is no longer sitting at his Father's right hand waiting. He is ruling as King, and soon he will eliminate all his enemies. (Hebrews 10:12, 13) What exciting developments then await us?

◇ After Jesus ascended to heaven, what did he do?

◇ When did "the Lord's day" begin, and what took place thereafter?

◇ Why do we have good reason to rejoice?

JESUS BRINGS PARADISE AND FINISHES HIS ASSIGNMENT

1 CORINTHIANS 15:24-28

Soon after Jesus' baptism, he faced an enemy who was determined to cause him to fail even before he began his ministry. Yes, the Devil tried repeatedly to tempt Jesus. Later, Jesus said about that evil one: "The ruler of the world is coming, and he has no hold on me."—John 14:30.

The apostle John foresaw in vision what lay ahead for 'the great dragon, the original serpent, the one called Devil and Satan.' That vicious enemy of mankind would be cast out of heaven, "having great anger, knowing that he has a short period of time." (Revelation 12:9, 12) Christians have good reason to believe that they are living during that "short period of time" and that soon "the dragon, the original serpent," will be abyssed and inactive for 1,000 years while Jesus rules in God's Kingdom.—Revelation 20:1, 2.

During that period, what will occur on earth, our home? Who will live here, and under what conditions? Jesus himself pointed to the answers. In his illustration of the sheep and the goats, he showed what future awaits righteous humans who are like sheep, who cooperate with and do good toward Jesus' brothers. He also made clear what lies ahead for those who do the opposite, those who are like goats. Jesus said: "These [the goats] will depart into everlasting cutting-off, but the righteous ones [the sheep] into everlasting life."—Matthew 25:46.

This helps us to understand Jesus' words to the criminal who was on the stake beside him. Jesus did not hold out to that man the reward that was promised to his faithful apostles, that of being part of the Kingdom of the heavens. Rather, Jesus promised the repentant evildoer:

• THE OUTCOME FOR THE SHEEP AND THE GOATS
• MANY WILL ENJOY PARADISE ON EARTH
• JESUS PROVES TO BE THE WAY, THE TRUTH, THE LIFE

139

"Truly I tell you today, you will be with me in Paradise." (Luke 23:43) Thus that man gained the prospect of living in Paradise—a beautiful park, or parklike garden. Logically, those today who prove to be like sheep and who enter "into everlasting life" will also be in that Paradise.

This harmonizes with the description that the apostle John gave of conditions that will then prevail on earth. He said: "The tent of God is with mankind, and he will reside with them, and they will be his people. And God himself will be with them. And he will wipe out every tear from their eyes, and death will be no more, neither will mourning nor outcry nor pain be anymore. The former things have passed away."—Revelation 21:3, 4.

In order for that criminal to enjoy life in Paradise, he will have to be raised from the dead. And he will not be alone in experiencing a resurrection. Jesus made that clear when he said: "The hour is coming in which all those in the memorial tombs will hear his voice and come out, those who did good things to a resurrection of life, and those who practiced vile things to a resurrection of judgment."—John 5:28, 29.

But what of the faithful apostles and the limited number of others who will be with Jesus in heaven? The Bible says: "They will be priests of God and of the Christ, and they will rule as kings with him for the 1,000 years." (Revelation 20:6) These who become corulers with Christ will have been men and women on earth. So they will certainly be compassionate and understanding heavenly rulers over those on earth. —Revelation 5:10.

Jesus will apply his ransom sacrifice to humans on earth and lift from them the curse of inherited sin. He and his corulers will raise faithful mankind to perfection. Yes, humans will then enjoy the life that God originally purposed for them when he told Adam and Eve to multiply and fill the earth. Even death that resulted from Adam's sin will be no more!

Thus, Jesus will have accomplished all that Jehovah asked of him. At the end of his Thousand Year Rule, Jesus will hand over the Kingdom and the perfected human family to his Father. Regarding this marvelous act of humility on Jesus' part, the apostle Paul wrote: "When all things will have been subjected to him, then the Son himself will also subject himself to the One who subjected all things to him, that God may be all things to everyone."—1 Corinthians 15:28.

Clearly, Jesus plays a vital role in accomplishing God's glorious purposes. And as those purposes continue to unfold throughout eternity, he will live up completely to the description he gave of himself: "I am the way and the truth and the life."—John 14:6.

◇ What does the future hold for mankind's great enemy, the Devil?

◇ Who will be able to enjoy Paradise, and under what conditions?

◇ By the end of the thousand years, what will Jesus have accomplished, and what will he then do?

TO IMITATE JESUS, BE...

COMPASSIONATE

As a perfect man, Jesus did not experience many of the distresses and concerns that other humans did. Yet he showed deep feeling for people. He was willing to go out of his way for them, to do things beyond what might have seemed necessary. Yes, compassion moved him to help others. Reflect on the examples in Chapters 32, 37, 57, 99.

APPROACHABLE

People of all ages—young and old—felt that they could approach Jesus because he did not have an air of aloofness or superiority. Sensing Jesus' personal interest in them, people felt at ease in his presence. To note this, see Chapters 25, 27, 95.

PRAYERFUL

Jesus regularly turned to his Father in earnest prayer, privately and when with true worshippers. He prayed on many occasions, not only at mealtimes. He prayed to thank his Father, to praise him, and to seek his direction before making serious decisions. Consider the examples found in Chapters 24, 34, 91, 122, 123.

UNSELFISH

At times when he could have benefited from some needed rest and relaxation, Jesus still put himself out for others. He did not have a me-first attitude. In this too, he provided a model that we can follow closely. Study how that model is reflected in Chapters 19, 41, 52.

FORGIVING

Jesus did more than teach about the need to be forgiving—he demonstrated forgiveness in dealing with his disciples and others. Meditate on examples found in Chapters 26, 40, 64, 85, 131.

ZEALOUS

It was foretold that most Jews would refuse to accept the Messiah and that his enemies would kill him. So Jesus could easily have been self-sparing in what he did for people. Instead, he zealously promoted true worship. He set an example of zeal for all his followers who face indifference or even opposition. See Chapters 16, 72, 103.

HUMBLE

Jesus was superior to imperfect humans in countless ways, such as in knowledge and wisdom. His perfection undoubtedly gave him physical and mental abilities beyond what anyone around him had. Yet he humbly served others. You will find lessons about this in Chapters 10, 62, 66, 94, 116.

PATIENT

Jesus consistently showed patience with his apostles and others when they failed to imitate his example or apply what he said. He patiently repeated lessons that they needed so that they could draw closer to Jehovah. Reflect on examples of Jesus' patience in Chapters 74, 98, 118, 135.

SCRIPTURE INDEX Numbers after the citations indicate chapters.

INDEX OF ILLUSTRATIONS (PARABLES)   Numbers indicate chapters.

INDEX OF BOXES

SOME MESSIANIC PROPHECIES

EVENT	PROPHECY	FULFILLMENT	CHAPTER
Born in Bethlehem	Micah 5:2	Luke 2:1-6	5, 7, 67
Flight to and return from Egypt	Hosea 11:1	Matthew 2:13-15, 19, 20	8
Mothers weep after their sons die in the attempt to kill young Jesus	Jeremiah 31:15	Matthew 2:17, 18	8
Proclaims liberty to captives	Isaiah 61:1, 2	Luke 4:17-21	21
Resides in Capernaum of Galilee	Isaiah 9:1, 2	Matthew 4:13-17	22, 67
Cures many who are sick	Isaiah 53:4	Matthew 8:16, 17	23
Does not quarrel on the streets	Isaiah 42:1-4	Matthew 12:16-21	33
Teaches by means of illustrations	Psalm 78:2; Isaiah 6:9, 10	Matthew 13:13-15, 34, 35	43
Enters Jerusalem riding on a colt	Zechariah 9:9	Matthew 21:1-9	102
Many do not believe in him	Isaiah 6:10; 53:1	John 12:37, 38	104
Trusted companion betrays him	Psalm 41:9	John 13:18, 21	117
Disciples scatter, abandoning him	Zechariah 13:7	Matthew 26:31, 54-56	118, 124
Hated without cause	Psalm 35:19; 69:4	John 15:24, 25	120
Soldiers divide up his garments	Psalm 22:18	John 19:23, 24	131
Thirsty while on the stake	Psalm 22:15	John 19:28	132
His body pierced after his death	Zechariah 12:10	John 19:34, 37	133
Bones not broken before he dies	Psalm 34:20	John 19:36	133

For more information, visit **www.jw.org** or contact Jehovah's Witnesses.

AUSTRALASIA: PO Box 280, Ingleburn, NSW 1890, Australia. **BARBADOS, W.I.:** Crusher Site Road, Prospect, BB 24012 St. James. **BRITAIN:** The Ridgeway, London NW7 1RN. **CAMEROON:** BP 889, Douala. **CANADA:** PO Box 4100, Georgetown, ON L7G 4Y4. **CENTRAL AMERICA:** Apartado Postal 895, 06002 México, D.F., México. **CURAÇAO:** PO Box 8150, Willemstad. **GHANA:** PO Box GP 760, Accra. **LIBERIA:** PO Box 10-0380, 1000 Monrovia 10. **NIGERIA:** PMB 1090, Benin City 300001, Edo State. **SOUTH AFRICA:** Private Bag X2067, Krugersdorp, 1740. **SURINAME:** PO Box 2914, Paramaribo. **TRINIDAD AND TOBAGO:** Lower Rapsey Street & Laxmi Lane, Curepe. **UNITED STATES OF AMERICA:** 25 Columbia Heights, Brooklyn, NY 11201-2483. **ZAMBIA:** PO Box 33459, 10101 Lusaka. **www.jw.org**